RICHARD WILKINSON AND KATE PICKETT

The Inner Level

How More Equal Societies Reduce Stress, Restore Sanity and Improve Everyone's Well-being

PENGUIN BOOKS

PENGUIN BOOKS

UK | USA | Canada | Ireland | Australia
India | New Zealand | South Africa

Penguin Books is part of the Penguin Random House group of companies
whose addresses can be found at global.penguinrandomhouse.com.

First published by Allen Lane 2018
Published in Penguin Books 2019
001

Set in 9.07/12.08 pt Sabon LT Std
Typeset by Jouve (UK), Milton Keynes
Printed and bound in Great Britain by Clays Ltd, Elcograf S.p.A.

A CIP catalogue record for this book is available from the British Library

ISBN: 978-0-141-97539-9

www.greenpenguin.co.uk

PENGUIN BOOKS

THE INNER LEVEL

Richard Wilkinson is Professor Emeritus of Social Epidemiology at the University of Nottingham and Honorary Professor at University College London and the University of York.

Kate Pickett is Professor of Epidemiology, University Research Champion for Justice and Equality and Deputy Director of the Centre for Future Health at the University of York.

Together, they founded the Equality Trust, which seeks to promote public understanding of the effects of inequality.

For

George and Annie Wilkinson

Sarah Colebourne and Helen Holman

And for the staff of The Retreat, York –
at the forefront of treating the mentally distressed
with respect since 1796

Contents

List of Figures

With the exception of figures 2.8 and 9.5, all the figures are either our own or have been redrawn from the original sources and, on condition that they are credited to the original publications, they can be reproduced without our permission.

The cartoon on page xvi is reproduced with kind permission of Steven O'Brien. All other cartoons are reproduced with grateful acknowledgement to www.CartoonStock.com.

Acknowledgements

This book has benefitted from three rounds of editing: from Shan Vahidy, Stuart Proffitt and Ben Sinyor. We felt very honoured by the quality and depth of thought each gave to our argument and how it could be expressed more clearly and elegantly. Rather than a few verbal comments and minor corrections to spelling and grammar from a quick read-through, each provided us with detailed notes on almost every page of our manuscript and a long list of more fundamental points to consider. At each stage we felt in good hands, guided to higher professional standards. Theirs are rare skills and we are extremely fortunate that our work received so much of their attention. We are deeply indebted to them.

At the University of York, Kate's research group read and commented on draft chapters, giving us great feedback while being gentle with us – it's not only students who fear their work being read by others! Thank you to Pippa Bird, Deborah Box, Alex Christensen, Holly Essex, Lorna Fraser, Stuart Jarvis, Ben Mallicoat, Madeleine Power, Stephanie Prady, Katie Pybus, Marena Ceballos Rasgado, Noortje Uphoff and Tiffany Yang. We are also particularly indebted to Sean Baine, Danny Dorling and Allison Quick for their thoughtful comments on early drafts, and to our many helpful academic colleagues and their families, too many to name, some of whom have given special support over the past few years. We thank Barbara Abrams, Christo Albor, Dimitris Ballas, Stephen Bezruchka, Karen Bloor, Jonathan Bradshaw, Baltica Cabieses, Helena Cronin, Martin Daly, Danny and Alison Dorling, Frank Elgar, Manuel Antonio Espinoza, Paul Gilbert, Hilary Graham, Sheri Johnson, Ichiro Kawachi, Sebastian Kraemer, Rosie McEachen, Annamarie Mercer, Jon Minton, Martin O'Neill, Annie Quick, Hector Rufrancos, Trevor Sheldon, Deborah Smith, 'Subu' Subramanian, Len Syme, Laura Vanderbloemen and John Wright. We also thank our 'bus family' who came together as part of an international expert working group in Bhutan, now part of the Wellbeing Economy Alliance (WE-All): Bob Costanza, Lorenzo Fioramonti, Enrico Giovannini, Ida Kubiszewski, Hunter Lovins, Jacquie McGlade, Lars Mortensen, Kristín Vala Ragnarsdóttir, Debra Roberts, Roberto de Vogli and Stewart Wallis – you have expanded our thinking and our world.

The graphs shown in our figures reflect the work of a large number of researchers in different countries. We are particularly indebted to those who sent us their original research data so that we could redraw their figures in a consistent format. They are: Richard Layte (Figure 2.1); Jonathan Burns (Figure 2.6); Steve Loughnan and Peter Kuppens (Figure 3.1); Paul Piff (Figures 3.3 and 3.4); Matteo Iacoviello (Figure 4.4); Frank Elgar (Figure 5.2); Lindsey Macmillan and Claire Crawford (Figure 6.3); Ida Kubiszewski (Figure 8.2); Colin Gordon (Figure 9.3); and Larry Mishel (Figure 9.4).

We are also grateful to current and former staff, volunteers, advisers, board members and trustees of The Equality Trust (www. equalitytrust.org,uk), with special thanks to our co-founder, Bill Kerry, the Chair of Trustees, Sean Baine, and Director, Wanda Wyporska, for campaigning and informing the public about inequality. Thank you to The Equality Trust's many supporters: individuals, affiliated local groups and funders, including the Joseph Rowntree Charitable Trust, the Network for Social Change, Tudor Trust, and the Barry Amiel and Norman Melburn Trust. Director Katharine Round and producer Christo Hird of Dartmouth Films created The Divide, a moving interpretation of our work, which reaches new audiences to tell the story of the impact of inequality: thank you both. Finally we thank everybody who has taken the time to read our work, invited us to speak, spoken encouraging words, or spread the message; we wish we could thank all of you individually, and hope you will continue with us on the journey.

O'Brien

Prologue

The story so far . . .

The Spirit Level, published in 2009, showed that people in societies with bigger income gaps between rich and poor are much more likely to suffer from a wide range of health and social problems than those living in more equal societies.[1] The evidence we presented in that book strongly implied that inequality has major psychological effects and that many of these problems are the result of increased social stress. In this new book we explore what these psychological effects and social stresses are: how inequality gets into our minds, how it increases anxiety levels, how people respond and what the consequences are for levels of mental illness and emotional disorders – how, in sum, living in a more unequal society changes how we think and feel and how we relate to each other. The picture we present is based partly on our own work but predominantly on a large body of research from academics around the world. The evidence drawn together here not only clarifies why more unequal societies are so dysfunctional, but also helps to identify the changes that would make social interaction better and improve everyone's health and happiness.

The Spirit Level provided the starting point for this book; so much so, that those unfamiliar with it may find it helpful to have a brief summary of its findings here. First, our earlier book showed that the populations of societies with larger income differences tend to have worse health: lower life expectancy and higher rates of infant mortality, mental illness, illicit drug use and obesity. Greater inequality also damages social relationships: more unequal societies experience more violence (as measured by homicide rates) and higher rates of imprisonment; people trust each other less and community life is weaker. Inequality also damages children's life chances; more unequal societies have lower levels of child well-being and educational attainment, more teenage births and less social mobility.

The same relationships between the scale of inequality and societal problems were evident whether we looked internationally at the scale of income inequality in different rich countries or when we analysed data for the fifty states of the USA. In both settings, bigger income differences correlated closely with worse outcomes.

The picture is remarkably clear and consistent. Take the USA as an example: compared to other rich countries it has the largest income differences between rich and poor and suffers from the highest homicide rates, the highest percentage of the population in prison, the highest rates of mental illness, the highest teenage birth rates, among the lowest life expectancy, low levels of child well-being and low maths and literacy attainment. Britain and Portugal, which during our research period were the next most unequal of the rich countries, also did very poorly on most of these outcomes. In contrast, more equal countries, such as the Scandinavian countries and Japan, did well. Figure 1 provides a simple summary of our findings for rich countries.

The identification of these patterns did not rest solely on our own work, but reflected findings from a large number of researchers in different academic disciplines in different countries. The first research papers showing that violence was more common, and health worse, in countries with bigger income gaps were published in peer-reviewed journals in the 1970s. Since then the number of published studies has grown and grown; there are now well over three hundred research papers that have examined health and homicide rates in relation to inequality in different parts of the world. Studies cover both developed and developing countries; some look at the relationship at a particular point in time, others at changes over time. Many have taken account of differences in average incomes and/or poverty, as well as other factors such as spending on public services. The vast majority show a consistent tendency for outcomes to be worse in more unequal societies.[2] The evidence is now such that these correlations between income inequality and both health and social problems must be regarded as causal, reflecting the ways greater inequality damages societies, harming human health and well-being.[3]

The step from evidence of correlation to evidence of causality is obviously a crucial one. Why do we think it can be made confidently? Epidemiology has been centrally concerned with statistical

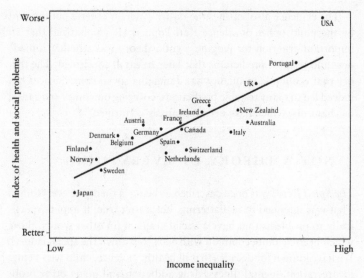

Figure 1: Health and social problems are more common in more unequal countries.[*][1]

evidence identifying the causes of disease and has therefore developed a set of criteria for judging whether relationships are likely to be causal. As well as the obvious point that causes must precede their effects, they also include the strength of the relationship, whether there is a 'dose-response' relationship – i.e., higher levels of inequality lead to successively worse outcomes – whether the relationship is biologically plausible, whether or not there are other likely explanations, and whether research results present a consistent picture. Judged on this basis, the evidence from several hundred research studies suggests that the relationship between larger income differences and a worsening of a wide range of health and social problems is indeed causal.[3]

* The Index of Health and Social Problems measures life expectancy, trust, mental illness (including drug and alcohol addiction), obesity, infant mortality, children's maths and literacy scores, imprisonment rates, homicide rates, teenage births and social mobility.

The evidence also satisfies the rather different criteria put forward by the philosopher of science Karl Popper. He emphasized that an important criterion for judging a good theory was whether it made new and testable predictions that later research confirmed. The theory that economic inequality has damaging social consequences has indeed led to many testable predictions, covering outcomes and causal mechanisms, which have been repeatedly confirmed.[3,4]

NOT A THEORY OF EVERYTHING . . .

The Spirit Level was once described as being 'a theory of everything'. That was intended to be flattering, but it isn't true. It applies specifically to problems that have a social gradient (in other words, those which become more common with each step down the social ladder). We have known for decades that ill health, violence, child well-being, incarceration, mental illness, drug addiction and many other problems have social gradients. Whether you compare rich and poor areas, high and low social classes, or people with more or less education, these problems all occur more often at each step down the social ladder. What *The Spirit Level* showed was in fact simple: that the many seemingly distinct problems which we know are related to social status (whether measured by income, education or occupation)* within our societies, get worse when bigger income differences make the status differences larger and more important. Position in the pecking order and the scale of status differences – inequality – play a causal role in problems with social gradients.

* We use the term 'social status' here in the generally accepted everyday sense, which coincides with 'social position' or where you are on the social ladder. Epidemiologists engaged in research on health inequalities used to spend time discussing whether it was best measured by income, education, occupation or the kind of neighbourhood you lived in. In the past, UK government statistics categorized occupations into social classes according to a rather subjective judgement of their 'general social standing'. Not only is no measure perfect, but the truth is that no one quite knows what an ideal measure would be. As will become clear later in this book, we believe that our judgements of social status are still coloured by our evolved psychological tendency, probably going back to how pre-human primates judged dominance and subordination in ranking systems.

One of our more surprising findings was that *inequality affects the vast majority of the population*, not only a poor minority. Although its severest effects are on those nearer the bottom of the social ladder, the vast majority are also affected to a lesser extent. This means that if well-educated people with good jobs and incomes lived with the same jobs and incomes in a more equal society, they would be likely to live a little longer and less likely to become victims of violence; their children might do a little better at school and would be less likely to become teenage parents or to develop serious drug problems. The issue is, therefore, not so much whether more unequal countries do or do not have more poor people, but the way larger income differences across a society immerse everyone more deeply in issues of status competition and insecurity.

It is because inequality affects most people that the differences in rates of health and social problems between more and less equal societies are often very large indeed. We found that mental illness and infant mortality rates were two or three times as high in more unequal countries.[1] Teenage birth rates, the proportion of the population in prison and, in some analyses, homicide rates were as much as ten times higher in more unequal societies.[1]

There is a widespread belief that the reason why so many problems tend to be more common lower down than higher up on the social ladder reflects the kinds of people who end up at either end – the idea that the capable and resilient climb up, while the vulnerable slip down into poverty and deprivation. The evidence of the effects of inequality presents a fundamental challenge to this view. Insofar as societies work as sorting systems, moving the fit upwards and the unfit downwards, that would obviously contribute to a greater burden of ill-health and other problems nearer the bottom of society. But shifting people up or down the social ladder would not, in itself, change the total number of people with any particular characteristic in society. If, for example, social mobility sorted people according to whether they had fairer or darker hair, that would of course create a social gradient in hair colour, but it would not change the overall proportion of people with either light or dark hair. The same is true if people were sorted according to their vulnerability to illness or tendency to violence.

However, the effect of changing inequality in a society is precisely to change the overall burden of almost all the problems with social gradients. Bigger income gaps not only make these problems worse, but, because they have a larger effect on the poor than the better off, they make the social gradients in different outcomes steeper. The implication is that social gradients in health, the incidence of violence and children's maths and literacy scores, among other measures, are not simply the result of a social sorting process. Something else must be going on. Our explanation is that these problems are driven by the stress of social status differences themselves, stresses which get worse the lower you are on the social ladder and the bigger the status differences. In effect, bigger income differences make status differences more potent.

By raising the stakes and making the differences more apparent, income and social position are seen as ever-more prominent indicators – measures almost – of a person's worth. Each step down the status hierarchy matters more as we come increasingly to judge each other by status. It is not surprising that problems which are sensitive to social status within our societies get worse when status differences increase.

MOVING ON

That, at its briefest, is where the evidence had led us almost a decade ago. We wrote *The Spirit Level* in 2007, sent it to our publisher in 2008, just as the global financial crisis was unfolding, and it was published early in 2009, with an additional chapter inserted in 2010 that responded to critics and gave a partial update. Since then the world has changed, rocked by economic crises, political polarization and populism, ideological conflicts, and the mass movement of refugees and economic migrants worldwide. Inequality has made no small contribution to all of these; and the need to combat climate change has become ever more urgent. At the same time, researchers from many different disciplines, including psychology, economics and environmental science, have added a rich body of new evidence on the impact of inequality. The result is that we can now see more clearly how inequality affects our values, our sense of self-worth, the way people feel towards each other and our mental health. In laying out in this book how inequality gets into our heads and our spirits, we also shed light on the causal processes that lead to a greater burden of health and social problems. This book brings together that new body of work and evidence to develop a vision of how we can create societies, economies and communities that focus on the sustainable well-being of people and the planet. Inequality may be entrenched in many of the societies we examine, but its current levels are neither inevitable nor irreversible. And despite the many challenges the last decade has brought, a better world is possible.

Note on Data and Figures

Most of the graphs we present in this book are charts linking income inequality to different health and social problems. Some show this relationship across different countries, others across the different states of the USA.

In our previous book, we aimed to present a consistent set of data by always using the same measure of inequality, the same set of countries and so on. As well as our own new analyses, in this book we present graphs and data that have been produced by researchers from all over the world. Each group of researchers has chosen, from official sources, the most appropriate measure of income inequality to use to answer their research questions, which countries or states and what years to include in the analysis, how to measure the outcomes they are interested in, how to analyse the data and draw the graphs. In each case, the researchers have carefully described their methods in the peer-reviewed journals and official reports that we use; all of these are included in the reference section at the back of this book and many are freely available online. Where possible, and when the data have been available publicly or through the kindness of other researchers, we have re-drawn graphs to be as easy to read as possible. All of the graphs we show come from reputable sources, almost all of them from academics publishing in peer-reviewed journals, and all of our own new analyses have also been peer-reviewed.

Although readers will see that there are differences in the countries studied, the years for which data are reported and the measures used, the most remarkable feature of this variation is that the overall picture we see is so consistent.

'It's a great party. Everyone here is more insecure than I am!'

I

This is Not a Self-help Book

> 'Many people of balanced mind and congenial activity
> scarcely know that they care what others think of them,
> and will deny, perhaps with indignation, that such care is
> an important factor in what they are and do. But this is an
> illusion. If failure or disgrace arrives, if one suddenly finds
> that the faces of men show coldness or contempt instead
> of the kindliness and deference that he is used to, he will
> perceive from the shock, the fear, the sense of being out-
> cast and helpless, that he was living in the minds of others
> without knowing it, just as we daily walk the solid ground
> without thinking how it bears us up.'
>
> Charles Cooley, Human Nature and
> the Social Order, 1902, p. 207[5]

In an article in Oprah Winfrey's O *Magazine*, her 'style coach', Martha Beck, discusses her experience of what she calls 'party anxiety'.[6]
When exposed to other people, she says the 'real enemies are shame,
fear, and cruel judgment'. Beck says she is 'one of the millions of party-
impaired people . . . social-phobes [who] dread party talk', who are
'petrified of saying something stupid, something that will reveal us as
the jackasses we are, rather than the social maestros we wish we were'.
She says that she felt she 'needed a whole armoury full of impressive
weapons to survive a party – things like cleverness, thin thighs, social
connections, and wealth . . . Every act, from choosing clothes to making small talk, is a fear-based defense against criticism.'

We treat our shyness, self-doubt and frequent inability to feel at ease with others as if they were purely personal psychological weaknesses, as if they were flaws built into our emotional make-up that we must cope with on our own as best we can. Because we tend to hide these insecurities from each other, we fail to see them in others. But, as we shall see, surveys suggest they are so widespread that few but the most confident escape them. Indeed, Alfred Adler, the Austrian psychoanalyst who broke away from Freud's circle early in the twentieth century, saw them as so fundamental to our human make-up that he developed the concept of the 'inferiority complex', and maintained that: 'To be human means to feel inferior.' Adler also saw what the statistics now demonstrate, that people respond to these feelings in two different ways – with shyness, low self-esteem and sometimes social phobia, or, alternatively, by hiding their insecurity under a show of self-importance, pomposity, narcissism and snobbery. He interpreted people's attitudes of superiority as a defence against underlying feelings of inferiority. The stronger the underlying sense of inferiority, the stronger Adler thought that defence was likely to be. 'Behind everyone who behaves as if he were superior to others, we can suspect a feeling of inferiority which calls for very special efforts of concealment.' 'The greater the feeling of inferiority . . . the more powerful is the urge to conquest and the more violent the emotional agitation.'[7] It is of course because these 'efforts of concealment' are effective that we underestimate how widespread these insecurities are, and imagine our own are a personal affliction.

What Adler could not see simply in his patients' psychologies, but which we can see with the help of modern statistics, is that these difficulties – and with them the different forms of concealment – are in fact much more common in some societies than others. This suggests that there are powerful external factors, which we may be able to identify, that make them better or worse for all of us.

Epidemiologists are trained to study the distribution and determinants of disease. They might, for example, try to identify the extent to which diseases like asthma and bronchitis are made worse by air pollution. Approaching the frequency of shyness, social anxiety and self-doubt in this way, as if they were caused – or at least made worse – by something in the emotional or social atmosphere, may enable us to identify those causes. Though we are all used to the idea that there are pollutants and carcinogens in the environment that have to be reduced in order to diminish the burden of physical disease, we are less used to the idea of tackling harmful emotional or psychological environments. Yet if the causes of heightened levels of social anxiety are the source of serious damage to social life and well-being, they surely warrant as much political and public attention as the air we breathe.

We are a social species, and our sensitivity to each other and our ability to avoid behaviour which might offend others are necessary skills. But a normal and beneficial sensitivity to people around us is being triggered so frequently and so strongly in everyday life today that for many it has become an intensely counterproductive reaction. Feelings of insecurity are often so great that people react defensively to even minor criticism; others are seemingly so nervous of social interaction that they isolate themselves. We also see endless signs of the desire for the trappings of status behind which people try to hide their insecurity. The widespread lack of confidence and sense of insecurity have reached a level of intensity that makes them perhaps the most important limitation on levels of happiness and the quality of life throughout many rich societies. The answer, as we will show, is not for us all to learn to become more like the most thick-skinned; it is instead to identify and deal with the factors in society that do the damage.

To understand the distinction between the components of shyness and self-consciousness which come from within and those which come from outside, imagine people running a hurdles race. If you wanted to know why some runners knock down more hurdles than others, you would look at individual differences between the runners – their ages, fitness, height, etc. But if you wanted to know why more hurdles were knocked down in some athletics meetings than others, you'd start by looking at whether the hurdles were higher in some than others. Similarly, if you wanted to know why some people could or couldn't do a bit of mental arithmetic, you would look at individual differences in their capacity and familiarity with arithmetic, but if you wanted to know why more people could solve one problem than another, you'd look at differences in how hard the problems were.

This is not a self-help book, and we will devote very little time to discussing the personal sources of individual differences in confidence and shyness. Our hope is that, by identifying why our social inhibitions are so easily triggered, we will have contributed to an improvement in the well-being of whole populations. Our primary focus is on the 'vertical inequalities' in society, on the effect of material differences from top to bottom of society, their implications for social hierarchy and status that lead us to value people differently and which feed into personal feelings of confidence or self-doubt. The so-called 'horizontal inequalities' between whole groups of people, whether defined by gender, ethnicity, class, disability, religion, language or culture, are experienced as major injustices because they involve the same issues of superiority and inferiority. Rather than concentrating on any of these particular group distinctions, our aim is to unravel the processes of dominance and subordination that are central to all such experiences of inequality. We begin by discussing our common vulnerability to them. In effect, we need to understand the receptors of social pain before we can recognize the structural causes of that pain.

Today we live in societies in which worries about how we are seen and judged by others – what psychologists call 'the social evaluative threat' – are one of the most serious burdens on the quality and experience of life in rich developed countries. The costs are measured not only in terms of additional stress, anxiety and depression, but also in poorer physical health, in the frequent resort to drink and drugs we use to keep our anxieties at bay, and in the loss of friendly community life which leaves so many people feeling isolated and alone. These insecurities are a cancer in the midst of our social life. Yet, despite this, they rarely if ever feature in measures of the quality of life.

Rather than discussing individual differences in genetics, early childhood experiences, or how people were treated at school, which might underlie differences in individual vulnerability, we instead treat this as a public health problem. Public health has always been highly political, from the provision of sewers and the Clean Air Acts to more recent battles over vehicle exhaust emissions. As the nineteenth-century German pathologist Rudolf Virchow said,

'Medicine is a social science and politics is nothing else than medicine on a large scale.' This book follows in that tradition.

SOCIAL ANXIETIES

Shyness is a very common sign of our feelings of vulnerability to how others see us. The most widely referenced survey of shyness is the Stanford Shyness Survey. It found that over 80 per cent of Americans surveyed said they were shy during some period of their lives, whether now, in the past, or always. One-third said they felt shy at least half the time and in more situations than not.[8] About a quarter regarded themselves as chronically shy. Although fewer than 20 per cent of respondents did not regard themselves as shy, most people even in this group reported that they sometimes experienced what are usually regarded as symptoms of shyness – blushing, a pounding heart or 'butterflies in the stomach'. These people appeared not to regard themselves as shy because they experienced shyness only in occasional situations. Only 7 per cent of those surveyed said they never felt shy.

Between 2001 and 2004, the US National Comorbidity Survey – Adolescent Supplement, surveyed over 10,000 American teenagers (13–18 years old). Asked to 'rate their shyness around people their own age who they didn't know very well', almost half regarded themselves as shy, but their parents reported that over 60 per cent of them were shy.[9]

Feeling shy means feeling increased self-consciousness, a sense of awkwardness and anxiety in relation to others, a lack of confidence in your social competence, which produce levels of stress which interfere with and interrupt thought processes. It makes it harder to interact with other people and enjoy their company, and harder to think and express yourself clearly – often to the detriment of careers and social life. Those who suffer high levels of shyness may be classified as suffering from social phobia, social anxiety or social anxiety disorder, but the clinical criteria for these conditions are designed to catch only the most severe end of the spectrum. People are only classified as having 'social anxiety disorder' when their fears and anxieties are 'grossly disproportionate to the actual situation' – and that is, of course, largely a reflection of what is regarded as normal.

A small minority of people find their lack of confidence so inhibiting, and social life such an ordeal, that they avoid contact with other people as much as possible. Many are so racked by social anxieties that the pleasure of meeting others is far outweighed by the stress. The following examples, from four different people, are all taken from the Experience Project website, set up to allow people to share their emotional problems.

> In social situations I shut down and I tend to be awkward because I'm scared of people judging me and not liking me so much that I just distance myself. I hear people laughing and I immediately think they're laughing at me (which is stupid) but I can't help it. Over the years I have learned to embrace the loner life style . . .

> Sometimes I avoid anyone and everyone because I can't stand the thought of them judging me.

> I'll have panic attacks over something as simple as going to the checkout at Walmart. I do self-checkouts so I don't have to talk to anyone.

> I am extremely shy around both people I know and don't know. It hinders my everyday life so much that people think I am making it up. I have no friends. It is hard for me to go anywhere. I always make sure I go shopping in the day – that way I can wear sunglasses or a hat. It is my security blanket from Social Anxiety Disorder. I get tongue-tied and sweaty, then I feel like they're looking at me like I am some sort of freak! It is a living hell I struggle with on a daily basis.

Accounts like these of self-imposed isolation leave no doubt as to the amount of pain felt by those afflicted or why normal life can become impossible for them. Many of those experiencing high levels of anxiety regard themselves as suffering from a mental illness; they seek medical help from professionals and are often prescribed anxiolytics (anti-anxiety medications) and other psychoactive drugs. Since 1980, social anxiety has been included in the American Psychiatric Association's classification of mental disorders – the *Diagnostic and Statistical Manual* (DSM). Unlike common levels of shyness, the prevalence of social anxiety has been carefully measured over time.

In the USA the number of those suffering from social anxiety disorder has increased over the last three decades from 2 per cent to 12 per cent of the population.[10-12]

RISING MENTAL ILLNESS AND STRESS

The rich developed countries have for some time been suffering from high and rising rates of mental illness. The better surveys take great care to make sure that they count only severe and disabling conditions and are not simply a reflection of changes in the awareness of mental illness among either the medical profession or the public. There are strict criteria for assessing the seriousness of conditions, designed to exclude minor mental and emotional upsets. One of the most respected and frequently cited studies, which measured the frequency of mental illness in the USA during the years 2001–2003, was the National Comorbidity Survey Replication. Using questionnaires designed and tested for their ability to identify people with mental disorders, trained research workers interviewed almost 10,000 people for an hour in their homes.[13] Among people aged 18–75, 46 per cent reported that sometime in their lives they had had symptoms which met the criteria for one or other mental disorder, not only in terms of symptoms but also in duration and the disabling effect of the disorder in question.

The biggest weakness in the way these statistics are compiled is that they mostly depend on memory. Studies that have compared retrospective surveys, which depend on recall, with ones that interview the same people repeatedly over time, find that people either forget some earlier episodes of mental illness or are reluctant to mention them. This means that wthe figures most commonly quoted – including that 46 per cent – are almost certainly substantial underestimates of the scale of the problem.

The evidence that rates of mental illness have been rising comes partly from comparing the experience of different age groups. Looking back over their lives, younger people seem to suffer higher rates of illness per year than are reported by older people. This is not just a reflection of poorer memory among the older age groups. That explanation is decisively ruled out by studies which have compared anxiety rates in successive samples of students and children over the years. One such study compared samples from all over the USA, spanning the years 1952 to 1993. It found dramatic increases in levels of anxiety among both the student and adult populations over that forty-year period, so much so that the report's author said that 'The average American child in the 1980s reported more anxiety than child psychiatric patients in the 1950s.'[14] In the UK, researchers from King's College London found that teenagers in 2006 had much higher levels of problems, particularly serious emotional difficulties, than teenagers just twenty years earlier.[15] The rising trend was true for boys and girls, and was found whether they lived in families with both parents or with single or step-parents, and whether or not they lived in poverty. An American Psychological Association survey in 2017 found that 80 per cent of Americans reported one or more symptoms of stress, such as feeling overwhelmed, depressed, nervous or anxious. When asked to rate how stressed they felt, on a scale from 1 (little or no stress) to 10 (a great deal of stress), 20 per cent rated themselves an 8, 9 or 10.[16]*

Although anxiety and depression disorders are the most common afflictions, there have also been rises in the other main categories of mental health problems, including other mood disorders, impulse-control disorders and substance abuse disorders. That they have all been rising together might lead us to expect some underlying common causes. It would be surprising if anxiety was not one of them.

It is difficult to assess how rates of shyness and social anxiety contribute to mental illness. The system for classifying mental illness, with few exceptions, categorizes by symptom rather than by cause. People can react to the same underlying anxieties in very different ways: if your social anxiety means you panic when you go out, you might be

* Since first publication of this book, a number of studies have confirmed that rates of mental illness continue to rise. In 2018 the Mental Health Foundation reported that 74 per cent of adults in the United Kingdom were so stressed that they sometimes felt overwhelmed and unable to cope. Thirty-two per cent had had suicidal thoughts, and half that number had self-harmed. In the same year, a nationwide survey of 6,700 adults in the USA found that 79 per cent felt stressed each day, 57 per cent to the point of feeling 'paralyzed' by stress. Twenty per cent of adults and 52 per cent of young people were found to have mental health problems severe enough to meet psychiatrists' diagnostic criteria for mental illness. And all this is among populations living in unprecedented standards of material comfort.

classified as suffering from agoraphobia; if it makes you depressed, then as depression; if over the years your attempts to steady your nerves develops into alcohol dependence, then alcoholism is itself classified as a mental disorder. If your worries about how you are regarded mean you are always trying to impress or are too concerned with what you look like, then, perhaps (with a few other contributing factors), you might be thought to be suffering from narcissistic personality disorder.

Just as risks of heart disease can be increased by many different causes, including lack of exercise, poor diet, smoking, stress, diabetes, obesity and high blood pressure, so numerous different factors can contribute to each kind of mental illness. However, not only are most physical and mental illnesses multi-causal, but most causes contribute to many different diseases – you could say these 'broad spectrum' causes are 'multi-diseasal'. For example, a list of diseases to which smoking contributes would include emphysema, chronic bronchitis, asthma attacks, lung cancer and cancers in at least ten other parts of the body, stroke, diabetes, heart disease, and a good many others.

Evidence that almost two-thirds of the population with social anxiety disorder suffer from other comorbid disorders, ranging from bipolar disorder to eating disorders and drug dependence, serves as a caution against thinking that shyness, rises in anxiety and increases in a wide range of mental illnesses are independent of each other. Feeling overly self-conscious, stressed and ill-at-ease when with other people, sometimes combined with almost overwhelming doubts about your self-worth, is a mix which strikes at the heart of our social existence. It would be hard to devise anything as psychologically damaging as circumstances that simultaneously undermine how we get on with other people and how we feel about ourselves.

Given that economic growth has brought us unprecedented luxury and comfort, it seems paradoxical that levels of anxiety have tended to increase rather than decrease over time. Being better off than previous generations should surely mean we have less to worry about compared either to our predecessors or to people in countries which have not yet enjoyed the same increases in living standards. However, the survey figures compiled by the World Health Organization (WHO) to provide a basis for international comparisons suggest that richer countries have substantially higher rates of mental illness than poorer countries.[13] WHO surveys conducted in the early years of this century found that the lifetime prevalence of any mental disorder was 55% in the USA, 49% in New Zealand, 33% in Germany, 43% in the Netherlands, but only 20% in Nigeria and 18% in China.

If anxiety has increased despite rising living standards, then that should shift the focus of any attempt to identify causes from material difficulties to social life. The greater prominence of the self-conscious emotions, including shyness and social anxiety, may be an important contributor to the rises in anxiety as a whole. But because material standards tend to play such an important role in our presentation of ourselves, they are not absolved from being a focus of anxiety. Instead of worrying primarily about keeping body and soul together, the balance has changed. Having (for the most part) reached a standard of living unthinkable a couple of centuries ago, we now worry much more about maintaining standards in relation to others – where we are in relation to the norms of our society and position within it. Our concern with living standards is closely related to the anxieties round self-worth and social comparisons mentioned earlier. There is, for example, a substantial body of research showing how well-being and satisfaction with our own pay depends substantially on how it compares with other people's pay, rather than whether it provides us with what we need.[17, 18] Our argument is not that there was a time when people did not make social comparisons, but that they have become more important to our sense of ourselves than they once were.

Worries about what others think of us often interact powerfully with judgements of and insecurities about social status. That means they may appear to depend on many factors that influence social status – everything from anxieties about exams, jobs, money and promotion, to worries about how your children behave in public.

APART TOGETHER

The press has greeted research reports about rises in anxiety and mental illness with a succession of alarming headlines: 'The Epidemic of Worry',[19] 'The Maddening of America',[20] 'The Anxiety Epidemic Sweeping Britain'.[21] In the words of commentators, 'The

United States has transformed into the planet's undisputed worry champion',[22] and 'Severe, disabling mental illness has dramatically increased in the United States'.[23] The data quoted from research on the scale of the increase in mental illness have been hardly less dramatic than the headlines: 'In 1980, 4% of Americans suffered a mental disorder associated with anxiety. Today half do.'[24] 'Anxiety epidemic affects 8.2 million in the UK'.[21] 'The tally of those who are so disabled by mental disorders that they qualify for Supplemental Security Income or Social Security Disability Insurance increased nearly two and a half times between 1987 and 2007. Among children there was a 35-fold increase during the same period.'[25]

There is no clear dividing line between people whose lives are drastically restricted by how stressful they find almost any social contact and those who experience levels of shyness more typical of the majority of the population. Those sharing experiences of incapacitating levels of social anxiety online, such as those quoted earlier, include women and men, young people, parents, soldiers and even people who find themselves struggling to do jobs which involve more than a minimal degree of social exposure and performance. No section of society is unscathed by social anxiety. We quoted at the beginning of this chapter Martha Beck's account of her 'party anxiety', which would have been recognized by many of her readers.[7] Famous for his outdoor survival skills, toughness and ability to deal with any eventuality, Bear Grylls' lifestyle could hardly differ more from that of a style coach. Yet in a TV programme on climate change with former US President Barack Obama, he admitted that what he most fears are not snakes or poisonous spiders, but cocktail parties.

Public appearances of course heighten these anxieties. In a Saturday column in the *Guardian* newspaper called 'How I Get Ready', celebrities described how they prepare to be seen – a process which usually takes several hours and sometimes starts a day before an appearance. Despite careful attention to hair, nails, make-up and clothes, both women and men mention their nervousness, and regard having a few drinks to steady their nerves as part of the preparation. Some also admit to cancelling a booking if they 'don't feel up to it'.

But even without having to appear in public, a great many of us show signs of feeling that in some way we are just not good enough.

When people are expecting visitors to their home, most (though perhaps fewer of those who employ someone else to do their housework) do extra vacuuming, cleaning and tidying before guests arrive. We prefer to hide how we really live – even from friends. Occasional exceptions are of course made for people who know us too well for pretences: we just hope that as they already know how we live they will accept us, warts and all. But with most other people – typically including our in-laws and relations – we try to present ourselves as having higher standards than we really do.

Although a large majority of the population probably clean and tidy before visitors come, we tend to do it rather secretively. We don't tell our guests that we only just managed to finish clearing up as they arrived at the door, even though most people admit that this is true of them too. It is such a widespread pattern that websites give advice on the quickest ways to clear up before guests arrive: tips on what makes most difference in the shortest time. According to one survey, people take an average of 28 minutes to tidy up in preparation for visitors.[26] Just how embarrassed people feel about their housekeeping is shown by the quarter of those surveyed who admitted to trying to prevent guests from entering their home and seeing their untidiness. In their hurry to clear up, people say they hide things away in the washing machine, tumble dryer or laundry basket. Fifteen per cent admit to hiding dirty dishes in the oven.[26]

People often disguise their motives for doing this even from themselves, saying things like 'I just think it's nice to have your home all pretty for your guests to make them feel comfortable during their time with you.' But the reality of feeling the need to hide a guilty secret shows through when the same person went on to say: 'No one needs to know what a slob I can really be; I'm certainly not proud of it. But . . . part of me does wish that I could let people into a normal day's mess without feeling anxiety or judgement.' She adds that that would feel 'quite freeing'.[27]

Signs of our concern for social appearance are everywhere. It is as if most of us fear being seen for what we are, as if acceptance depended on hiding some awful truth about ourselves: what we really look like, our ignorance, signs of ageing, unemployment, low pay, incipient alcohol dependence, humourlessness, inability to make small talk – in fact anything which might make others view us less positively.

For most people these feelings are not usually serious, but they are nevertheless a mild source of additional stress in a great many spheres of life. As such, they increase our vulnerability to other difficulties. For example, to stiffen your nerve, you might get used to drinking more than you should, or become oversensitive to what people say, or start to be seen as 'touchy'. Nervousness can make you more inhibited. Some become depressed by a sense of failure. In the absence of easy and enjoyable interaction with people, you become more prone to having slight paranoia about others. When these difficulties seem to be piling up it would be tempting – for example – to start feigning sickness, and taking extra days off work. You might comfort eat, or find it harder to stop smoking. These behaviours could themselves become additional things to hide from others, or reasons to avoid them altogether, so making you more socially isolated.

FRIENDSHIP AND HEALTH

Being cut off from each other by high levels of social anxiety is very damaging. Over the last thirty or forty years, a large number of studies have shown that having a network of close friends, good relationships and involvement with others is extraordinarily beneficial to health. As well as its direct effects on health, anxiety also makes a powerful additional contribution to illness and reduced life expectancy because it reduces friendship, weakens community life and increases social isolation.

The best summary of evidence on the health benefits of friendship comes from a 2010 research report combining data from almost 150 different peer-reviewed studies, which together included individual data on more than 300,000 people.[28] The report concluded that having lots of friends, enjoying good relationships and being involved with others is not just an attractive idea: it is at least as important to health and longevity as not smoking. Although the long-term sick may lose friends, the studies found that having fewer friends led to poorer health.

Many of the studies of friendship and health were observational: they asked initially healthy people about their friendship patterns and followed them over time while taking differences in education, income or class into account to ensure that they compared like with like. But there have also been experimental studies. One involved making blister wounds on the arms of volunteers. It found that they healed more slowly among people who had more hostile relationships.[29] Another, in which volunteers were given nasal drops containing cold viruses, found that after the same measured exposure to infection, people with fewer friends were four times as likely to develop colds, even after taking account of prior antibody levels and a number of other factors.[30]

Causes of health and illness which stand out most clearly in population data are likely to be those which at least some people have too much or too little of. For example, the effects of vitamin deficiency were most obvious when many people were short of nutrients. Scurvy couldn't be ignored on long sea voyages when people were short of fresh fruit and vegetables, but in well-nourished populations the evidence that particular nutrients are important for health is much less obvious. It is the same with friendship. Because studies depend on comparisons, what makes it possible for so many studies of large random samples of the population to provide evidence that friendship and social networks are so protective of health, is that each sample contains not only people with good social networks but also a large number whose networks fall below some level of adequacy. It is an odd paradox that in our modern, densely populated urban societies, there is a shortage of friendship and good relationships; people are together, but separate. Recognizing the importance of social bonds to health, people in Germany sometimes refer to them as 'vitamin B' – for *Beziehungen*, meaning 'relationships'. To remember the health benefits of friendship, English speakers would do well to remember the importance of vitamin F.

Much of the effect of friendship on health is likely to be rooted in reduced stress and increased social ease which means that people are less likely to 'keep themselves to themselves'. The health differences between people who are more and less sociable will partly reflect differences in the stresses and anxieties that make us either welcome or avoid social contact in the first place. Even people who experience only mild levels of shyness or self-consciousness will sometimes feel social contact involves too much of an effort and would prefer to stay at home than go out. Those more susceptible to social anxiety will often find social gatherings so stressful that they regard them as an ordeal to be avoided whenever possible.

Sustained over long periods, stress is damaging to health. It interferes with many different physiological processes, including the immune and cardiovascular systems. When prolonged, its effects are similar to more rapid ageing: people become vulnerable to the effects of old age – including the risks of degenerative diseases and death – earlier than they otherwise would. And if even fairly low levels of stress continue for months and years, the evidence shows (Figure 1.1) that death rates are raised and lives shortened.[31]

But although the number of friends people have is sometimes an indication of how stressful they find social contact, that is not the only reason friendship and health are related. At its heart it is about whether people feel liked or disliked, valued or devalued, by others. Having friends who value you makes you feel better about yourself and increases confidence, just as feeling excluded and unwanted has the opposite effect. It's a two-way relationship: whether or not you have friends is partly a reflection of how easy or difficult you find

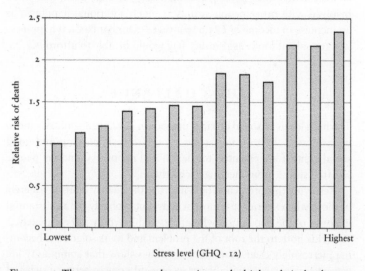

Figure 1.1: The more stress people experience, the higher their death rates. Data include 8,365 deaths among 75,936 people (aged 35 years and older living in England) whose levels of distress were surveyed using measures of anxiety, depression, social dysfunction and loss of confidence.[31]

social contact, but having friends increases feelings of self-efficacy and confidence.[32, 33] It is, after all, almost impossible to remain self-confident if you feel excluded by others.

There are few sources of pleasure as important as time spent chatting and joking with friends, and it would be surprising if having friends and good social contacts was not also a key to happiness. In his book *Happiness: Lessons From a New Science*, the economist Richard Layard outlined the evidence showing how marriage, friendship, involvement in community life and voluntary work are all powerful contributors to happiness.[34] A more recent 2014 study, using data on almost 50,000 people in 25 European countries, confirmed that social interaction and feeling you can trust others makes an important contribution to happiness.[35] Human beings are more fundamentally social animals than is often recognized, and our enjoyment of relaxed social contact is a pleasure that is too often overlooked. If you had to choose between more money and more contact with other people, the data suggest that becoming more involved with other people brings as much additional happiness as an increase in income of £85,000 a year.[36] On that basis, if happiness was for sale, it looks as if rather few would be able to afford it.

THE CHALLENGE

The high levels of social anxiety in modern developed countries mean we are faced with an important conundrum. Friendship and good social contact are essential for health and happiness, and yet people so often shrink from meeting each other.

Resolving this problem would improve the quality of life not merely of those who experience it most acutely, but probably for a substantial majority of the population who are less inhibited by it. Fortunately, a vital clue both to the root of the problem and to its solution is becoming increasingly clear. A number of studies show that community life is weaker in societies with bigger income differences between rich and poor. Societies with smaller income gaps have repeatedly been shown to be more cohesive. People in more equal societies are more likely to be involved in local groups, voluntary organizations and civic associations.[37] They are more likely to feel they can trust each other, are more willing to help one another, and rates of violence (as measured by homicide rates) are consistently lower.[38-40] People get along with each other better in more equal societies.

Since before the French Revolution, the idea that inequality is divisive and socially corrosive has been widespread.[41] Now that we have sufficient data to compare inequality – as measured by income differences between rich and poor – in each country, it has become clear that this intuition is emphatically correct, perhaps more so than we ever imagined. Rather than a private hunch, it has – as hundreds of studies now show – become an objectively demonstrable truth.[2, 3] Figure 2.7 in the next chapter shows the international association between income inequality and participation in local organizations and groups. In *The Spirit Level* we showed similar relationships between inequality and measures of trust.

We thought that the most likely explanation for why community life is stronger in more equal societies might be that people are more at ease with each other in those societies; greater equality might make mixing easier if it meant there were smaller differences in perceptions of personal worth. Most people do, after all, tend to choose their friends from among their near equals. Although that is certainly true, the causal processes are not quite so simple: social anxiety does not just affect people when in the company of those who are better off than them. People worry about failing to create a good impression even among near equals.

The implication (and the explanation best supported by the evidence) is that the more hierarchical a society is, the stronger the idea that people are ranked according to inherent differences in worth or value, and the greater their insecurities about self-worth. This is true despite the fact that there is, as we shall see in Chapter 6 and in Figure 6.7, less social mobility in more unequal countries. Irrespective of individual differences in skills and abilities, in such countries people's social position is taken even more as indicating their worth as superior or inferior. Inevitably this exacerbates the 'social evaluative threat' and people's status anxieties. Social comparisons become more fraught, increasing insecurities about self-worth.

Rather than being confined to issues of status as conventionally understood, insecurities and social comparisons spread to include every personal characteristic that can be seen as positive or negative. Everything from physical attractiveness and intelligence to leisure activities, skin colour, aesthetic taste and consumer spending take on greater social meaning in terms of rank and worth. If social comparisons have their evolutionary roots in comparisons of relative strength in animal ranking systems, then they have become much more multifaceted and less one-dimensional among humans.

In the next few pages we will provide brief, thumbnail illustrations of how people's sense of self-worth, and their belief that they are inherently superior or inferior to others, can be affected by different kinds of structural change in the nature of the society they live in. These issues are crucial, not only for those who experience varying degrees of social anxiety, but for all of us, who, as the quotation from Charles Cooley at the beginning of this chapter makes clear, are affected by how others see us.

EGALITARIAN ORIGINS

Although inequality is central to the differential values we place on each other, and so to the worries about how people judge us, it only began to develop in human societies with the comparatively recent beginnings of agriculture. Fully stratified class systems became entrenched even more recently. These began to appear around 5,500 years ago in more densely populated agricultural societies in the Tigris and Euphrates valleys; in many parts of the world they are even more recent than that.[42, 43] Before the development of agriculture, humans lived as hunter-gatherers in remarkably egalitarian communities. Living in small groups, reliant on whatever could be hunted or foraged, might seem an almost animal-like existence. But early human societies avoided the hierarchical structures seen in many animal species, in which the strongest eat first and the dominant males monopolize access to females. As we shall see in Chapter 5, for more than 90 per cent of the time we have been 'anatomically modern' (that is to say, looking as we do now, with brains their current size), equality was the norm in human societies. The anthropological evidence suggests that equality in early human societies was maintained by what have been called 'counter dominance strategies': people who behaved in domineering ways were put in their place fairly systematically by being ignored, teased or ostracized, as others tried to maintain their autonomy.[44]

The modern anthropology of recent hunting and gathering societies shows that being embedded in a community of equals did not mean that people failed to recognize or value differences in individual skills, knowledge and abilities. More talented individuals would be respected and valued, but that did not give them power over others. There was no sense of a social system in which people became richer or poorer, living in comfort or hardship, according to some hierarchy of status and personal worth.

STATUS HIERARCHIES

In almost any hierarchical society, the way we see and relate to each other is pervaded not simply by the idea that people vary in their personal worth, but by the assumption that they are ranked from the best at the top to the least valuable at the bottom, from most able to least able, from the most admired to the least admired. And the lower you are in the hierarchy, the more stigmatized you are likely to feel. It's hard to think of anything better calculated to exacerbate all your insecurities about whether you appear as successful or as a failure, interesting or dull, clever or stupid, well-educated or ignorant, than being ranked by class.

What other people think of us is filtered through our expectations, fears and tensions about where we come in the scale of personal worth. And as we shall see in Chapter 7, a great many aspects of individual preferences and behaviour – such as aesthetic taste, pronunciation, table manners, knowledge of the arts – serve as markers of status, almost as if they were designed to trip and expose the unwary. Even the issues of body image and weight, about which so many agonize, are drawn into the same arena because people know they affect selection for jobs and marriage: that attractive people are more likely to move up the social ladder.[45, 46]

But class distinctions work in different ways in different societies.

Haddon Hall, in Derbyshire in England, dates from the twelfth century. It is advertised as 'probably the finest example of a fortified medieval manor house in existence'. When visitors are shown the main hall, they are told that everyone – including the members of the noble family who owned the Hall and all their servants – would have lived and slept (usually on the floor) in this one huge room. A community of perhaps fifty people would have shared a level of intimacy which we now rarely experience even within the family home. Though normal for the period, this level of mixing and exposure between classes later became unacceptable. At Haddon, a wall was erected some centuries later to separate off rooms where the family owning the Hall could enjoy more privacy. This would have added strongly to the sense of social division between superiors and inferiors.

By the nineteenth century the degree of social class separation throughout society had become even more pointed. Although almost all upper-middle-class families had servants living in their houses with them, they tried to ensure that contact with them was reduced to a minimum. Servants slept in cramped attic rooms at the top of the house and worked in the kitchen and scullery, usually situated in the basement or ground floor of urban houses. To allow them to get from attic to basement without meeting their employers, these houses usually had a narrow servants' staircase, as well as a grander main one. The aim was to enable different classes to live in the same house while interacting as little as possible. For the same reason, as well as the front door, they had a separate servants' and tradesmen's entrance. And, of course, going with these social distinctions went an ideology that higher classes had breeding and refinement built into them which set them apart from what seemed to be the rough-hewn or 'common' nature of those who made up the lower social classes.

LOSS OF SETTLED COMMUNITIES

Part of our increased anxiety about what others think of us reflects the fact that most of us no longer live in settled communities with people who have known us all our lives. Instead, for much of the course of daily life we are surrounded by relative strangers. The result is that where the way we were defined in each other's eyes was once formed over a lifetime and hard to change, there is now a sense that who we are, and how others see us, is always more fluid and subject to constant reassessment. In a society of strangers, outward appearances and first impressions become more important.

Rarely meeting people outside the immediate community made for a less self-conscious culture in other ways as well. The relative stability of identity and lack of anxiety about social status to be found in close-knit communities is immediately apparent even to outsiders. This was evident in the peasant farmhouses in a French village which one of us (Richard) got to know a generation ago. People were almost entirely without affectation or adornment, unselfconsciously practical. In the absence of outsiders to impress, there was little or nothing inside their farmhouses which was bought or displayed simply for show. This contrasted with the urban culture of families who, despite often living in cramped accommodation, nevertheless tried to keep a 'front room' especially for visitors.

This is not to say that living your whole life in a settled community without modern transport and little geographical mobility is without its limitations. Not only are opportunities restricted, but it is also much harder to change people's view of you, to reinvent yourself or escape any stigma. When one of the farmers in the same village was asked what it was like to live in the same small community knowing the same people all his life, he thought for a moment and said wryly: 'You get to know their faults.'

The modern high rates of geographical mobility mean that, whether we like it or not, our identity is no longer settled, maintained and confirmed by other people's lifelong knowledge of us. How others see us does not become less important, only less stably embedded in others' minds. Secure only in the minds of a few close friends and family members, it is endlessly open to question. As a result, our sense of ourselves becomes less well anchored, more prone to ups and downs, and more at the mercy of passing moods. Without the stabilizing effect of an identity held in the minds of a community of people, it is as if each encounter demands that we try to implant a positive version of ourselves in others' minds. To them we are simply unknown, and whether we create a good or bad impression is up to us.

SOCIAL MOBILITY

How everyone understands and experiences their relatively superior or inferior position in society also differs according to whether people normally remain in the class or caste they (and often previous generations of their family) were born into, or whether their social position can change. This is the distinction between what sociologists call 'ascribed' and 'achieved' social class. In societies where there is little or no social mobility, class is seen simply as an accident of birth and, although your class or caste may be seen as inferior, there is little sense that you are personally culpable for your low social status: you can't be blamed for your parentage. But in societies where people are regarded as moving up or down the social ladder according to individual merit and effort, status appears much more as a reflection of personal ability or virtue, so making low social status appear as a mark of individual failure.

The belief that modern market democracies are 'meritocratic', and that class position therefore reflects ability, implies that these societies are in some sense fair: that differences in status are justified. The result is that low social status appears even more as if it were a mark of personal inadequacy and failure. It strengthens the widespread tendency to assess people's ability and intelligence on the basis of their social position, so making low social status still more demeaning. Nor are these tendencies confined to how we judge others. They also raise or lower people's belief in their own intelligence and ability.

The belief that social status reflects personal worth is cemented and heightened at school by our experience of exams and assessments designed to rate us by ability in comparison to others, a process which leaves permanent psychological scars in some, and feelings of superiority in others. And beyond school, whether you went to university, how prestigious it was and what class of degree you got, are all sometimes seen as indications of personal worth. In adulthood, overt processes of social comparison continue through interviews and assessments of many different kinds. One of the benefits of retirement is the knowledge that you will never again have to go through the process of being formally assessed and ranked in comparison to others. But the informal processes by which people assess each other's position in the hierarchy remain.

INCOME INEQUALITY

The scale of income and wealth differences in a society is not just an additional element in status and class differentiation; it now provides the main framework or scaffolding on which markers of social status are assembled. In effect, bigger income differences make the social pyramid taller and steeper. In his book *Distinction*, the French sociologist Pierre Bourdieu showed how much we use income to express status – not only through cars, clothing and housing, but also through things which demonstrate 'taste', like the books, restaurants and music we choose.[47] That tendency means that bigger income differences both enable and motivate more obvious status differences. With that goes the tendency for people who are richer to be regarded as superior and to think they are better than other people. (The reasons for this connection in our evolved psychology will be discussed in Chapter 5.) Greater inequality makes money more important as a key to status and a way of expressing your 'worth'.

In *The Spirit Level*, we showed that income differences make class and status more powerful.[1] The problems related to social position, like poor health, violence and low educational performance, which all become more common at each step down the social ladder, also get worse in societies with wider income gaps. The larger the disparities in income, the bigger the differences in lifestyles which express class position, and the more invidious and conspicuous inferior status feels.

Material differences are a crucial key to status in almost all societies. Ranking systems are fundamentally about gaining access to resources, and that is true whether we are talking about the importance of money in modern life, of land holdings in feudal societies, or even the way dominant animals gain first access to food. Power matters because it ensures privileged access to all the necessities, pleasures and comforts of life. Although it is easy to confuse the trappings of status for its fundamentals, if you either make or lose a fortune it will eventually affect your social position. Even when, in the nineteenth century, people imagined that class was a matter of good breeding, people who drank or gambled their money away may have been regarded as 'genteel poor' for a generation, but by the next generation the family was just poor. Similarly, if you made substantial sums of money you might initially have been regarded as 'nouveau riche', but by the time your children and grandchildren had picked up a modicum of class culture, they would be accepted among their financial equals. Although it is hard to identify or measure the processes by which the socially mobile become integrated into their new class, the impression is that – at least among the rich nations – they have accelerated over the past century. It is therefore perhaps clearer now than it once was that the scale of differences in income and wealth in a society is a powerful determinant of whether the class social pyramid is very tall, with big social distances between rich and poor, or whether it is much broader and shallower with smaller social distances between people.

In rich market societies today there is little masking of the importance of money in how we are seen and how we try to influence people's judgements of us. Few of the most obvious markers of status – from houses and cars, to holidays, brands of clothing and electronic gadgetry – do not involve expenditure. And the more expensive they appear to be, the better they serve the purpose.

It was the American economist and sociologist Thorstein Veblen who, in 1899, first put forward the concept of 'conspicuous consumption' to draw attention to how people use purchases to express their social status aspirations.[48] Modern research shows clearly that as people get richer, they choose to increase their expenditure more on goods and services that express status and can be seen by others, than on ones which don't and can't. So, as people become better off, they spend more on what can be seen in public: up-market mobile phones, pedigree dogs, watches, jewellery and cars rather than home furnishings. As we vie for status, what is less publicly visible matters less.[49]

Veblen lived during what has been called the 'Gilded Age', when differences in income and wealth between rich and poor were very large, and men like Andrew Carnegie and John D. Rockefeller built their fortunes. His death in 1929 came at the beginning of a long period of narrowing income differences. That narrowing continued until the late 1970s. Since then, however, income differences have widened almost continuously and we have now returned to levels of inequality not seen since Veblen's day. These long-term changes in income inequality can be seen in Figure 9.1 in the last chapter.

All the progress towards greater equality which was made in the intervening decades has been lost, and the inflated salaries and bonuses of many bankers and company CEOs have allowed them to found new dynasties in which their children and grandchildren will be able to live on unearned income in perpetuity. In the same way as the yawning gap between rich and poor led to the conspicuous consumption of Veblen's day, so the rise in inequality since the end of the 1970s has intensified status competition and consumerism in our own societies.

While low incomes limit what poorer people can buy, they leave status aspirations undiminished – or even heightened – by the desire to escape the stigma of low social status. That is why it was particularly designer-label clothes and high status electronic goods that were stolen by young people who rioted almost simultaneously in many different places in England during the summer of 2011.[50]

How strongly we are affected by social hierarchy is increased or decreased not only by the scale of income differences between rich and poor, but also by the ever-widening range of goods that can be used to express status. Both factors make income and status differences more visible. Outward wealth is so often seen as if it was a measure of inner worth. And as greater inequality makes social position more visible, we come to judge each other more by status. With more social evaluation anxieties, problems of self-esteem, self-confidence and status insecurity become more fraught.

The CEOs of many large multinational corporations are now paid three hundred or four hundred times as much as the least-well-paid full-time workers in the same companies. In a society in which status is increasingly defined by relative income, it is hard to imagine a more powerful way of telling a large swathe of the population that they are almost worthless than to pay them a quarter of 1 per cent of what someone else in the same company is paid. The suggestion made by some commentators that the poor lack self-esteem, as if that was a cause rather than an effect of their circumstances, underscores the strength of the connection between income and status.

EQUALITY RE-ENVISIONED

Perhaps because people tend to imagine that human beings have always lived in hierarchical societies, we rarely, if ever, stop to imagine what it would be like to belong to a community of near equals, free of the insecurities caused by class and status divisions. We assume that the only way to regain the confidence and social ease which we lack would be to increase our own status, to be better educated, more affluent or successful, or to live a more interesting and enviable life.

There are, however, some intriguing indicators that living in much more egalitarian communities may make rather fundamental differences to human relationships and stress levels. A few recent studies show the physiological effects of 'modernization' – the shift from traditional rural cultures to developed urban societies. For example, it is well known that blood pressure tends to rise among people frequently exposed to stress.[51, 52] Partly as a consequence of that, it is taken as entirely normal in developed countries for blood pressure to rise as people get older. However, in tribal societies without settled agriculture, in which people live in non-hierarchical communities, several studies have found that blood pressure shows no tendency to rise with age.[53-55] In the Intersalt study, which measured blood pressure in 10,000 people across 32 countries, average blood pressure from the samples in developed countries was almost always between 12 and 25 points (systolic blood pressure, in mm Hg) higher among 60-year-olds than among 20-year-olds. The only two examples to show no age rise in blood pressure were the Xingu and the Yanomami foraging tribes in the Amazon rain forest.[54] That was true even when comparisons were adjusted for the effects on blood pressure of things like diet, salt intake and obesity.

That members of these tribes live together almost naked, without private areas in their huts, indicates levels of exposure to, and familiarity with, each other which would feel very uncomfortable to modern populations. Presumably if most people had felt a strong need to keep substantial areas of personal life hidden from each other, the custom would have been to erect internal walls or screens to provide privacy, rather as the owners of Haddon Hall did to separate themselves from the communal sleeping area. Just how appalling this way of living seems to those in developed societies is a measure of the fundamental changes which have taken place in the nature of human relationships even at the most personal level.

Another angle is provided by a study that recorded changes in blood pressure among nuns living in a closed order in Italy. Though they were eating much the same diet as the rest of the local population, the study found they had no rise in blood pressure as they aged during a twenty-year follow-up period. The study's authors attributed this to living in a stress-free, closed, monastic environment 'characterized by silence, meditation, and isolation from [outside] society'.[56]

It is difficult to guess what human psychology might be like in such different contexts and societies. Perhaps our hunter-gatherer ancestors did not feel that they would only be valued and accepted by others if their less attractive characteristics remained hidden. What is clear is that our modern belief that privacy is a legal right would have been alien to them. But the point of raising these issues here is not simply to glimpse what might once have been. It is instead to understand the debilitating strength of the heightened social evaluative threat we all face, how it contributes to our present social and psychological problems, and how it can be reduced. Not only does a larger area of privacy increase the potential for anxieties about what others would think if they knew what was hidden, but, as honesty has always been associated with what is done 'above board', 'out in the open' and 'for all to see', it also gives more scope for mistrust and paranoia.

The chapters ahead progress from an analysis of the problem towards ways in which it might be solved. In Chapter 2 we show that people living in countries with bigger income differences between rich and poor are more prone to status anxiety. Regardless of individual income levels, people in more unequal societies become more worried about how they are seen and judged. We also outline research which shows that those kinds of anxieties have particularly strong effects on people's levels of stress hormones. Greater inequality almost inevitably increases the tendency to regard people at the top of society as hugely important and those near the bottom as almost worthless. The result is that we judge each other more by status and become more anxious about where other people think we fit in.

There seem to be two contrasting responses to the way inequality increases the 'social evaluative threat'. High levels of social anxiety make some people feel that social life is a constant battle with low self-esteem. Lacking in confidence and overcome by extreme shyness, they tend to withdraw from social life and often become depressed. Chapter 2 also shows evidence that this kind of response is more prevalent in more unequal societies. It also provides evidence that some other common categories of mental illness involving feelings of superiority or inferiority also become more common in societies with bigger income differences.

The other common response is almost the opposite. Instead of withdrawing from social life, we show in Chapter 3 that many people respond to the status anxieties and increased worries about how others see them by projecting an exaggeratedly positive view of themselves, apparently to conceal their self-doubt. Modesty about personal abilities and achievements tends to be replaced by narcissism and a kind of self-enhancement or self-promotion. For most people this second strategy is a matter of putting on a brave face, putting their best foot forward and trying to hide their insecurities. But there are probably also people with thick skins and apparently impervious egos who feel secure in a belief in their inherent superiority. Chapter 3 provides evidence that narcissism and self-aggrandizement increase with inequality.

Working in the early twentieth century, without the benefit of statistical evidence, Alfred Adler had, as mentioned earlier, made important progress in understanding these responses to social anxieties. Whether people are overcome by a low sense of self-worth or hide it under a narcissistic cover, higher levels of social anxiety mean that they feel the need for various props to put themselves at ease, to bolster confidence or to reduce self-conscious inhibitions. The result is that people resort to drink, drugs and large numbers of prescribed psychoactive drugs to help themselves deal with high levels of anxiety. Consumerism often provides another prop to keep social anxieties and status insecurities at bay. Because a heightened social evaluative threat means that appearances matter more, people become more consumerist in an attempt to create a positive image of themselves. These responses, along with other props to boost self-confidence, are discussed in Chapter 4.

We explore the evolutionary origins of social anxiety and the powerful place it has in the human psyche in Chapter 5. The discussion there focuses on our vulnerability to each other and the extent to which good social relations have always been determinants of human well-being. Likewise, we show that ignoring how others see and react to us has also always been a serious mistake. Monitoring how people respond to us has been essential to well-being because other people have the potential to be either the greatest source of help, co-operation and assistance of every kind, or our most formidable adversaries and rivals for all the necessities of life.

In Chapter 6 we show why it is mistaken to think that the hierarchy in the societies we analyse is meritocratic, ordering people by inherent ability from the most able at the top to the least able at the bottom. The belief that people are genetically endowed with substantial differences in intelligence and ability, which determine where they end up in the social hierarchy, is almost the opposite of the truth. Brain-imaging techniques, and our growing knowledge of the malleability of the human brain, have made it clear that the most important differences in ability result *from* an individual's position in the social hierarchy, rather than being determinants of it.

We discuss in Chapter 7 how the cultural markers of status, which flesh out – or clothe – the crude differences in income and wealth, have developed to maintain visible class distinctions. Aspects of the cultural differences between classes seem to exist primarily to provide tests of status, almost for the purpose of identifying those who can be devalued and excluded.

The point of trying to understand these issues is to see what can be done to change them. In the last two chapters we suggest how we can move towards a society which will cease to generate such intense and counterproductive feelings of insecurity and self-doubt by fostering a radical egalitarianism in terms of income, class and power. However, as we show in Chapter 8, it is no longer possible to make suggestions for radical reform of the way our societies work without also taking account of the urgent need for them to become environmentally sustainable. The challenge is to combine a transformative reduction of inequality with progress towards an environmentally sustainable way of life. Fortunately, just as inequality is inimical to sustainability, we shall see that greater equality is a pre-condition for living within our planetary boundaries. But rather than having to tighten our belts and accept a deterioration in our real quality of life, we show that the key is to replace materialism – as a false source of well-being – with a way of life more fundamentally consistent with our human sociality. We believe that it is possible to achieve a more equal and sustainable society that will improve the quality of life for all. In Chapter 9, we show that this objective can be achieved not simply by some marginal redistribution of income, but by embedding greater equality more deeply into the structure of social relations to produce a better quality of life for all of us.

PART ONE
Inequality in the Mind

'Like to sample an antidepressant, sir? Brighten your day
a bit? . . . Free antidepressant, ma'am? . . .'

2

Self-doubt

'Do other people feel like this? Or is there something really wrong with me? . . . I do feel I hide the real me from people.'

Posted online, 2012, on internet chat
site I Just Want To Be Left Alone

THE ANXIETY EPIDEMIC

To test whether, as we had hypothesized, income inequality really does make us all more anxious about status and how others see us, sociologists Richard Layte and Christopher Whelan looked at levels of status anxiety in more and less unequal societies. They used data on the 35,634 adults in 31 countries (27 European Union member states, plus Norway, Croatia, Macedonia and Turkey) that took part in the European Quality of Life Survey in 2007.[57]

Respondents were asked to what extent they agreed or disagreed with the statement: *Some people look down on me because of my job situation or income*, which seems a reasonable measure of whether or not people are more or less concerned with social status and status competition in different societies. The researchers found big differences between countries in the proportion of the population who either agreed or strongly agreed with the statement. In all countries, status anxiety increased as people's income rank decreased and, as you would expect, those at the top of the income hierarchy were consistently less worried about their status than those at the bottom. But status anxiety was higher *at all income levels* in more unequal countries. Bigger income differences do, as we had predicted, increase everyone's social evaluation anxieties. Inequality makes everyone more worried about status and how they are judged by others.

In Figure 2.1, the top solid line shows the level of status anxiety in the more unequal countries, running from the poorest tenth of people living in those countries on the left, to the richest tenth of people on the right. The middle line shows the same thing for medium inequality countries, and the bottom dashed line shows the same thing for the most equal countries. Whether you are in the highest or the lowest income group, you are more likely to suffer status anxiety if you live in a more unequal country. Among the countries in this study, status anxiety was highest in more unequal countries such as Romania, Poland, Lithuania, Latvia, Portugal and Macedonia, and lowest in more equal countries such as the Czech Republic, Denmark, Norway, Sweden, Slovenia and Malta. Most of the other Western European

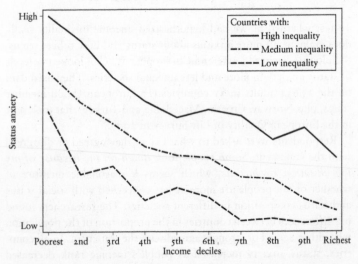

Figure 2.1: Status anxiety is higher at all levels of income in more unequal countries.[57]

countries came within the medium inequality group. Perhaps the most likely explanation of why inequality increases status anxiety across entire societies is because it increases the sense that people at the top of the social ladder are extremely important and those at the bottom almost worthless, and, as money becomes more entrenched as a measure of people's worth, it makes us all more worried about where we come in the hierarchy.

Differences in status anxiety are important. Social evaluation anxieties have been found to be a particularly powerful source of stress. There have been many studies of how levels of stress hormones respond when you have to do something stressful. Typically they measure levels of cortisol (a central stress hormone) in the blood or saliva of volunteers before, during and after a stressful task. Different studies have used different activities to make people feel stressed. Some asked volunteers to solve mathematical problems – sometimes with the additional embarrassment of having to announce their mark publicly. Others were asked to write about an unpleasant experience they had had, or were given tasks which involved verbal interaction, or being videoed, or having to put up with a loud noise. Because so many different kinds of tasks were used as stressors, Sally Dickerson and Margaret Kemeny, psychologists at the University of California, were able to go through the data to see what kind of task most reliably raised levels of cortisol.[58] They analysed results from 208 such studies and found that what pushed up stress hormones most dramatically were 'Tasks that included social-evaluative threat (such as threats to self-esteem or social status), in which others could negatively judge your performance.' Rises in cortisol were over three times as high for tasks which involved some threat of social evaluation compared to tasks which did not. Dickerson and Kemeny suggest that what is at stake is your social (as distinct from physical) self-preservation, which they say is a matter of your social value, esteem and status, based largely on other people's perception of your worth.

These findings mean that the higher levels of status anxiety across all income groups shown in Figure 2.1 are almost certainly an indication of an important increase in stress throughout the populations of more unequal countries.

ARE WE ALL GOING UNDER?

In 2010, we published an article in the *British Journal of Psychiatry*, showing that – at least in rich countries for which data was available – greater income inequality is associated with higher rates of mental illness.[59] We showed that the more unequal countries had three times as much mental illness as the more equal ones: in Japan and Germany, for example, fewer than 1 in 10 people had experienced any kind of mental illness in the past year; in Australia and the UK it was more than 1 in 5; and in the USA more than 1 in 4. The data are illustrated in Figure 2.2.

A more recent study published in 2017, which combined the data for twenty-seven separate studies, concluded that rates of mental illness are indeed higher in societies with bigger income differences.[60] But when our article came out, it received an irate response from a consultant psychiatrist.[61] His quarrel was not with us – he didn't

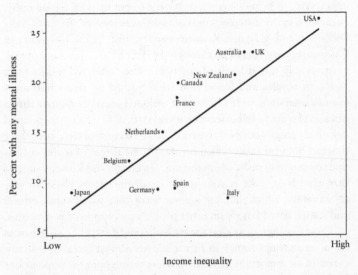

Figure 2.2: The prevalence of mental illness is higher in more unequal rich countries.[59]

question the link between inequality and mental health – but with the high rates of mental illness shown in the data we had used. How, he asked, could we take at face value such outrageous figures? One million British school children mentally ill? More than a quarter of the American adult population? He said that such figures seemed 'preposterous' to him, as a doctor and as a citizen, and represented the increasing medicalization of everyday life, a tendency to label distress, discomfort and difficult emotions as illness.

The data we had used came from the World Health Organization's World Mental Health Survey Consortium and similar epidemiological surveys of mental illness.[62-65] In all such surveys, the most commonly reported mental illnesses are depression and anxiety; the World Health Organization now estimates that depression alone affects 350 million people worldwide. Depression is the leading cause of disability in the world, as it can affect people's ability to take care of themselves and carry out their day-to-day responsibilities. Women are particularly affected, and in rich and poor countries alike depression is the number one cause of women's burden of disease, far more prevalent than the next leading causes, HIV/AIDS and tuberculosis. Unlike most physical illnesses, depression often strikes at a young age. At its most severe, depression can lead to suicide; 1 million people take their own lives every year. Suicide is a leading cause of death among people aged between eighteen and thirty years old, and contributes to rising mortality rates among middle-aged Americans.[66, 67]

So, who is right? The surveys, which suggest a heavy burden of mental illness? Or our irate psychiatrist, who deplores the modern tendency to give pathological labels to normal human emotions? Is the world suffering from an intolerable burden of disease, or are we simply mislabelling valuable human emotions and responses as illness, pathologizing sadness and anxiety, and turning everyday experiences into medical problems?

The psychiatrist's reason for not believing the evidence from carefully constructed scientific surveys stemmed from his surprise at the high rates of mental illness they suggest. The numbers are shocking. But casting our minds over family, friends and acquaintances, we can easily count episodes of depression, anxiety, self-harm, eating disorders, addictions, bipolar disorder and more which are broadly compatible with the data. As we shall see, the ways in which inequality affects mental illness rates are tied up with incentives for people to conceal their suffering and blame themselves for it – perhaps this is why we seem to regard mental illness as less common than it actually is.

LABELS AND CUT-OFFS

Before we consider *how* inequality might create depression and anxiety, we do need to be sure that the statistics we're relying on are valid and appropriate for comparing levels of mental illness in different populations. Few countries have the kinds of health-care systems and data storage that would let us compare hospital admissions or outpatient treatment rates for mental illness. In any case, these measures would be skewed by the variance in access to medical care, and the degree to which mental illness is stigmatized in different cultures and societies. For the same reasons, we can't simply ask people in a survey whether or not they have ever been treated for mental illness, or told by a doctor that they have a mental illness.

If we want to know whether a particular *individual* has a mental illness, we can refer them to a psychiatrist for a careful (also lengthy and expensive) diagnostic interview. The psychiatrist will consider his or her assessment of the patient against a system for classifying different types of mental illness. But if we want to know about the level of depression in the whole *population*, rather than in a particular individual, or examine trends in depression over time, or compare different countries, then we obviously need a method that is quicker and cheaper than the gold-standard psychiatric interview, but which nevertheless remains accurate and reliable. For these purposes, researchers use 'diagnostic interview schedules', developed in the United States in the late 1970s for large-scale surveys of mental illness in the population. They are highly structured interviews that lay out very precisely the questions that the interviewer must ask, with a substantial number of questions related to symptoms of each mental illness. Once someone has answered all the questions, their answers can be scored to decide whether or not they meet the criteria for one or more disorders. The reason these interviews can be used in large-scale surveys, despite being rather lengthy, is that they can be carried out cheaply by non-clinician interviewers with minimal training.

There have been a huge number of studies that evaluate how these interviews compare to the gold-standard psychiatric assessment, and the interviews have been refined and improved over time. The general feeling in the academic psychiatric literature is that, while they may slightly overestimate 'clinical' levels of mental illness, they allow us to reliably compare levels of mental illness over time and across different societies. The main criticism of the technique comes from those concerned about thresholds: are we labelling too many people as 'ill', when all mental health conditions exist along a continuum?[68] Some people are severely depressed, some are moderately depressed, some are mildly depressed, some have been depressed for long periods of time, others for short episodes – where should the cut-offs fall?

WHY ARE SOME GROUPS SO VULNERABLE?

To some extent, these questions about cut-offs and labels are red herrings. If we accept the consensus of experts that the surveys are reliable and reasonably accurate, then the question is not whether it is 23 per cent of British adults suffering from mental illness, as opposed to, say, 20 per cent, or whether a particular score should put you into the category of severe depression versus moderate depression, but rather: why do some societies have much higher levels of mental illness, particularly depression and anxiety, than others? And why do those levels change over time? In some countries around a quarter of the population suffers mental distress each year. If almost one in four of us feels sad, unhappy, fatigued, suicidal, traumatized, guilty, lonely, anxious, nervous, unconfident, etc., what is it about those environments or societies that produces such feelings, and why are we so vulnerable to feelings that can cause us to withdraw from our family, be incapable of work, and unable to involve ourselves with friends and community?

When faced with such questions, we should look for a pattern. We can begin to move towards some answers by looking at the relationship between mental illness and where people fall on the social ladder.

As with so many other health and social problems, people at the bottom are more affected than those at the top: mental illness is a socially graded issue. A 2007 national survey of mental illness in England showed that people whose incomes put them into the lowest 20 per cent of household incomes were more likely to have a 'common mental disorder' than those with incomes in the top 20 per cent, and that this pattern was particularly striking for men.[69] Men in the lowest income group were three times more likely to have a mental health problem compared to men in the highest income group, after taking age into account. Specifically, depression showed the most extreme gradient: men at the bottom were thirty-five times more likely to have depression as men at the top (Figure 2.3). But as with so many other health and social problems, mental illness isn't restricted to the least well off; even men in the *second richest* income group were substantially more likely to have depression than those in the richest group.

DOMINANCE AND SUBMISSION

Psychologists are now uncovering the role of both evolution and experience in creating regular responses to and interactions with features of our day-to-day environments. Some systems of behavioural

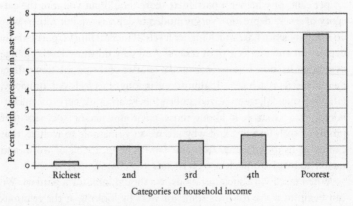

Figure 2.3: There is a social gradient in depression.[69]

responses can be recognized in animals as well as in humans. One such system that casts an important light on our understanding of mental illness is the *Dominance Behavioural System*, or DBS.[70] Because issues of dominance and subordination are key to the conduct of social life in all animal species with ranking systems, the brain has evolved systems for understanding them, making judgements of rank and producing appropriate behavioural responses.

In the words of Sheri Johnson, a psychologist at the University of California at Berkeley, and her colleagues, the DBS can be 'conceptualized as a biologically based system which guides dominance motivation, dominant and subordinate behavior, and responsivity to perceptions of power and subordination'.[70] The DBS affects how we react to superiors and inferiors and ensures that we know our own position. Crucial in social interactions, it helps us learn the best social strategies for meeting our own needs while avoiding unwinnable conflict and defeat. If competition leads to misjudged aggression, there can be huge costs, both for individuals and for the group, so we have evolved a capacity for judging rank, deciding when to play dominant or subordinate roles.

Although the DBS is a system with a long evolutionary history, it is shaped by our environment and experience. As children, we learn from experiences of power and powerlessness, and develop a working model which shapes our thoughts, emotions and actions related to power. We learn, for example, that if we are aggressive towards other children, maybe we can snatch a desired toy, but that doing so often leads to conflict and consequently we have nobody to play with; if we share a toy, sometimes others might share with us. We learn from past success and failure. Some people develop a strong motivation for dominance; others try to avoid it. People who have a high motivation for dominance might act more aggressively than others, they might assert their authority, display over-confidence in their abilities or opinions, or they might try to gain dominance by aligning themselves with others, ingratiating themselves with those who have authority or power. Psychological researchers have tried to capture some of this complexity in the model we draw below (Figure 2.4): we all act somewhere along a continuum from dominant to submissive behaviour, but in addition we can act in social (warm) or antisocial (hostile) ways to achieve our goals.

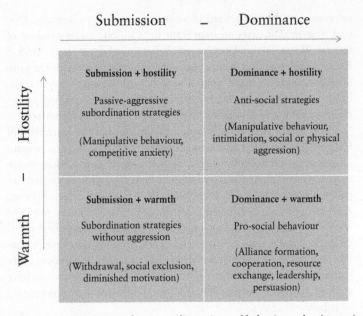

Figure 2.4: Humans act along two dimensions of behaviour: dominance/submissiveness and warmth/hostility.

In our modern world, most of us are not seeking access to scarce food or shelter (although we still, of course, seek access to sexual partners); we're trying to access esteem, praise, attention, respect and power, whether cultural, political or economic. When we have power* our emotions are more positive, we are more confident, we think faster and are less behaviourally inhibited, which means that sometimes we're less sensitive to others than we could be.[70] On the other hand, when we're powerless, we feel vulnerable and inhibited, we are sensitive to threats and fearful of being disliked or rejected.

The Dominance Behavioural System relates to our emotions, specifically the self-conscious ones: feelings of pride on the one hand

---

* Researchers working on the DBS define power here as the ability to control material and social resources, regardless of whether this is achieved using aggressive, coercive or prosocial strategies.

and shame on the other. We feel pride when we're doing well in the eyes of others, when we have their respect and attention. We feel shame when we feel devalued by others, when we feel inferior and unattractive, when our confidence is low. The experience of loss of face and humiliation is often a trigger to violence when people try to defend themselves against being shamed.

We can measure different aspects of the human Dominance Behavioural System – dominance motivation, dominance behaviour, power, pride and shame – which means we can see how it relates to mental illness and to inequality. We can measure it in children as young as pre-school age, rating how they interact with others, whether they are aggressive or submissive in a conflict and so on. In addition, biological measures, such as levels of testosterone in the saliva or blood, can be usefully correlated with other measures of dominance motivation and behaviour. For example, in a study of almost seven hundred men in prison, those with a history of violence had higher levels of testosterone than those with a history of property crime.[71] This link between testosterone levels and dominance is reinforced by studies which show that people with low levels of testosterone show signs of distress when they are temporarily placed in a high-status position in psychological experiments. Other hormones, such as dopamine, serotonin and cortisol, all intimately related to our emotional reward system and stress responses, are also linked to power and the kind of social defeat – losing in any kind of confrontation – that invokes shame.

STUCK IN SUBORDINATION

In what ways is our Dominance Behaviour System linked to mental illness? In a remarkable review of many hundreds of psychological research papers on experimental, observational, biological and self-reported aspects of mental illness, Sheri Johnson and two colleagues found evidence that a number of different kinds of mental illness and personality disorders were related to the DBS.[70] They report:

> Extensive research suggests that externalizing disorders, mania proneness, and narcissistic traits are related to heightened dominance

motivation and behaviors. Mania and narcissistic traits also appear related to inflated self-perceptions of power. Anxiety and depression are related to subordination and submissiveness, as well as a desire to avoid subordination.

Externalizing disorders include disorders characterized by disruptive behaviour. Mania includes conditions with heightened arousal and mood and is part of bipolar disorders and depression, as well as psychotic mood disorders and schizophrenia.

When this paper was written in 2012, the authors had assumed that the scale of the social class pyramid which would raise issues of dominance and subordination involving the DBS was much the same in most societies. But it is now clear that most of the conditions to which the authors drew attention are actually more common in more unequal countries. We shall see in the course of this chapter and the next that depression, psychotic symptoms, schizophrenia and narcissistic traits are all significantly more common in more unequal societies. Given that people with these disorders are at one end of a continuum of much more widespread but less severe problems, the evidence points to the very serious costs of greater inequality across entire populations, in terms of the personal anguish which so many suffer. The conclusion that these forms of psychopathology involve the DBS, and that greater inequality strengthens issues to do with dominance and subordination which trigger the DBS more strongly is hard to avoid.

It is sometimes suggested that the lower burden of mental illness in more equal societies may not result from the psychological effects of inequality, but could instead reflect higher public expenditure on services which could help prevent or treat illness.[72] A study was specifically designed to test this using data on over 35,000 people from 30 European countries. It found no support for explanations involving public spending, but did find support for what the author called the 'psychosocial hypothesis'[72]: more equal countries seemed to have better mental health at least partly because their populations are less anxious about status and are more involved in social networks that involve reciprocity, trust and co-operation. A similar study that sought to see if lower public expenditure contributed to the relationship between higher inequality and higher levels of violence reached the same negative conclusions.[73]

Inequality, then, damages mental health because it affects how we feel and the nature of our social relationships, not because of the amount a country chooses to spend on its health system. We should therefore continue to follow up the issues to do with dominance and subordination related to inequality. First we'll concentrate in this chapter on the pathways involving *submission and subordination* running from inequality to status anxiety, to depression and anxiety. In the next chapter, we'll consider what happens when inequality heightens *dominance* behaviours.

Researchers increasingly consider involuntary subordination and submission to be a pathway into depression. Submission involves signs of defeat. In our evolutionary past, this would be how we avoided physical injuries, even death: submissive behaviour served to end fights with superiors and avoid future conflict. Even when competition and aggression is rarely physical, submissive behaviours can still make sense; they may help us to avoid ongoing conflict or trigger assistance from others.

That our stress responses to subordination still reflect the fear of physical conflict is shown by studies of levels of a blood clotting factor called fibrinogen. Fibrinogen levels rise in response to stress so that blood clots faster in the event of injury. In a study of almost 3,300 middle-aged men and women working in the British civil service, fibrinogen levels were found to be higher in both sexes at each step down the office hierarchy.[74] The blood of subordinate civil servants appeared to be prepared for the kind of attacks which, for example, a subordinate baboon might risk from dominants.

The theory linking depression to submission and subordination suggests that it results from an inability to stop, or escape from, a submissive situation or defeat. A growing body of research supports this idea. Across more than twenty research studies, it has been found that people with depression were more likely to report feeling inferior, or experiencing shame.[70] Twenty-three studies have found that low testosterone levels are related to depression and depressive symptoms, and in an experiment where men were given testosterone-lowering drugs, 10 per cent developed depressive symptoms, compared to none in the group receiving a placebo drug. In another study, people without depression who were given antidepressant medication became less submissive, when assessed by the people they lived with, and more dominant when interacting with strangers in a psychological laboratory.

Anxiety and depression often coincide, and anxiety is also closely related to powerlessness, lack of control, subordination and social defeat. People seem to be particularly susceptible to social anxiety as a result of rejection and childhood experiences of insecure attachment, which lead to a heightened sensitivity to social comparisons and attempts to avoid ostracism and harmful attention. Anxious individuals are constantly monitoring social rank, fearful of humiliation, and perceive themselves as lacking power. As with depression, studies of anxiety show that it is correlated with feelings of shame and submission, and people with anxiety are prone to comparing themselves unfavourably to others. Some studies suggest that anxiety is most common in individuals with high levels of dominance motivation who experience threats to social power – a situation slightly different from depression, where people are more motivated to avoid conflict. But, overall, the desire to avoid inferiority seems to be stronger in those with anxiety disorders than among those trying to achieve dominance. When shown images of angry faces, which psychologists consider a potent social signal of hostility or dominance, people with social anxiety disorder react more strongly than others.[75]

This large body of research evidence linking the Dominance Behaviour System to the self-conscious emotions (including sensitivity to social threats and low self-esteem, as well as to symptoms or clinical diagnoses of depression and anxiety), makes the links between inequality, worries about how we are judged and mental illness very clear. We have built-in strategies – not necessarily conscious ones – for dealing with situations that might require us to adopt either a dominant or submissive tactic, or a balance of both.

Paul Gilbert, a pioneering clinical and research psychologist at the University of Derby, who has extensively studied these patterns of behaviour, their evolutionary basis and links to mental illness, describes in his book, *The Compassionate Mind*,[76] the human need to be cared for in infancy and childhood. Through our long evolutionary history, maternal caring protected us from predators, provided food and comfort and calmed us when we were upset or anxious. When an infant or child is cut off from this care, it protests through crying and communicating distress, trying to elicit help, protection and support. But if help or the return of the mother doesn't happen quickly, these signals could quickly become dangerous – noise can attract danger, it's better to be silent. Gilbert describes despair as 'a form of behavioural deactivation when protest does not work. Positive emotions and feelings of confidence and the desire to explore, search and seek out must be toned down.'

There are so many life events or situations that can trigger this 'deactivation' strategy – defeats and setbacks, being dominated, bullied or rejected. While initially protective, such a response involves feeling less (or nothing), turning off our positive as well as negative emotions, and some of us get stuck, unable to turn off this 'coping' strategy when it is no longer helpful. Feeling cut off from other people, we can get stuck in a self-reinforcing cycle of rumination, trying to work out why we feel such a failure and driving ourselves further into depression. This chain of events, from rejection and defeat to depression, seems to be activated on the scale of an epidemic in the modern world: as mentioned earlier, according to the World Health Organization, depression is the major cause of disability globally.[77] We might be trapped in a situation, at school or work or at home where we are bullied, put down or made to feel inferior. We might hate our job but need the money, so continue in a situation where we feel stressed every day. We are often trapped, and it is this entrapment in a submissive or subordinate response that is at the root of depression. The following were all posted on an internet chat site, I Just Want To Be Left Alone:

> I don't think I have always been someone who hides . . . I do believe it is because I am somehow ashamed. I take on every fault that is turned my way as my own. I think if an injustice is done to me that I must have caused it somehow. (Posted 2009)

> Too much concern about what other people think. I hide away not only because I think others will think poorly of me, but because I care a lot about their opinions. (Posted 2008)

> The real person in my head, whom I'm trying to let out [is] not . . . quiet, boring, always thinking and having anxiety from every little

aspect of his life. Being shy is destroying my life. I love people but I have no clue how I could interact with them to the extent that they will be my friends. (Posted 2009)

Psychologists have developed a measure of our sensitivity to subordination called the 'striving to avoid inferiority scale'.[78] This measures fear of rejection or criticism for 'not keeping up' with others; the pressure to compete to avoid inferiority. Researchers have found that some people exhibit what they call *insecure striving*, a fear of rejection, of being overlooked and losing out, linked to a tendency to seek validation from others, feel inferior, shame and submissive behaviour – and increased stress, depression, anxiety and self-harm.[79]

Self-harm is perhaps the most shocking example of how low self-esteem and perceived lack of control can manifest as a health problem. The numbers are staggering. Representative surveys of health behaviour in England, carried out in schools under exam conditions, suggest that 22 per cent of children aged fifteen have self-harmed at least once, and 43 per cent of those said they harmed themselves once a month.[24, 80] Figures from an Australian study, based on telephone interviews, suggest that one in twelve (2 million people) self-harm sometime during their lives.[81] This figure is likely to be an underestimate resulting from a low response rate (38 per cent) caused mainly by parents refusing to give permission for children under eighteen to be interviewed. The USA and Canada consistently report that somewhere between 13 and 24 per cent of school children self-harm.[82] Young people, some as young as seven years old, are cutting, scratching and burning themselves, pulling out their hair, bruising themselves and deliberately breaking their own bones.

It's hard to imagine the mental anguish that makes life seem so painful that inflicting bodily pain comes as a release, and provides a (very temporary) sense of control, but those feelings are what many young people and adults consistently report. Self-harm is more common in people who are very self-critical and have feelings of shame; early experiences of abuse, trauma or neglect can, unsurprisingly, play a part, but the recent epidemic rise of self-harm suggests that something has changed in our societies to make this problem worse.[83]

It may be that for those unable to reach 'socially desirable goals or self-images', the ensuing sense of shame turns into anger and harm towards oneself. Self-harm as a response to social pain may also reflect the very close connection between physical and social pain. Brain scans show that the pain of feeling excluded by others activates the same areas of the brain as physical pain.[84] The connection between the two is so deep that doses of common pain-killing drugs like acetaminophen / paracetamol (marketed as Tylenol and Panadol) have been found to reduce not only the physical aches and pains we normally use them for, but also the emotional upsets and anxieties that come, for instance, from the experience of rejection.[85]

Looking back at Figure 2.3, at the gradient in depression from rich to poor, it is hard to avoid the conclusion that this is partly a reflection of a gradient in the freedom of action to escape from entrapment in a stressful situation; and then, looking at the pattern in Figure 2.1, that more unequal societies increase this kind of threat for all of us. We need to link our understanding of individual vulnerability to what might be damaging characteristics of whole societies or cultures to gain an understanding of the modern epidemic of depression and anxiety.

Depression and anxiety are so much a part of our human development, so much a part of our evolutionary heritage, that they feel like programmed responses we can't shake off. Understanding the Dominance Behavioural System helps to explain why we are so sensitive to the way that others see us, why we are attuned to rank and status, and why some of our individual experiences – such as poor attachment in infancy, rejection and bullying in adolescence or not feeling valued by people round us – might trigger submission and subordination in some people.

KEEPING UP WITH THE JONESES, LOOKING DOWN ON THE SMITHS

In more competitive, unequal and materialistic societies, where hierarchy matters more and people are more prone to compare themselves with others, doing well in others' eyes and having all the trappings and characteristics of success becomes the main meaning of achievement.

The Dominance Behaviour System helps us understand how we have evolved to be sensitive to situations of social threat. From this, we can hypothesize that situations in which our social status is higher, where we feel in control of our lives and more appreciated by people round us, will lead to less depression and anxiety, and situations where we are at greater risk of low social status and feel less in control will lead to more.

There is a common belief that as people ascend to positions of leadership and face increasing demands and responsibilities, they will experience higher levels of stress. If, however, leaders also have an increased sense of control as a result of their higher status, leadership should actually be linked to *lower* levels of stress.

Researchers studying people enrolled in an executive education programme at Harvard University compared leaders (defined as people who managed others) with non-leaders.[86] After taking into account age, sex, education, income and mood, they found that the leaders had lower levels of the stress hormone cortisol, and reported lower levels of anxiety than the non-leaders. Then, looking only at the leaders, the researchers studied the interplay between leadership, a sense of control, and stress. Higher leadership (managing more people, having more people directly reporting to them and more authority) was linked to lower cortisol levels and lower levels of anxiety. Higher leadership predicted a greater sense of control, and this in turn predicted lower cortisol and lower anxiety. The higher the rank that people held and the more power and control they had, the less stressed they were.

An additional insight into the importance of rank comes from psychologist Alex Wood, from the University of Stirling, and his colleagues.[87] They argue that if social rank is important for mental well-being, then income should be related to mental health through the way it acts as a proxy or marker for rank: the *amount* of income you have should matter primarily for *where it places* you in the social hierarchy.

Taking a very large sample of 30,000 people in the UK, they used a statistical model that allowed them to compare the effect of *absolute* level of income to income *rank*. They found that in terms of predicting mental distress, rank trumped absolute income, even when accounting for age, gender, education, marital status, house owner-ship and other factors. The researchers were also able to show that a person's income rank at a given time was related to changes in mental distress over the next year – whatever their mental state to begin with. The same was true for people thinking about or attempting suicide: where people ranked in the income distribution was more important than how much money they had.[88] The same pattern was confirmed by research in the United States, which showed that, over time, a per-son's income within a social comparison group, rather than their income itself, predicted the development of depressive symptoms.[89]

The effects of rank go beyond distress, depressive symptoms and even suicidal thoughts; income rank leaves a physical mark on our bodies as well. Woods's research team has shown that income rank trumps absolute income for predicting biological markers of disease such as levels of cholesterol, blood pressure, body fat and blood sugar control.[90]

A similar study used data on psychological (e.g., feeling low or nervous) and physical (e.g., headache) symptoms in more than 48,000 adolescents in 8 countries. It looked to see whether the frequency of symptoms among children was most affected by actual family income or by how their income compared with families of other children attending the same school or living in the same area. Once again, income rank compared to other families was related to the adoles-cents' symptoms more strongly than absolute levels of affluence or deprivation.[91] These findings are reinforced by a study of eleven-year-olds in the UK, which found that, as expected, children had higher self-esteem and life satisfaction if family incomes were higher. In addition, young people who viewed their family as poorer than those of their friends were more likely to have worse well-being, even when actual family incomes were the same.[92]

As we have seen, people in positions of leadership tend to suffer less stress, and where we stand on the social ladder seems to matter more for both mental and physical health than the actual amount of money we have. If income is important mainly because of where it locates you in the social hierarchy, it doesn't mean that differences in the level of inequality wouldn't matter. In any given society income differences could be made either bigger or smaller without moving anyone up or down the rank order of incomes. But if the differences between people's income become very small indeed, we would be almost unaware of the differences – we would all appear and feel much the same in status. If, however, the income differences were huge, we would be unable to ignore them. Everyone's position in relation to others would be immediately apparent and the status differences would be obvious. So the size of income differences makes income rank, social position or status either much more or much less important.

THE EVIDENCE GROWS

We started this chapter by showing the strong link between income inequality and levels of status anxiety and mental illness in different societies. With a clearer understanding of how inequality increases the importance of the social evaluative threat, and how this activates the Dominance Behavioural System, we can begin to understand the consequences of greater inequality for mental illness. There are now several studies showing that some of the disorders that Sheri Johnson and her colleagues found to be related to the DBS are indeed more common in more unequal societies.

Researchers from the Inter-American Development Bank used data from more than 80,000 people from 93 countries who responded to a 2007 Gallup Opinion Poll.[93] Although this study is limited by having only a self-reported measure of depression, its findings are still thought-provoking: overall, almost 15 per cent of people reported feeling depressed the previous day. Significantly, some countries had much lower, and others much higher, rates. These differences were unrelated to average incomes but correlated closely with income inequality. The effect of inequality seems to have been felt more keenly by people living in cities, rather than in rural areas. Some studies have looked at particular population groups. Higher income inequality was linked to higher depression scores among 17,348 university students from 23 high-, middle- and low-income countries, after controlling for family wealth and other factors.[94] In a 2008 study of 251,158 people, surveyed in 65 countries by the World Health Organization from 2002 to

2003, income inequality was related to depression in high-, but not middle- and low-income countries.[95] In a study conducted across forty-five US states,[96] there is a clear relationship between income inequality and higher rates of depression (see Figure 2.5), and this is borne out by another study by Amy Fan and her colleagues,[97] and one of depression among older adults.[98] Another study found that depression was more common in those European societies where people judged social status differences to be larger.[99]

The questions used to identify the prevalence of depression shown in Figure 2.5 would have included most cases of bipolar disorder. Before the revised official categorization of mental illness introduced in 2013, bipolar disorder was treated as a sub-classification of depression. Bipolar disorder, in the past also called 'manic depression', is characterized by dramatic mood swings. Over periods that can vary from a few days to a few months, people can move from depression to a very positive, even euphoric, mood and back again. A paper by Johnson and Carver reports the results of a series of experiments which found that

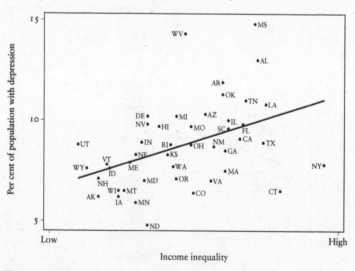

Figure 2.5: Income inequality and prevalence of depression across forty-five US states.[96]

people in the manic phase showed numerous signs of dominance motivation, and high assessment of their own power in terms of both dominance and prestige.[100] They also showed signs of hubris and pride in themselves. Other research has suggested that these characteristics tend to go with overly positive social comparisons, high self-esteem and sometimes delusions of grandeur. But bipolar disorders are also related to self-harm, substance abuse and suicide. It looks as if the growing understanding of the Dominance Behavioural System may shed light on both the depressive and manic phases of bipolar disorder.

Several studies have shown a tendency for schizophrenia to be more common where income differences are greater. The largest collected 107 measures of the prevalence of schizophrenia from 26 countries, and found that rates were higher in more unequal countries.[101] The authors suggested that an explanation for the link might lie in the loss of social cohesion and heightened comparisons of rank in more unequal societies.

Another large multinational study analysed data on psychotic

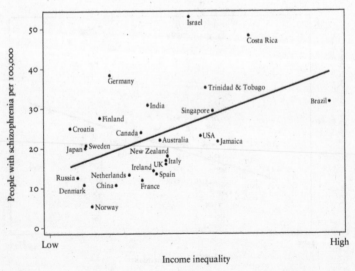

Figure 2.6: Income inequality and incidence of schizophrenia, 1975–2001.[101]

symptoms collected as part of a World Health Organization dataset that used diagnostic interviews with representative samples (totalling almost 250,000 people) in 50 countries.[102] These symptoms included hearing voices, having feelings that people were 'too interested in you' or were plotting to harm you, and that your thoughts were being controlled by another person or by strange forces. Because more repressive governments might increase these kinds of fears of persecution or of being controlled, the study took into account the number of years of democratic government in each country. It found a significant tendency for these symptoms to be more common in the more unequal of the fifty countries. An increase in the share of income going to the richest 1 per cent of the population in each country was associated with increases in people experiencing hallucinations, delusional moods, delusions of thought control and with the total number of these symptoms suffered by people.

Feelings that other people or external forces control your thoughts could perhaps be seen as the extreme end of a continuum from what psychologists call 'external locus of control' to 'internal locus of control'. People differ in how far they regard what happens to them, and how their life pans out, is down to luck, fate and other people (i.e. external factors), and how far they believe that what happens to them depends on their own actions, choices and efforts (internal factors). For over fifty years psychologists have been looking at how far people have an internal or external 'locus of control'. Measures are based on people's responses to twenty-three contrasting pairs of statements, such as 'People's misfortunes result from the mistakes they make' versus 'Many of the unhappy things in people's lives are partly due to bad luck.' Professor Jean Twenge collected all the data she could find from measures of external versus internal loci of control among samples of children (nine to fourteen years old) and of college students over the years 1960 to 2002 in the USA.[103] She assembled measures from forty-one samples of children and ninety-seven samples of college students. When she looked at changes over time she found that there had been a large decline in how much control young people felt they had over their lives. According to Twenge, 'the implications of increasing externality are almost uniformly negative'. People with an external locus of control are more anxious and more likely to be depressed, and in childhood they do less well at school. She says that the rise in external locus of control measures reflects a growth of cynicism, distrust and alienation.

The rise in income differences in the USA from the later 1960s, and which continued well beyond the end of Twenge's study period, is at least consistent with the idea that increasing inequality might have contributed to the trend towards this feeling of external locus of control. We found only one study that looked to see if there is a relationship between locus of control and inequality. Using data for forty-three countries, it found – as expected – that people in more unequal countries felt they had less control over their lives.[104] The same study also showed that there was an increase in external locus of control at each step down the income scale, from the richest with most sense of control to the poorest with least.

The reality is that inequality causes real suffering, regardless of how we choose to label such distress. Greater inequality heightens social threat and status anxiety, evoking feelings of shame which feed into our instincts for withdrawal, submission and subordination: when the social pyramid gets higher and steeper and status insecurity increases, there are widespread psychological costs. Status competition and anxiety increase, people become less friendly, less altruistic and more likely to put others down.

Research continues to confirm that in varying degrees it is not simply a few individuals but whole societies that are damaged by these processes. As well as causing us distress, struggling to keep up also seems to make us less compassionate towards others. An important consequence of greater inequality is the damage it does to social cohesion. Using a very large sample of volunteers taking part in an internet personality survey, Robert de Vries, a sociologist at the University of Kent, and colleagues tested the hypothesis that inequality creates a more competitive, less cohesive social milieu.[105] They measured how people scored on an 'Agreeableness' scale – a measure of people's attitudes and behaviours towards others, including being helpful, considerate and trusting rather than tending to find fault with others, being aloof, rude or quarrelsome. The researchers looked to see whether people living in more unequal societies would respond to more hierarchical structures by scoring lower on the

Agreeableness scale. This is exactly what they found, even after taking into account age, sex, education, urbanization, average income and the percentage of people belonging to ethnic minorities. People living in less equal US states had significantly lower levels of Agreeableness than those living in more equal states.

Consistent with this finding are the results of a study by Marii Paskov, a sociologist at the University of Oxford. She found that in more unequal European countries both poorer and richer people were less willing to help neighbours, older people, immigrants, and the sick and disabled.[39] Paskov and colleagues have also found that, rather than striving harder for status, it looks as if people are instead discouraged by the greater obstacles put in their way by inequality.[106] A further study using data from twenty-four European countries showed that civic participation (belonging to groups, clubs or organizations, including recreational, political, charitable, religious or professional groups) is significantly lower in more unequal countries (see Figure 2.7), and we have known for a long time that levels of trust are lower in more

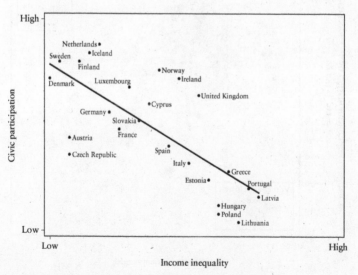

Figure 2.7: Civic participation decreases in more unequal European countries (income inequality measured by the Gini coefficient).[37]

unequal places.[107] Evidently, social cohesion is reduced in more unequal societies.

The single most important reason why participation in community life declines with increased inequality is likely to be the increased social evaluative threat: people withdraw from social life as they find it more stressful. More unequal societies become more fragmented as social distances increase. People become more withdrawn, less neighbourly and more worried about appearances and giving the wrong impression, they prefer to 'keep themselves to themselves'. And when some people feel excluded or threatened, the same processes which affect so many individual minds and bodies also affect the political process.

Responding to a Twitter challenge to find factors that predicted the electoral swing to Donald Trump in US counties in the 2016 Presidential election, *The Economist* published Figure 2.8. It reported

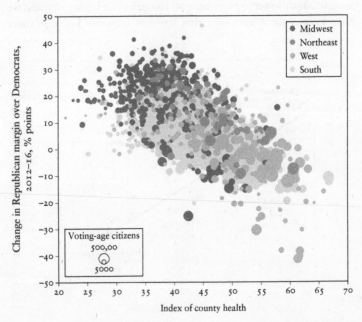

Figure 2.8: There was a bigger swing in the vote towards Donald Trump in counties with worse health.[108]

that a combined measure of obesity, diabetes, heavy drinking, lack of physical exercise and low life expectancy – all of which are made worse by income inequality – was the best measure they could find. Economists at the European economic think tank Bruegel confirmed this: Donald Trump performed more strongly in states with higher income inequality.[109]

"GRANDPA, BEFORE SELFIES AND SOCIAL MEDIA, HOW DID PEOPLE SELF-PROMOTE?"

3

Delusions of Grandeur

*'I'm an opportunist, I don't really get attached to people,
I live for myself and everything I do is seen in terms of
"how will this event/person/thing be of use to me?"'*

*'I crave respect. I lack the talent, beauty and skill to get it
one way . . . then I will fight for it the other way. With the
only weapons I know, lies, deceit, pain and torture.'*

> Posted online in 2012, on the internet
> forum I Am A Narcissist

PUTTING ON A GOOD FACE

A few years ago, searching for new academic studies comparing
levels of income inequality and health in different countries, we came
across an interesting phenomenon. Our search uncovered nine recent
studies of this kind in rich, developed countries. Of these, the seven
that used objective measures like death rates, or life expectancy, confirmed that health is worse in more unequal societies.[1] The two that
came to a different conclusion looked instead at income inequality in
relation to 'self-rated health', based on surveys that ask people to
assess their own health on a scale running from excellent to poor.

This immediately piqued our curiosity: if objective measures of
deaths and illness are related to income inequality, why wouldn't
measures of self-rated health show a similar correlation? Geogra-
phers Dr Anna Barford and Professor Danny Dorling have since
found, counterintuitively, that average levels of self-rated health are

actually higher in countries where life expectancy is lower.[110] In Japan, for example, a more equal society, only 54 per cent of people rated their health as good, compared to 80 per cent of Americans. Yet Japan has almost the highest life expectancy in the world (topped only by tiny Monaco), at eighty-two years in 2005, whereas the USA is at the bottom of the life expectancy league for rich countries, with an average of seventy-seven years. It appears that in more unequal countries people want to present a more positive view of their own health, and that people in more equal societies are more modest or willing to admit imperfections.

Clearly, there are cultural differences in how people view and describe their health that are unrelated to their actual risk of illness and death. But the correlation we found suggested that there was a relationship between self-reported health and income inequality – just not the way round that we expected. In more unequal societies, with more status competition, the data imply that it is more important to appear tough and self-reliant. Asserting that you have excellent or very good health might be part of maintaining your self-image in a more competitive environment. In more equal societies, people seem to be more modest and less inclined to rate themselves at the top of a scale. And this phenomenon doesn't just apply to health; in Japan, it is much less common to report that you are satisfied with your life or happy than in the USA, where it is expected that people at least say they are satisfied and happy.[34, 111] We wondered whether growing up in a more egalitarian society might mean that people are less likely to claim to be 'the best' or 'excellent'.

THE 'LAKE WOBEGON EFFECT'

In 2011, this intuition was confirmed in a study by Australian psychologist Steve Loughnan and his colleagues.[112] They studied what psychologists call 'self-enhancement bias', or 'illusory superiority' – people's tendency to emphasize or exaggerate their desirable qualities, relative to other people. This is the phenomenon we all laugh about when we hear that almost everyone believes they are a better driver than average. It's also known as the 'Lake Wobegon effect', after

American comedian Garrison Keillor's fictional town where 'all the children are above average'. It's a well-known effect, demonstrated time and time again across many different areas of performance. For example, almost 70 per cent of academics at one university rated themselves in the top 25 per cent for teaching ability,[113] and 25 per cent of American students rated themselves in the top 1 per cent for getting along with people.[114]

Although self-enhancement bias has been found all over the world, and in relation to all kinds of characteristics and abilities, the degree to which people exaggerate their talents varies from culture to culture. While over 90 per cent of Americans think they are better than average drivers, less than 70 per cent of Swedes feel the same way.[115]

Most explanations of these differences have focused on notions of individualism versus collectivism: the idea that some cultures emphasize individual autonomy, independence and assertiveness, whereas others emphasize the needs of, and relationships within, groups such as families, communities and workplaces. Western cultures are more individualistic and have higher levels of self-enhancement bias, compared to Eastern cultures.

Partly to test our argument about the effects of inequality, Dr Loughnan, working with an eighteen-strong international team, tested whether self-enhancement was related to inequality.[112] He reasoned that 'in unequal societies, individuals are strongly motivated to stand out as superior to others. One expression of this desire may be to engage in stronger self-enhancement. In societies with more economic equality, the benefits of superiority diminish, and people's tendency to see themselves as above average should weaken.' In a study of fifteen different countries, Loughnan and his colleagues show that self-enhancement is strongly related to income inequality. They found that income inequality was a much stronger predictor of self-enhancement bias than a measure of individualism vs collectivism in these fifteen countries (Figure 3.1).

Psychological research shows that this picture, both of increased self-enhancement in more unequal countries and the paradoxical tendency for self-rated health to be better in countries where death rates are actually higher, reflect responses to increased social evaluative threat. There is a robust body of evidence which shows that

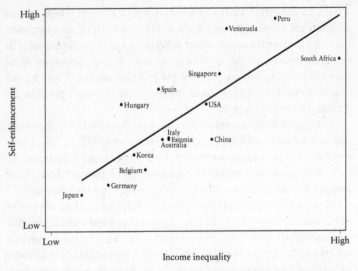

Figure 3.1: Income inequality is related to higher levels of self-enhancement bias.[112]

people's tendency to self-enhancement increases when they are faced with a greater social evaluative threat.[116–118] In a typical psychological experiment, people are told that either a higher or lower proportion of their fellow students thought they were likeable. They were later asked to rate themselves compared to their peers on various characteristics, such as how stingy they were, how jealous, messy or bossy. Just as in other experiments, those who had been led to believe they were regarded as less likeable rated themselves more positively compared to others. In the research literature this is usually seen as a form of ego-defence, but it could be seen as analogous to the way dogs raise their hackles, or other animals try to look bigger, when threatened.

We saw in the last chapter (Figure 2.1) that status anxiety increases with inequality. The evidence that self-enhancement also increases in more unequal societies provides additional confirmation that inequality does indeed raise the social evaluative threat. We tend to big ourselves up as a consequence.

WHAT DO WE MEAN BY
SELF-ESTEEM?

Are these tendencies to self-enhancement just amusing cultural dif-ferences, allowing us to poke fun at boastful Americans and po-faced Japanese, or do they reflect a more dangerous, insidious effect of inequality, harmful to individual well-being and to social cohesion? Isn't it a good thing, if people view themselves positively, believe in their capabilities and have strong self-esteem?

Modern popular psychology places a high value on the concept of self-esteem. Feeling good about ourselves is considered the bedrock of mental health and well-being, a necessary underpinning for achieve-ment and success. It gives us the confidence to realize our potential; if we believe we're special, we'll *become* special. But will we?

It now seems that what we think we mean by self-esteem is prob-ably not what we are measuring when we think we're measuring it. Psychologists used to think that there had been a paradoxical ten-dency for rising trends in anxiety to be accompanied by rising trends in self-esteem. In the 1950s, only 12 per cent of American teenagers agreed that they were a very important person; by the 1980s, 80 per cent of them were sure of their own importance.[119] At the same time, their levels of anxiety were rising dramatically.

The standard measure of self-esteem was for decades the Rosen-berg scale. It asked whether people agreed or disagreed with ten statements, such as: 'I feel that I'm a person of worth'; 'I am inclined to think that I am a failure'; 'I wish I could have more respect for myself'; 'I take a positive attitude toward myself'; and so on. But it failed to distinguish between 'secure self-esteem', based on a realistic appraisal of one's own efficacy and capabilities, and defensive or pro-tective self-enhancement – saying that you are OK when you are not – sometimes called 'insecure self-esteem'. And so we arrive at the apparent paradox of increasing anxiety levels at the same time as self-esteem appears to rise.

There is also the additional puzzle of high rates of self-esteem being found in groups that actually experience more low social sta-tus, discrimination and prejudice, which you'd think were damaging to self-esteem. Numerous studies have shown over the years that African American men appear to have higher rates of self-esteem than white men (the same pattern is true for women, although the differences are not as marked). In a 2011 poll conducted by the *Washington Post* and the Kaiser Family Foundation, 72 per cent of black men had high levels of self-esteem, compared to 59 per cent of white men.[120] This was despite the fact that, in the same survey, black men were much more worried than white men about losing their jobs, not having enough money to pay their bills, not getting the healthcare they needed, getting HIV or AIDS, being the victim of a violent crime, being a victim of discrimination, and providing a good education for their children.

The clue to this disjunction lies in the answers to the survey questions that asked about respect.[120] Seventy-two per cent of black men said it was very important to be respected by others, compared to only 55 per cent of white men, but black men were much more likely to say they had been treated with less respect than other people, received poorer service than other people in restaurants and stores, and felt ignored or overlooked. Twenty-eight per cent of African Americans thought it was a bad time to be a black man in America.

Of course it's natural, and probably psychologically sensible, for any group experiencing low social status, lack of respect, discrimination and prejudice to maintain their self-respect as much as possible, and to do all they can to avoid sinking into the insecurity of self-doubt. Rising inequality seems to have resulted in a heightened need for people to defend their self-worth in the face of increasing status competition and worries about how they are seen by others. Inequality might be expected to increase this defensive self-esteem, but not the genuine article.

THE DARKER SIDE OF
LOVING OURSELVES

If we are to use the term to mean what we think it means, we need to drop our blunt measures of 'self-esteem' and find one that separates realistic confidence and self-appraisal from a defensive, narcissistic, presentation of self. We need a scale on which people score high if they have a positive, but reasonably accurate, view of their strengths in different situations, and a different scale for narcissism.

Having confidence in ourselves, feeling a sense of self-worth, is obviously a good thing if it is realistic and goes along with empathy and good relationships with other people. But if empathy is lacking, if people deny rather than recognize their weaknesses, if they react badly to criticism, or are excessively preoccupied with themselves, with success and with their image and appearance in the eyes of others, then self-regard is dangerous.

This pathological, unhealthy brand of what can look like high self-esteem is narcissism. Narcissistic characteristics include attention-seeking, reacting badly to criticism, self-importance, a tendency to exaggerate your own talents and achievements, a lack of empathy and a willingness to take advantage of others.

The Narcissistic Personality Inventory (NPI) was developed by psychologists at the University of California at Berkeley in the 1980s. People are given forty paired statements and asked to choose which one describes them best; they are not told that the test measures narcissism. For example, people are asked to choose between:

A. I am no better or worse than most people
         or
B. I think I am a special person

And:

A. I prefer to blend in with the crowd
         or
B. I like to be the centre of attention

Some of the paired statements seem to offer a weird choice, where neither seems quite right. It is easy to imagine, for example, that many will feel neither of the statements *I like to look at myself in the mirror* or *I am not particularly interested in looking at myself in the mirror* quite describe how they feel about mirrors. Many will enjoy looking at themselves in a mirror when dressed in something nice, on a good hair day, with flattering lighting, but prefer not to look in many other circumstances. Indeed, we may not be embarrassed to find ourselves agreeing that if we *ruled the world it would be a much better place* (or at least a bit better), while at the same time agreeing that *the thought of ruling the world frightens the hell out of us.*

Evidently, the two types of self-regard outlined above can be difficult to tell apart, but quibbles aside, most research on narcissism uses the Narcissistic Personality Inventory and it has been shown to be a valid measure of narcissistic attitudes, values and behaviours, capable of identifying insecure self-esteem. It measures gradations in a personality trait, *not* a psychiatric disorder. (Narcissistic Personality *Disorder*, as diagnosed by a psychiatrist, is a pathological long-term diagnosis for a constellation of self-centredness, self-importance and lack of empathy.) Although most people can be a bit narcissistic at times, the Narcissistic Personality Inventory is a valuable tool because, just as with the diagnostic interview schedules we described in Chapter 2, it can be used to measure levels of narcissism in populations. This means we can assess whether some societies and cultures are more narcissistic than others, and whether or not levels of narcissism change over time, and why.

THE NARCISSISM EPIDEMIC

Professors Jean Twenge and Keith Campbell are psychologists who research self-esteem and narcissism. We referred to some of Twenge's work showing dramatic rises in rates of anxiety in Chapter 1. Their 2009 book, *The Narcissism Epidemic: Living in the Age of Entitlement*, describes a worrying rise in narcissism in America.[119] It is full of stories of self-esteem gone mad, from the bride whose wedding cake was in the shape of herself, to the company called Celeb4ADay, where you can hire fake paparazzi photographers to follow you around, taking pictures and shouting your name. Chapters on vanity, relationship troubles and antisocial behaviour show the extent to which narcissism has spread through American culture. As the authors say, 'The fight for the greater good of the 1960s became looking out for number one by the 1980s.'

Twenge, Campbell and their colleagues drew together eighty-five studies that had used the Narcissistic Personality Inventory in samples of the American population between 1982 and 2006.[121] They found a steep rise in narcissism over that period – 30 per cent more people showed narcissistic tendencies in 2006 than in 1982. Given the relationship between self-enhancement and inequality, and the evidence that a defensive self-esteem contributes to narcissism, we expected narcissism to reflect changes in inequality. The period in which Twenge found a steep rise in narcissism was also a period which saw substantial rises in income differences in the USA. In Figure 3.2 we plot both trends together, using income inequality data from the World Top Incomes Database.[122]

We had predicted that narcissism and self-enhancement would be related to greater inequality because inequality makes social status more important. Where some people are 'worth' so much more than others, we judge each other more by status. Narcissism is the sharp

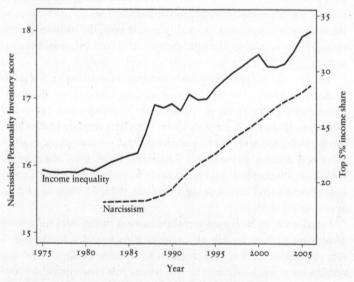

Figure 3.2: College students' Narcissistic Personality Inventory scores over time appear to reflect the rise in US income inequality.[123]

end of the struggle for social survival against self-doubt and a sense of inferiority. It is a reaction to the same kind of environment that produces social anxiety, shyness and lack of confidence. Twenge and Campbell write that competition and status-seeking have increased in American society, along with 'a growing perception that people have to claw their way up, or risk being mired in poverty'.[119] The connection between inequality and narcissism is supported by research on how growing up poor is associated with status-seeking, and growing up wealthy with narcissism. Feeling wealthy, self-identifying as rich and having a higher income have all been associated with a higher likelihood of being narcissistic. Using data collected from active soldiers in the United States Army, Sean Martin of Boston College and his colleagues found that parental income was positively related to later narcissism.[124] Soldiers from wealthier families were more likely to agree that they were 'special because everyone keeps telling me so' and that 'group activities tend to be dull without me'.

Another sign of the connection between rising inequality and people's desire for status comes from survey data showing the rise in the income levels people aspire to. In the decade from the mid-1980s to the mid-1990s, as income inequality rose steeply, the incomes people thought they would need to fulfil their dreams doubled, from $50,000 to $102,000.[125]

Twenge and her colleagues have compared the attitudes and goals of different generations at the same age, including 'Baby Boomers' (born 1946–1961), those in 'Generation X' (born 1962–1981) and 'Millennials' (born after 1982). Those born later thought that money, image and fame were more important, and self-acceptance, affiliation and community were less important. Over time, and in years with higher income inequality, wanting to make money was a more important motivation for going to college than wanting to gain an appreciation of ideas.[126, 127]

Faced with an increased social evaluation threat stemming from greater inequality, we are all between a rock and a hard place – succumbing to anxiety and depression, or attempting to claw our way up via self-enhancement or narcissism. Just how intense the conflict is between these two alternatives is shown by the frequency with which people suffering from conditions such as schizophrenia or the manic phase of bipolar disorder, develop delusions of grandeur. As many as half of those with these conditions come to believe they actually are famous celebrities, political or religious leaders or the CEOs of major multinational corporations. While these delusions appear to provide a defence against low self-esteem and depression, the adoption of an illusory identity is a high price to pay to resolve the conflict between the desire for fame and fortune and the short-comings of reality.

RESHAPING OURSELVES

Some of the characteristics of narcissism include self-obsession, the need for constant attention and flattery from others, and having unrealistic fantasies of success, beauty or romance. So as status anxiety and competition drive increases in narcissism, we not only see our temperament, personality, success, etc. through each other's eyes, we're also more likely to compare our bodies with others', worry about how they see us, and confuse how we look with personal worth.

Journalist Leora Tanenbaum has described how women undertake cosmetic surgery to erase the 'flaws' they perceive in their faces and bodies, so that they can fit in with a limited, supposed ideal, of how a woman should look.[128] Plastic surgery has its roots in the nineteenth century, when Jewish men tried to eliminate racialized facial characteristics to escape discrimination in their business and professional lives. The power of contemporary pressure on women to conform is in some ways not dissimilar: the images of women that we are all bombarded by every day, whether in magazines, advertisements, films, on television or the catwalk, suggest that women need to conform to the ideal and self-enhance to be valued. The effect of these pressures becomes clear as soon as girls reach puberty. The Millennium Cohort Study found that the proportion of girls in the UK with emotional problems – as reported by their parents – rises from 12 per cent among eleven-year-olds to 18 per cent among fourteen-year-olds. When, at the age of fourteen, children reported their own symptoms, 24 per cent of girls said they suffered from depression.[129]

Men are not immune either. In movies, TV shows, music videos and men's magazines, the ideal man is broad shouldered, sculpted and muscular. Just as women have been pressured by idealized images of female beauty on billboards and screens, now men are also constantly confronted with larger-than-life images of washboard abs and bulging biceps, whether it's underwear or cars that are on sale. The pressure on men to look fit is reflected in the vast amount of shelving given over to bodybuilding supplements in ordinary supermarkets, the rise of eating disorders among men, and increasing numbers of men waxing, bleaching, using Botox and undergoing other cosmetic procedures. As the tabloids put it, it's as difficult to look like Ken as it is to look like Barbie.[130]

In 2013, almost 2 million Americans had plastic surgery, and around 14 million had non-invasive cosmetic procedures, such as Botox injections or wrinkle fillers.[131] Most popular were breast augmentation, nose reshaping, eyelid surgery, liposuction and facelifts. Among the procedures growing fastest in popularity were breast lifts (up 70% since 2000), tummy tucks (up 79%), buttock lifts (up 80%), lower body lifts (up 3417%) and upper arm lifts (up 4565%). A different professional association – the American Society for Aesthetic Plastic Surgery – adds labiaplasty (reshaping the folds of skin surrounding the vulva) as an increasingly fashionable operation.[132] In the same year in the UK, 50,000 cosmetic surgeries were performed, with breasts, noses, eyelids and faces the most popular areas for correction, just as in the USA.[133] Liposuction procedures, the sucking out of excess fat, rose over 40 per cent in just that one year.

Should these statistics worry us? Perhaps going under the knife, or allowing yourself to be injected with toxins, reflects a reduced stigma around such interventions, and more people choosing to fulfil a healthy desire to look the way they want. A study published in 2012 suggests not, however.[134] It followed teenage girls in Norway for thirteen years, collecting information on their satisfaction with their appearance, their mental health and their use of cosmetic surgery. Symptoms of depression and anxiety, a history of self-harming, feeling suicidal and illegal drug use were predictive of those young women choosing to have cosmetic surgery. Young women who had surgery during the study period had an increase in symptoms of depression and anxiety, eating problems and alcohol use compared to those who didn't have surgery. An earlier American study showed that cosmetic surgery patients were five times more likely to have a history of psychiatric illness, compared to patients having other surgery; in fact, 18 per cent of the cosmetic surgery patients were using psychiatric medications at the time of their surgical consultation.[135] Trends in cosmetic surgery are not something we should be complacent about, as they are so clearly a reflection of insecurity, anxiety and unhappiness. And if this is about social comparisons it is surely a zero-sum game – we can't all look more attractive compared to each other.

FEELING SPECIAL

Let's return to the issue of whether or not it's important to love and feel good about ourselves. Don't we need to do this in order to feel confident, to get ahead, to have the courage to 'make something of ourselves'?

The reaction to Twenge and Campbell's work in America was mostly positive, but they describe receiving some 'harsh criticism', as those immured in the cult of self-esteem and positive thinking asked 'should we all just hate ourselves instead?' One student protested in the media: 'But we are special. There's nothing wrong with knowing that. It's not vanity that this generation exhibits – it's pride.' Nobody likes to be accused of self-centredness, and research shows that young people especially dislike being labelled as entitled and narcissistic, even as they admit to being a more narcissistic generation than their parents.[136]

As Twenge and her co-authors point out, narcissists lack empathy, which in the long-term means they have difficulty maintaining mutually loving relationships and friendships. They also show that there isn't a correlation between narcissism and performance on intelligence tests, that narcissists are no more physically attractive than non-narcissists, and narcissism does not lead to sustained success. Narcissists are more likely to drop out of college, have too high a tolerance for risk in business, are unpopular as bosses, and work poorly in groups. Narcissists aren't really better than the rest of us; their admiration for themselves isn't based on real qualities or achievements, and their behaviour can cause real suffering to their family, friends and colleagues. Narcissism is another consequence of the 'each against all' logic, of the way inequality replaces co-operation with status competition.

PSYCHOPATHS AT THE TOP

All societies like to think of themselves as ones in which honest, law-abiding, hard-working citizens can make a living, contribute to society and find fulfilment. We expect our institutions – whether schools, businesses or governments – to reward moral, ethical behaviour, hard work and co-operation. However, inequality and the heightened status competition and individualism which go with it seem to contribute to a culture in which 'greed is good', risk-taking is admired, and the differences between overly dominant behaviour and leadership are elided.

In such a climate, it is perhaps no wonder that individuals with a personality disorder characterized by lying, manipulation, deceit, egocentricity and callousness can often be found at the very top of modern corporate structures. Psychologists Paul Babiak and Robert Hare call this phenomenon 'snakes in suits', documenting how 'snakes' with psychopathic personalities have thrived, at the expense of others, in the fast-paced, competitive world of modern business corporations.[137]

Greater inequality not only causes psychopathic tendencies to manifest in more people, it provides the cut-throat environment in which those tendencies come to be seen as admirable or valuable, and competitiveness as more important than co-operation. The idea that the upper reaches of the business world are increasingly peopled by those with psychopathic tendencies has caught the attention of psychologists and the public alike. Journalist Jon Ronson's 2011 book, *The Psychopath Test*,[138] describes how he learned to spot psychopaths, applying Robert Hare's Psychopathy Checklist. A diagnosis of psychopathy depends on a high score on this checklist rather than on having every single characteristic; so it doesn't depend on having a criminal record or a history of behavioural problems in childhood. It is plausible, therefore, that in a culture that values *some* expressions of *some* of these behaviours, people with more of these traits might do rather well, at least in the short-term.

Ronson recounts his meeting with Al Dunlap, a former CEO of Sunbeam-Oster, a US firm that made electrical home appliances such as toasters and waffle irons. Dunlap was known as a business turnaround specialist and professional downsizer; according to Wikipedia, he was known as 'Chainsaw Al' and 'Rambo in Pinstripes' for his ruthless methods. Despite some initial reluctance, Dunlap agreed during their meeting to go through Hare's revised Psychopathy Checklist with Ronson. He agreed that many of the items applied to him, but saw them as positives. He claimed to be 'totally charming', saw grandiose self-worth as important – 'you've got to believe in yourself' – and saw manipulation as 'leadership':

> And so the morning continued, with Al redefining a great many psychopathic traits as Leadership Positive. Impulsivity was 'just another way of saying Quick Analysis. Some people spend a week weighing up the pros and cons. Me? I look at it for ten minutes. And if the pros outweigh the cons? Go!' 'Shallow affect' stops you from feeling 'some nonsense emotions'. A lack of remorse frees you up to move forward and achieve more great things.[138]

Over lunch, Dunlap tells Ronson supposedly funny stories about firing people, his wife laughing at each one, and Ronson speculates on 'what a godsend to a corporation a man who enjoys firing people must be'.

Of course, Dunlap wasn't a godsend to many of the long-term and loyal employees of Sunbeam-Oster. Widespread plant and factory closures and mass firings might have been popular with shareholders, but they caused enormous human suffering and devastated many small-town economies. And in the long-term, Sunbeam-Oster itself suffered badly from Dunlap's grandiose sense of self-worth, cunning and criminal versatility – he used fraudulent accounting methods to make shareholders believe that the company had been turned around and was making huge profits. He was sued by the Securities and Exchange

Commission in 2001, and in 2002 Sunbeam-Oster filed for bankruptcy. Closer investigation showed that he had a history of such irregularities and of being fired for his aggressive management style. John Byrne, the editor of business magazine *Fast Company* who wrote a book about Dunlap, claimed never to have come across an executive as 'manipulative, ruthless, and destructive as Al Dunlap'.[139]

Is Dunlap a bad apple, one of a very few? Are there really more psychopaths at the top of the corporate world than lower down the ranks? British psychologists Belinda Board and Katarina Fritzon compared the personality traits of 39 senior business managers (all men) to a sample of 768 patients from Broadmoor High Security Hospital. All of the Broadmoor patients had received a legal classification of either mental illness or psychopathic disorder and either been convicted of serious crime or found unfit to plead when tried for such crimes.[140] The businessmen scored higher than the diagnosed patients on several negative traits, including histrionic (superficial charm, insincerity, egocentricity, manipulativeness), narcissistic (grandiosity, lack of empathy, exploitativeness, independence), and compulsive (perfectionism, excessive devotion to work, rigidity, stubbornness and dictatorial tendencies) features.

In Chapter 2, Figure 2.4 showed how people can be classified along two dimensions of behaviour: between dominance and submissiveness and between warmth and hostility – people with narcissistic and psychopathic tendencies are in the top right quarter of the diagram, where dominance and hostility meet. Whether they achieve success through manipulative and ruthless business practices or end up in prison for violent and aggressive offences, may depend in large part on whether chance landed them in family and social circumstances that enabled them to climb up the ladder of business – snakes in suits – or whether poverty and difficult early circumstances hampered their ability to avoid aggression, and they ended up at the bottom.

Babiak and Hare describe the corporate climate that developed in the USA in the late 1970s as one of takeovers, mergers and acquisitions, downsizing and break-ups, the shedding of bureaucracy, rapid change, speed and innovation. What was lost was an appreciation of corporate or institutional loyalty, and the social contract between employer and employee, between business and society. This transformation of business was a consequence of the political and economic ideologies of the time. The belief in unfettered individualism and free markets also marked the onset of the widening of income differences and the rise of status competition throughout society. In fact, so closely do modern corporations resemble the narcissistic and psychopathic individuals they often embrace that there is a full-length 2003 documentary feature film about this, *The Corporation*, based on a book by law professor Joel Bakan.[141] Corporations have gone from being legal institutions with public functions, to having the legal rights of personhood, giving them some of the rights of individual humans (including making political expenditures). Bakan therefore examines the corporate structure as a personality – and diagnoses it as psychopathic. In 2003 this could be seen as darkly humorous, but since the global financial crisis of 2007–8, book after book, and films such as *The Four Horsemen* and *Inside Job*, have traced the damage caused to millions worldwide by the corporate risk-takers and socially irresponsible rogue businesses.

Philosopher Simon Blackburn, discussing rising inequality and the vast salaries and bonuses of the top 1 per cent in his extended essay on self-love, *Mirror, Mirror*, asks: 'How can they look [at] themselves in the mirror, walk down the street? Have they no sense of decency, let alone fellow feeling with the rest, whom they have robbed and continue to rob?'[142] The answer, as he goes on to discuss, is that such people have come to believe that they are 'worth it because of their exceptional abilities, judgement and intelligence. Anything less than, say, 300 times the average income of workers in their companies would be unjust, a simple failure to reward their astonishing gifts adequately.' Never mind, points out Blackburn, that it requires no extraordinary genius to pay bank customers 1 per cent interest, lend to borrowers at 16.5 per cent interest, and pocket as much of the difference as they can get away with.

How, in an unequal world, can we hope to transform business to once again foster the values most of us share? We will argue in Chapter 9 that to uphold and prioritize a social contract above shareholder value requires the development of all forms of economic democracy. Employee-owned companies, co-operatives, employee share-ownership schemes, strong trade unions and employee representation all help to curb runaway top incomes and the bonus culture. But economic democracy can also act as a curb to the excesses and ruthlessness of narcissistic and psychopathic business 'leaders', constraining their freedom to manipulate and bully, take too many risks, and cover up mistakes. It's possible for business leaders accountable to employees to achieve status by combining positive dominance strategies with warmth, so sitting in the lower right-hand side of our Figure 2.4 – using their skills and expertise for alliance-building and co-operation, demonstrating true leadership through persuasion and conscientiousness, inspiring rather than intimidating people, and taking authentic pride in creating and growing businesses that serve, rather than exploit, people and society.

THE RICH REALLY ARE DIFFERENT . . . INEQUALITY AND SENSE OF ENTITLEMENT

Most people aren't narcissists, even if there is suggestive evidence that there is a rise in narcissism caused by inequality, and only a very tiny proportion are psychopaths, even though such people cause disproportionate amounts of emotional and criminal damage at the top and bottom of society. But narcissism and psychopathy are the tip of the iceberg. There is huge damage to society from people simply feeling that their superior position makes them more deserving than others.

Paul Piff, a social psychologist at the University of California, Berkeley, has carried out a remarkable set of experiments focused on social hierarchy, emotions, relationships between social groups and what psychologists call 'prosocial' behaviour – that is, actions that benefit others or society as a whole, such as sharing, volunteering, co-operating and helping others.

In the first set of experiments, Piff and his colleagues looked at the prosocial behaviour of people in 'lower social classes' – defined as people whose life circumstances (with less education, less money, lower rank and more of the problems related to deprivation, including stressful family relationships) typically lead to a low sense of personal control.[143] They wanted to know if, despite (or perhaps because of) their social position, people in this group are more concerned with the needs of others and more willing to help others than people with higher incomes, more education, etc. They already knew that, in America, poorer households give a larger proportion of their income to charity than richer households (perhaps a reflection of their own experience of having to rely on social bonds and networks to get by).[144] In experimental conditions in which they took account of age, ethnicity and religious tendencies, the researchers found that, in economic games, people in the lower class group allocated more money to a partner, were more trusting, believed that a higher proportion of a family's income should be donated to charity, and were more helpful to a partner in a controlled situation set up to make them believe that the partner was in distress.

Not only were people in the lower social class group more prosocial, they were also more ethical. In a second set of tests, Piff and his colleagues again used laboratory experiments and observational studies of car drivers at an intersection and a pedestrian crossing.[145] They found that drivers of higher status (more expensive) vehicles (based on make, age and appearance) were more likely to cut in front of other drivers instead of waiting their turn, and less likely to yield to pedestrians waiting to cross the road (Figure 3.3).

Piff also looked at a sense of entitlement among upper- and lower-class subjects.[146] The upper-class group scored higher than lower-class subjects on psychological measures of entitlement (sample question: 'I honestly feel I'm just more deserving than others'), on the Narcissistic Personality Inventory, and were more likely to spend time looking at themselves in a mirror when they were left alone and thought they were unobserved.

In controlled experiments, after reading scenarios in which characters took something or benefitted from something they were not entitled to, those in the upper-class group were more likely than people in the lower-class group to say that they would do the same. Although this might simply have indicated that the upper-class group cared less about what the researchers thought of them, they were more likely to actually deceive others in a scenario where they could choose to withhold the truth from an imaginary job applicant. They were also more likely to cheat in a dice game. And they were more

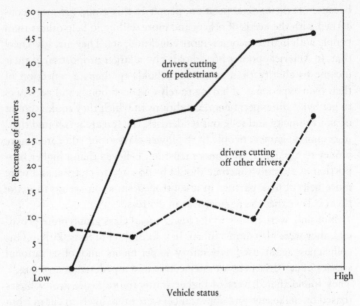

Figure 3.3: Percentage of cars that cut off other vehicles at an intersection and pedestrians at a crossing, by vehicle status.[145]

likely to take sweets that they had been told were intended for children in a nearby laboratory.[146]

Piff's research suggests that we can change people's tendency to behave in unethical, antisocial, narcissistic ways by appealing to their better nature. When subjects were primed to think about the statement 'greed is good' by having to write down three benefits of equality, differences in unethical behaviour between the upper- and lower-class groups disappeared. The researchers concluded that the groups didn't differ in their capacity for unethical behaviour, but did differ in their general default tendencies towards it. And the researchers similarly were able to reduce the upper-class subjects' narcissism by getting them to think about egalitarian values. The subjects were split into two groups before completing the Narcissistic Personality Inventory. One group ('Egalitarian') was asked to write down three benefits of treating other people as equals; the other group ('Control') simply wrote down three activities they did on a typical day. In the control group, there was the expected excess of narcissism among upper-class individuals, but in the group who had been asked to think about egalitarian values, the narcissism of the upper-class individuals was significantly reduced (Figure 3.4).

There are two plausible explanations of Piff's finding that higher-status people appear to behave worse towards others. One is that people who are more strongly motivated to maximize their own status may also, by nature and temperament, be more antisocial. The other is that we might all behave badly to those below us on the social ladder; high-status people might then differ only in seeing *more* of us as their inferiors.

The real explanation, though, seems to be that it is inequality itself that creates the climate in which richer, higher-status people behave badly, rather than some inbuilt characteristic. Piff's observations and experiments were all conducted in the USA. It now looks as if the tendency for better-off people to behave in more antisocial ways is not found in more equal societies. Researchers have found that in the

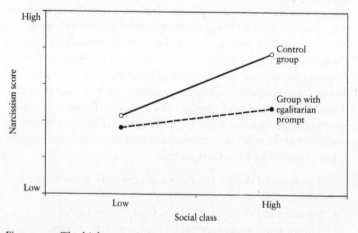

Figure 3.4: The higher narcissism scores of upper-social-class people are reduced when they are primed to think about egalitarian values.[146]

Netherlands, Germany and Japan, all much more equal than the United States, richer people are no less likely than poorer people to be trusting or generous.[147] Further evidence from that 2015 study found a tendency for higher-income individuals in the United States to be less generous only in more unequal states.[147] Researchers used a nationally representative survey that gave participants an opportunity to donate to others, and found that in the most unequal US states, higher-income people were less generous than those with lower incomes, whereas in the least unequal states, higher-income individuals were more generous. They also set up an experiment in which levels of economic inequality in participants' home states were described as either relatively high or low. In this case, higher-income people were less generous than lower-income people if they had been told they lived in a more unequal place, but not when they were told they lived in a more equal place.

NARCISSISM TRUMPS GOOD LEADERSHIP

Perhaps none of this would matter if higher-status individuals in more unequal societies were effective leaders, despite being less trusting, less generous, etc. When we started writing this book, we had no idea that someone with pronounced narcissistic tendencies could be elected to the highest political office, but the leadership qualities of President Trump are now a matter of great concern throughout the world. It is impossible to diagnose someone solely though their pronouncements on social media, but Donald Trump's incessant tweeting suggests self-grandiosity, callousness, poor sense of control and many of the other characteristics of narcissists and psychopaths. A few examples of his Tweets include:

- 'I understand things. I comprehend very well, better than I think almost anybody.'
- 'I understand the tax laws better than almost anyone.'
- 'I know more about renewables than any human being on Earth.'

- 'Nobody knows banking better than I do.'
- 'Nobody in the history of this country has ever known so much about infrastructure as Donald Trump.'
- 'There's nobody bigger or better at the military than I am.'

And perhaps most amusingly (or sadly):

- 'The new Pope is a humble man, very much like me.'

Narcissists tend to be regarded as effective leaders on short acquaintance, probably because we value the confidence they exude. However, in the longer-term narcissists become increasingly unpopular, as their arrogance and aggressiveness come to the fore.[148, 149]

In the study of active US soldiers that we referred to earlier in this chapter, coming from a richer family was linked to a higher risk of narcissism, and the researchers also found that this link led to less effective leadership.[124] If, as many have suggested, income inequality has exacerbated the social divisions that underpin the present rise of populism, it can also throw up leaders with such a sense of entitlement and narcissistic self-belief that they cannot lead effectively, or with humility and compassion.

EMPATHY: HOW SOCIETIES MIND THE GAP

Just as important as the impact of inequality on narcissism, psychopathy and a sense of entitlement, are the effects on empathy. Understanding and sympathizing with each other's feelings underpins community life and social relationships. It's not just an important human quality; many social animals exhibit empathy, for it is what allows them to maintain relationships within social groups. Among our nearest animal relatives, monkeys and apes show attachment to one another and share emotions, becoming excited when other members of the group are excited, or comforting another animal that appears frightened or sad. Primatologist Frans de Waal cites examples of chimpanzees and bonobos throwing a chain to another animal stuck in a zoo moat, or bringing water to an animal unable to obtain it for itself.[150] Empathy is key to survival because co-operation is so essential.[151]

Empathy in individuals, including children, can be destroyed by neglect or abuse. Mary Clark, an expert on conflict resolution, calls the compassion that arises from empathy the *primary characteristic* of humans.[151] Loss of empathy, what psychiatrist Simon Baron-Cohen calls 'turning people into objects', puts us into 'I mode' and this lack of empathy underpins cruelty.[152] Baron-Cohen's book *Zero Degrees of Empathy* gives examples of individuals acting without empathy from many different cultures, and examples of gratuitous cruelty. He defines empathy as occurring when 'we suspend our single-minded focus of attention, and instead adopt a double-minded focus of attention', which allows us to 'identify what someone else is thinking or feeling, and to respond . . . with an appropriate emotion'. As inequality renders whole societies less empathetic, we are less able to bridge the widening differences and social distances between groups; we increasingly lose any sense of being in this together and of the necessity of protecting the most vulnerable and the voiceless.

Susan Fiske, a psychologist at Princeton University, describes how psychological experiments that induce people to feel powerful also cause deficits in their ability to understand others' emotions and thoughts, because powerful or dominant people can ignore others with impunity.[153] As she says, 'power may allow scorn', and, as she also shows, scorn is harmful to both the scorned and the scorner, creating barriers to shared experiences. She calls scorn a moral hazard of high status, causing everything from casual thoughtless disregard to the dehumanization of those who are scorned. Envy of others, the flip-side of scorn, is also corrosive for both the envier and the envied; enviers feel shame, resentment, anger; the envied are perceived as cold, calculating and threatening.

Beyond the personal experiences which shape our own empathy and compassion, does inequality shape our collective, societal empathy? As we have already described, income inequality increases the social distances between us and heightens the salience of status and competition for status. In the very first two sentences of her book *Envy Up, Scorn Down*, Fiske says: 'we are divided by envy and scorn, brought on by the status concerns that pervade our society. Income inequality, now at historically high levels, aggravates these status divides.'[153] Until very recently, however, there was no real evidence that empathy is affected by different levels of income inequality. Two studies, both published in 2012, now go some way to addressing that.

The first, from psychologist Federica Durante of the University of Milan and her colleagues, was a global study across thirty-seven countries of the ways in which people stereotype 'others'.[154] The researchers wanted to understand how, given the extensive problems it causes, populations don't actively oppose inequality, and instead acquiesce in the maintenance of the status quo. They suggest that being able to view 'other' groups in ambivalent ways – allowing those groups to have both good and bad characteristics – might be a way in which people are able to rationalize inequality. For example, if we felt all rich people were selfish and mean, we might not tolerate the inequality that allows people to become very rich; but if we believe the rich are especially capable and do good things for the economy, then we would tolerate their existence.

We all, to some degree, hold stereotypes about 'others', and view different groups as having different strengths and weaknesses. Some of the characteristics by which we stereotype groups of people include whether or not we believe they are of high or low status, more or less competent, competitive or collaborative, warm and friendly as opposed to cold and hostile, etc. Durante and her colleagues hypothesized that holding *ambiguous* stereotypes about others, for example holding the paternalistic view that women are warm but incompetent, or that the rich are competent but cold and calculating, would be more common in more unequal countries. This was borne out by their findings: in more unequal societies people tended to view others more ambivalently. As income inequality increases, so does the need to justify and rationalize it, to think that the rich contribute something good, even if they are selfish, or that the poor are kind to one another, even if they have failed to get on in life – otherwise the whole social structure would feel unjust and intolerable. We rationalize inequality by seeing different groups as more or less deserving or moral. As the authors say, 'the more income inequality, the more social groups need to be rewarded'. Inequality changes the way people think about others.

Do such stereotypes matter? After all, the study simply measured how people think about others (in fact, how they think other people think about others), rather than how they act, and indeed interact, with other people. Surely the truer sign of empathy is how people actually behave towards one another, their willingness to act compassionately rather than coldly, collectively rather than competitively?

In Chapter 2, we mentioned a study by social scientists Marii Paskov and Caroline Dewilde, who used data from the European Values Survey to look at income inequality and solidarity.[39] They defined 'solidarity' as people's willingness to contribute to the welfare of others, an important aspect of empathy. People in twenty-six European countries were asked: 'Would you be prepared to actually do something to improve the conditions of: (a) people in your neighbourhood/community; (b) elderly in your country; (c) sick and disabled people in your country; (d) immigrants in your country?' The analysis controlled for each country's average income, spending on social protection and type of welfare regime, and for each respondent's gender, age, marital and employment status, whether they were an immigrant or religious, as well as their education and income.

Taking all these things into account, the researchers found a significant tendency for people in more equal countries to be more willing to help others. The strongest reasons given for helping others were moral duty and sympathy, rather than the general interest of society or self-interest. People were much more willing to help the sick, disabled and older people, and less willing to help immigrants, but the differences between countries were substantial. In Sweden, 85% of people were willing to help the elderly, compared to only 54% in Great Britain, and 33% in Estonia; 68% of Swedes would help immigrants, whereas only 14% of British people and 4% of Lithuanians were willing to do so. The effects of inequality on social cohesion, segregation and trust are well known[1, 155]; many separate studies have shown that increased inequality erodes trust. What Paskov and Dewilde have shown is how levels of trust and social cohesion might translate into actual solidarity and neighbourliness: regardless of their own income level, people in more unequal countries were less willing to help others.

*

In this chapter, we've traced the evidence that shows how inequality pressures people to feel a greater need to present themselves as better than others; how a modern epidemic of narcissism reflects growing inequality; how business has paved the way for people with psychopathic tendencies to rise to the top of the corporate world; and how people are more anxious about their status in more unequal countries. We've seen how the rich can be encouraged to be less antisocial, more ethical, and feel less entitled when they are asked to think about egalitarian values. And we've seen evidence that empathy and willingness to help others is eroded by income inequality.

What this suggests is that greater societal inequality makes status, self-advancement and self-interest more powerful influences on us – as if the only way to respond to a competitive, unequal world is through self-aggrandizement, through competing to claw our way up. But there is also evidence that self-enhancement and narcissism can mask great insecurity, and inhibit people from happy and fulfilling relationships. Feelings of scorn and envy up and down the social hierarchy are bad for well-being – whether you scorn or are scorned, envy others or are envied.

Empathy is a keystone of human social relationships and well-being. Simon Baron-Cohen describes it as a universal solvent: interpersonal problems and marital difficulties, problems at work or with neighbours, political deadlock and international conflict can all be solved when immersed in empathy. Empathy is free, and the exercise of empathy cannot oppress anyone. Despite its erosion by inequality, the potential benefits of unleashing and optimizing empathy by reducing inequality should give us enormous hope that we can create a better world.

'Actually, I don't consider myself a have or a have-not.
I'm more of a have-to-have.'

4

False Remedies

'Every night I lay in bed and say never again. "Tomorrow
will be different" but no . . . it's always the same, it never
stops, I'm worthless, I can see how my friends are so happy
and I'm just sort of there. Not a part of it. I'm in my own
world, looking in at this life I could have . . . I should have.'

Posted online, 2014

'I have that hole again, the one in my stomach that begs to
be filled. Not that it is food I am hungering for.

'A touch, a caress, would be a good start. But none for
me, not tonight.

'I guess I'll go eat after all . . .'

Posted online, 2014, on the internet
chat site I Have An Addiction

Shopaholic, alcoholic, workaholic, chocoholic, sexaholic, gizmoholic.
It seems we can be addicted to anything and everything. Many claim
to be obsessed with the latest video game or television series, others
say they are addicted to bacon, sleep or cupcakes. The online Urban
Dictionary rather sniffily claims that the 'holic' suffix is 'always
improperly used unless referring to an addict of alcohol', but a lot of
people are clearly willing to admit to an overwhelming involvement or
an obsession with something that, when indulged, makes them feel
temporarily better about themselves and about their lives.

As we have seen, trying to maintain self-esteem and status in a more unequal society can be highly stressful. Whether a person's confidence collapses and they feel defeated by intensified social comparisons, or whether they brazen it out in a struggle to convince the world that they are managing successfully (usually on the basis of fairly fragile egos), this experience of stress can lead to an increased desire for anything which makes them feel better – whether alcohol, drugs, eating for comfort, 'retail therapy' or another crutch. It's a dysfunctional way of coping, of giving yourself a break from the relentlessness of the anxiety so many feel.

Many professionals who work with people addicted to drugs or alcohol object to the language and labels of addiction being applied to any other kind of behaviour, but here we adopt a definition offered by psychologist Bruce Alexander, famous for a series of experiments known as the Rat Park studies. These studies showed that rats housed in social groups took far less opioid drugs than those housed in isolation, leading Alexander to suggest that the characteristics and qualities of the drugs themselves – their inherent addictiveness – explains only a small part of the 'drugs problem'. He demonstrated that addiction is as much a social as an individual problem, and this perspective is borne out by the evidence we examine in this chapter. In his overview of the history of addiction, *The Globalization of Addiction: A Study in Poverty of the Spirit*, Alexander defines addiction as 'an overwhelming involvement in any pursuit whatsoever that is harmful to the addicted person, to society, or to both'.[156] This is a broad definition, inclusive of all the ways in which people might become trapped in repetitive behaviours that endanger themselves and others, and one which allows us to consider addiction at a societal level and ask why people increasingly engage in addictive behaviour and to so many different things.

Alexander sees addiction, in this broad sense, as a by-product of modernity. He believes that free market economies break down social cohesion, creating *dislocation*, which he also calls 'poverty of spirit'. In his view, addictions are ways that we adapt to feeling dislocated, alienated, disconnected. By 'dislocation' Alexander means feeling out of place, excluded, disconnected from good social relationships, unhappy in ourselves. In modern, free market societies, he argues, dislocation is not a pathological state confined to a few individuals, but a general condition propagated by the antisocial conception of 'economic man'. This is the idea that human nature makes us act with rational self-interest, pursuing individualistic goals with no thought for the common good – an idea that has become entrenched over the last half century. Alexander points out that material poverty can be borne with dignity, but that poverty of spirit, or dislocation, cannot, and it cannot be overcome with material things.

Alexander's interpretation of the roots of addiction is based on some long-standing psychological thinking about what it means to be a healthy individual. Healthy people maintain a balance between their individual needs for autonomy and achievement and their equally vital need for social connection and belonging.[157] According to Alexander, 'free market society can no more be free of addiction than it can be free of intense competition, [and] income disparity'. Individual competition is overemphasized at the expense of social cohesion, and (as we have seen) increasing levels of inequality heighten status anxiety. Under these conditions, people struggle to achieve psychosocial integration and turn instead to a variety of addictive crutches. That these behaviours are generally self-defeating in varying degrees only cements the mental distress which motivated them in the first place.

ESCAPING OURSELVES

If sustaining our psychosocial integration with others and having a resilient sense of identity is increasingly difficult in free market societies,[158] and also heightened by the constant social evaluative threat of social media and the digital world, then our need to belong and to feel valued is more important than ever. In his 1991 book, *Escaping the Self*, Roy Baumeister, professor of psychology at Florida State University, points out the range of things we do to maintain our self-image and our image as we present it to others[159]:

> We struggle to gain prestigious credentials. We read books and take courses on how to make a good impression. We discard clothes that are not worn out and buy new, more fashionable ones. We work hard

to devise self-serving explanations for failures or mishaps and fight to make others take the blame. We go hungry to make ourselves fashionably thin. We rehearse conversations or presentations in advance and ruminate about them afterwards to try to imagine what went wrong. We undergo cosmetic surgery. We endlessly seek information about other people so we can have a basis for comparing ourselves. We engage in fistfights with people who impugn our respectability or superiority. We grope desperately for rationalizations. We blush and brood when something makes us look foolish. We buy endless magazines advising us how to look better, make love better, succeed at work or play or dieting, and say clever things. Maintaining self-esteem can start to seem like a full-time job!

Living with high levels of social evaluative threat is exhausting; an almost impossible, Sisyphean task, and one that can only be getting harder with the added effort of constant self-curation of our online identities. Baumeister describes the kinds of things that make us want to escape ourselves and the effort of maintaining a good front in the eyes of others – not just calamities but also the chronic burden of other people's expectations. Before the Renaissance, people tried to conform to standard or ideal models of *conduct*; now we seem increasingly concerned with a more superficial ideal, with conforming to standards of beauty and owning the right things.

And when we feel looked down on by others, and we start to feel worthless, incompetent and rejected, drugs, alcohol, immersion in the fantasy worlds of video games and television, comfort food, retail therapy or the possibility of a big win become more alluring and draw so many of us in. We are endlessly tempted with products which promise to create for us the identities we desire, with activities and purchases that provide short-term fixes for our chronic stress and anxieties but nothing more.

REPLACING PEOPLE WITH THINGS

The idea that addiction and compulsive behaviour involve 'replacing people with things' has been around since the late 1980s. The phrase was originally coined by psychotherapist Craig Nakken and it features prominently in journalist Damian Thompson's book *The Fix*, which describes the ways in which we're increasingly obsessed by our mobile phones, sugary cupcakes, video games, frozen coffee drinks and online shopping.[160]

Thompson tells the story of how vast numbers of American GIs in Vietnam took up heroin to cope with the lonely, stressful and frightening situation they found themselves in, but almost all kicked the habit once freed from that context and safely back home. For Thompson, modern consumers, with their addictive-like behaviours, 'are like soldiers drafted to Vietnam – disorientated, fearful and relentlessly tempted by fixes that promise to make reality more bearable. You don't have to be ill to give in; just human.' The analogy is troubling because we are already 'home', and if we are to escape the destructive patterns he describes we need to understand what it is about unequal societies, in particular, that pushes us into them.

START AS YOU MEAN TO GO ON

Although the terms 'preloading' and 'predrinking' are fairly new, they describe an already widespread trend. They simply mean drinking large quantities of alcohol before going out socially, a practice that has changed the typical pattern of young people's drinking. Instead of starting in the pub and going on to a club, they start drinking at home, with typically one-third of a night's alcohol consumption taking place before they've left the premises. In all studies of this kind of drinking, the prime motivation given by young people is to save money. By drinking cut-price supermarket alcohol at home before they head out to pubs, bars and clubs, they can achieve their preferred level of drunkenness at a much lower cost – although of course many of them also concede that going out drunk is not actually conducive to sensible spending later in the evening. But another strong motivation for preloading is social anxiety. For many young people, going out drunk means not having to cope with the social evaluative threat of starting a night out cold sober. As girls in a research study[161] said: 'I get scared in clubs so drinking before I go out gives me the courage to face it', and 'Pubs don't work for me and my mates until we're pissed and ready to face the chaos.' In a New Zealand study, the researchers describe how 'everyday inhibition, extreme shyness and a sense of actually finding the night-time economy just too unpleasant if sober, were all given as personal motivations for pre-loading to intoxication'.[162]

Socializing has always been fraught with anxiety for young people; they are unsure of their own identity while at the same time they're looking for friendship groups, relationships and sexual partners, and feel constantly exposed to the judgement of others. But is this worse in more unequal modern societies? We saw in Chapter 2 how status anxiety is increased, across the social spectrum, for people living in more unequal countries, and we know that anxiety and depression and the use of alcohol and drugs to self-medicate go hand-in-hand[163, 164]; but do we know for sure that anxiety and income inequality increase preloading, binge drinking, alcoholism, drug use and other addictive behaviours? Are people living in more unequal societies more addicted to gambling, video games or cupcakes than their counterparts in more egalitarian countries?

MEASURING THE SOCIALLY UNACCEPTABLE

In our previous book, we showed that a measure of mental illness that included addictions was significantly related to income inequality in rich countries, and inequality was also related to a combined index of drug use, such as heroin, cocaine and amphetamines. Among US states, the most unequal have higher rates of drug addiction and more deaths from drug overdoses.[1] And studies of New York City neighbourhoods found that those with the most income inequality had higher rates of marijuana smoking[165] and deaths from drug overdose.[166] The connection between inequality and illicit drugs is clear and robust, but alcohol use has more complicated social patterns. In the UK and the USA, drinking *any* alcohol at all is more common higher up the social ladder, but *problematic* drinking is more common further down. People's own reports of the amount of alcohol they drink are suspect, and studies comparing alcohol use between different countries have often used data on sales of alcohol rather than self-reported alcohol consumption because of these concerns. It's not just that some people prefer not to disclose how much they drink, but also that people don't have an accurate assessment of their intake – there is understandable confusion over how many 'units of alcohol' are present in a large glass of wine, or a half pint of beer, or a double gin and tonic.

Nevertheless, income inequality has been linked to more frequent drinking in New York City neighbourhoods,[165] heavier drinking and drunkenness among adolescents in rich countries,[167] per capita alcohol consumption in thirteen European countries,[168] and (in a complicated pattern) to deaths attributable to alcohol in Australia.[169] However, not all studies have straightforward results. For example, the study of thirteen European countries found links between inequality and heavier alcohol consumption but none with alcoholic liver disease. Among US states, one study found that race-related income inequality (poor minority groups compared to white people) was more closely related to higher levels of alcohol problems than an overall measure of inequality.[170] In sum, the evidence that income inequality is related to risky alcohol consumption is complex but substantial and, taken alongside the studies of drug use and addiction, is another piece in the puzzle that depicts how inequality, mediated by social anxiety, causes harm.

As for gambling, video gaming and cupcakes, there is little good, comparable data on how prevalent these behaviours are in different societies. We know that obesity is higher in more unequal countries and states, as we showed in *The Spirit Level*, and we might view this as some kind of proxy measure for compulsive overeating – indeed, calorie intakes per person are higher in more unequal countries.[171] There is now a substantial body of evidence from observational and careful experimental studies that anxiety, including the increased anxiety resulting from inequality, contributes both to the drive to eat and to a preference for less healthy foodstuffs high in sugars and fats.[172, 173] That comfort eating is a deep-seated response to stress is suggested by the fact that the same tendencies have been demonstrated in animal studies, and sugars and fats have been shown to be calming and to reach the same areas of the brain as opiates.

Gambling and gaming are comparable to drinking in that they are not problems per se but certainly can be addictive and problematic, so knowing how many bets are placed or games are played in different places doesn't tell us much: we need to know how many people gamble or play compulsively. Luckily, a report was published in 2012 with the results of painstaking effort to calculate the percentage of people engaged in problem gambling, adjusted for the age make-up of the population.[174] We found a strong and significant relationship between these estimates and income inequality. Figure 4.1 shows the correlation between problem gambling and the ratio of the richest to the poorest 20 per cent of households in each country (as reported in the United Nations Human Development Reports, 2007–2009).*[123]

There do not seem to be enough reliable estimates of video game addiction to look at its association with income inequality across different countries, but, to give an idea of the scale of the problem, a 2009 study in America estimated that 8 per cent of young gamers show symptoms of pathological video game behaviour.[175] Other recent studies suggest figures of 9% for Singapore, 12% for Germany and 8% in Australia,[176] but less than 1% in Norway.[177] Some countries, like South Korea and Japan, now view video game addiction as a public health problem, but it is hard to be sure about its scale and severity.[178]

The absence of an association between income inequality and cigarette smoking among adults in rich countries is puzzling. Perhaps because smoking provides only the very mildest feelings of psychological escape or diversion from one's self, it may do little to diminish feelings of powerlessness, inadequacy and impotence which are heightened by social inequality, whereas depressants like alcohol, stimulants like cocaine and activities like gambling and gaming can

* Although the USA as a whole has exactly the level of problem gambling which its level of income inequality would lead us to predict, we didn't find the same relationship across individual US states, presumably because of the particular variations in the legality of gambling in America. Before 1964, gambling was legal only in Nevada; even today Utah and Hawaii still prohibit gambling, and in many states, the casinos established by sovereign Native American tribes on reservations, allowed since 1987, have concentrated gambling in these areas, nearly all of which are located in the generally more equal northerly mid-western and western states.

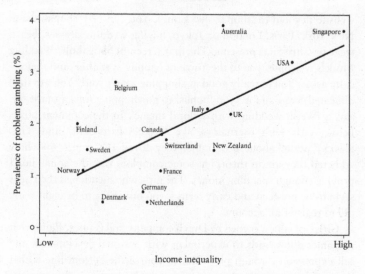

Figure 4.1: Income inequality is related to higher levels of problem gambling in rich countries.[123]

make us feel powerful or competent, and provide an escape from social fear and helplessness.[179] However, studies show that for young people in middle- and low-income countries, buying and smoking cigarettes is a status symbol, and here income inequality *is* linked to higher rates of smoking.[180] As we shall see, buying things, particularly status goods, is also shaped by the status anxiety and the intense competition fuelled by income inequality. The deeper the inequality in society, the higher the value we seem to attach to self-regard and the tougher the consequences of being disregarded by others.

SHOPAHOLICS

The internet site GirlsGoGames.co.uk specializes in downloadable games and apps aimed at young girls. There are kissing games, beauty games, dressing up and fashion makeover games, games focused on cupcakes and doughnuts, and an entire section of the website devoted to 'shopaholic' games. You can be a shopaholic in New York, Paris, London or Tokyo, buying wedding dresses, beach wear or Christmas presents. The first screen of Shopaholic Wedding Models welcomes you to the 'town of happily ever after' and rhetorically asks: 'You're really good at shopping aren't you?' You are then allocated $700 and a $500 'bonus' to go shopping for an outfit for, say, a 'Welsh wedding with a floral theme'. In the comment boxes below, girls with usernames like 'PrincessFairyCake' and 'Giggles123' write about how much they loved the games and how addicted they are to them, but some complain that the game didn't provide enough spending money. The girls who mentioned their ages seem to be pre-teen and early teens – you only have to be eight years old to register an account.

GirlsGoGames, owned by Dutch company Spil Games, claims that its games allow 'girls to experiment with personal development and self-expression through play'. But of course the bottom line is that these girls are a great target for potential advertisers, because the online platform gets 39 million unique visitors each month. 'From youngsters, through to teens, to women: we've got you covered', Spil Games tells advertisers. When these girls grow up, they can move on to the series of best-selling, ambiguously satirical Shopaholic books, written by Sophie Kinsella and featuring anti-heroine Becky Bloomwood, a spoiled, entitled woman with an out-of-control consumerism habit and commensurate debt problems.

In his book *All Consuming*, political commentator Neal Lawson describes the culture of shopping that developed in the UK in the decades leading up to the global financial crisis as 'turbo-consumerism'.[181] Fuelled by the relaxation of trading hours, easy credit, cheap imports and online commerce, shopping – and the products we acquired – increasingly became the way we defined ourselves, the way we spent our time, and more and more of our money. We became locked into a cycle of spending, dissatisfaction, and more spending – we could never keep up and the goalposts were constantly shifting. Published in 2009, Lawson's book captures a moment in time when it looked as if all this might change. High street chains were closing daily, wallets were shrinking, jobs were insecure and it looked as if everything might have to shift; we'd need a 'new normal', structured by an alternative kind of economy and different values. Despite the scale and seismic effects of the financial crash, this change was not forthcoming, and the hopes Lawson expressed were quickly dashed. 'The crash changes everything,' he wrote. 'I believe there is an alternative and that it's worth fighting for ... we can tip the balance against lives that are all-consuming and define a new normality based on having the time and space to find genuine and lasting happiness.'

Lawson's book, rather like Jean Twenge's on narcissism (see Chapter 3), is full of stories that shock and amaze: the amount that people will spend on handbags, the amount they will spend on eBay for a *used* carrier bag from an exclusive store so that they can pretend that they shop there, the girl who says she thinks that the brands a boy wears are more important than what he looks or is like, the amount the nation is spending on storage units to stash all the stuff we keep on buying but don't have room for. But just as with narcissism, the human feelings and motivations that lie behind the staggering stories are painful. We buy things to belong, to join the tribe, and we buy things to show we're good enough. And for the poor, their inability to keep up, to buy the latest goods, seems to mark them out as failures. Second-rate goods are seen as marking out second-rate people.

Of course we enjoy having nice things. The fillip which follows a good purchase, whether it's because we've scored a bargain or chosen quality over quantity or obtained something we've coveted, is universal. It is, however, not always easy to identify where the pressure to shop is coming from. Increasingly, people feel tempted to revamp their houses, even if everything works perfectly well. The compulsion to 'do it up' often has nothing to do with function and everything to do with the impression that it looks 'dated'. You can easily construct a case for renewing everything (the sink has fiddly bits that are difficult to clean, etc.) but really the temptation owes more to subliminal and overt messages picked up from Sunday supplements and television programmes, the recently renovated bathrooms of relatives, and so on, which make what we have seem tired and tawdry. None of us really likes to admit how much we're driven to purchase things for status reasons, how much of our spending is about keeping up. However, advertisers endlessly exploit our anxieties about status, already heightened by inequality, because they know it works.

SPENDING SECRETS

We seem to have quite an appetite for books and programmes that tell us what the stuff we buy says about us. These range from fun social commentary, such as 2013's *Consumed* by journalist Harry Wallop,[182] which contrasts the spending habits of 'Asda Mums' and 'Wood Burning Stovers', to the slightly more serious, such as anthropologist Kate Fox's *Watching the English*[183]; from the openly condescending (*Chav! A User's Guide To Britain's New Ruling Class* by Mia Wallace and Clint Spanner[184]) to those based on lifetimes of scholarly work (*Empire of Things* by Frank Trentmann[185]). All make it clear that how we spend our money labels us in other people's eyes: the food we eat, the clothes we wear, what we read and listen to, where we go on holiday, what we plant in our gardens. Harry Wallop argues that how we spend our money has become a more important indicator of social class than how we earn it, and that it is 'a cause of great social anxiety as well as financial hardship' for some.[182] Spending money need not be frivolous, of course: many people spend large amounts of money, even when it causes them some hardship, on things like private education and health care, believing that the free equivalents – state schools and the NHS – are not only inferior services, but that using them would mark them out as inferior people.

But wherever you direct your cash, trying to improve your social status through your spending is an uphill struggle. As the French sociologist Pierre Bourdieu has theorized, it is the possessors of 'cultural capital', those with education and other social assets, who determine what good taste is in any society at any time.[47] Any attempts by those in lower classes to define their own aesthetics and tastes is condemned by those higher up the social scale. And if the middle, and then the lower classes appropriate upper-class tastes and aesthetics, then whatever they have favoured becomes unfashionable and loses any social cachet.

Type 'the rise and fall of the Ugg boot' into Google and you'll pull up pages of stories about the changing fortunes of this distinctive Australian brand of sheepskin boot. Dating back to the 1930s, Uggs had a steady following among those who like their feet to be comfortable, but in the early 2000s they suddenly became uber-fashionable, seen on the feet of so-called A-list celebrities, such as film star Cameron Diaz and model Kate Moss. And then they (and endless cheaper copies) were everywhere. As soon as they were adopted by the masses, they were dropped by the top celebrities, losing their fashion mojo and seen only on C- or D-list reality TV stars. By 2012, sales were falling, and Ugg was working hard to keep the brand buoyant, even introducing bridal Uggs (white with a pale blue sole and a diamante crystal button). This decline of brands from their desirable and exclusive status has been snobbishly named 'prole drift', and if you're trying to maintain or raise your social status it can become necessary to monitor their rise and fall through magazines, newspaper fashion columns or blogs. The process never stops and you have to keep on spending if you want to try and keep up. It's not entirely linear; brands can regain their distinction and once again represent a tasteful or fashionable purchase. But if you're lower down the social scale, then however much you spend, and whatever you buy, you are likely to be scorned and looked down on for your choices.

In rich consumer societies, shopping has become an everyday way in which we replace people with things. We define ourselves through other people's eyes and we see them looking not at what we're like inside, but at the impression of us that our stuff creates. People are compelled to go on shopping until they drop – or credit limits are reached. Until the conditions that induce this anxiety and competition for status are addressed, until we reduce the inequality which drives compulsive consumption, this state of affairs – with all its consequences for our finances, health and, as we shall see, planet – will continue.

HOW TO BE A VERY IMPORTANT PERSON

Material goods are not all we buy to elevate our status. Daniel Briggs, from the University of East London, has studied working-class British tourists on holiday in Ibiza.[186] Briggs highlights the excessive and reckless drinking, drug use, sex and violence which characterize their behaviour and the impact this has on them and on the holiday resort. But more importantly, he shows how their behaviour and choices are shaped by the culture of their native country and by the exploitation of their social anxieties once they arrive on the island. Although they go on holiday to 'live the dream' and 'be who they want to be', their behaviour is in fact an exaggerated extension of their weekend lives back home. Briggs describes their actions as having been 'already structurally conditioned, socially constructed, packaged, repackaged and marketed to them – and it is this commercial pressure which is aggressively foisted on them during their holiday in the resort.'

For these people, their holiday is a space and time outside their daily routines, where they can enjoy the sun, sea, sand and freedom from the everyday restrictions of work and relationships back home. For that short period, they escape their low status back home; just as in the medieval days of the lords of misrule, for a brief space of time the rules of social stratification are suspended. For the young people Briggs spends time with, their hedonistic, consumerist lifestyle is a marker of status: it shows that they count for something, that they have an approved social identity among their peers. To be able to go to Ibiza shows that you can afford the good life, and will experience the good times. Sadly, all too many are injured, harassed, raped or die each tourist season. But their choices, behaviour and spending are shaped by commercial interests and pressures. The tourist industry and the media, particularly reality TV, create and reinforce the idea that you can only have fun if you spend more. You'll have a better time if you bring a different bikini to wear every day, or are showing off an expensive watch or pair of jeans. You'll have a much better time if you buy 'extras' – a boat party or a sunset cruise, entry into a more exclusive club or a jet ski experience, a tequila tasting or entry to a private beach club. Briggs describes parties of young people running through their cash long before the holiday is over and having to fall back on credit to make it through. But despite going home in debt, they're eager to come back next year, with more money, so they can 'do Ibiza properly'.

Doing it properly means paying for more exclusivity: a VIP sun lounger, or entry into the VIP area of a super-club. But you can always spend more, and there is always a class of more exclusive space and facilities if you spend *even* more – so the question is always, what level of VIP privilege can you afford, and if you come back next year can you buy even more status than you've managed to buy this year? Briggs labels this 'extreme capitalism', a commercial profit-making marketing process that pulls in young people made vulnerable by their low-paid, unfulfilling working lives, and incites exaggerated hedonism and overspending.

SELLING THE DREAM

Many researchers and commentators have drawn attention to the sophisticated ways in which the designers and purveyors of consumer products target our neurological reward systems and lure us into relationships with things, providing short-term fixes to our chronic stress and anxieties that might be better soothed through relationships with people. We have evolved to survive in environments where food, sex and comfort are scarce and must be pursued, but are rather less good at exercising restraint in the face of plenty, leaving us vulnerable to the modern world.

In *Affluenza*, his book on overconsumption, psychologist Oliver James quotes a Danish newspaper editor who says:

> Multinationals have learnt that there is no market for luxury goods here. When a new type of product comes out, for a few years it doesn't penetrate at all because it's too expensive and we don't like to be ostentatious, so only freaky playboys have one. But when the price comes down, so that middle-class Danes can afford it, then within eighteen months it reaches 70 per cent of the population.[187]

James comments that consumption of luxury goods is not a source of status for Danes; their greater equality of income, as well as greater equality between men and women, means that they are less susceptible to advertising and to pining after flashy cars and other prestige goods. Can this be true? Do advertisers really try less hard in more equal societies?

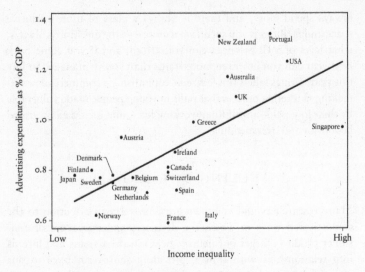

Figure 4.2: Spending on advertising, as a percentage of GDP, increases with greater income inequality.[123]

It would seem so. Looking at spending on advertising as a proportion of Gross Domestic Product (GDP), in relation to our usual measure of income inequality (Figure 4.2), we found that spending increased significantly as inequality increased.

BORN TO SHOP

The evidence increasingly suggests that materialism and status consumption are profoundly affecting the well-being of children in unequal societies. In 2007, the British public were shocked to learn that the UK ranked bottom in a report from UNICEF on child well-being in rich countries.[188] In two research papers, we showed how that index of child well-being (in both 2007 and 2013) was tightly correlated with income inequality (Figure 4.3).[189, 190] The response of the Labour government in power in 2007 was to criticize the UNICEF report for using out-of-date statistics (although this is always a problem with reports – it takes time to collect, process and analyse data – and applied equally to all countries included in the index), and claim that child well-being in the UK was improving. The Children's Commissioner for England hoped that the 'report [would] prompt us all to look beyond the statistics to the underlying causes of our failure to nurture happy and healthy children'.[191]

Recognizing that call for more in-depth understanding of children's lives, UNICEF UK commissioned a further study, of family life in three countries: Sweden, which had low inequality and high child well-being; Spain, with mid-range inequality and high well-being; and the UK, with high inequality and low well-being.[192] The study aimed to 'dig beneath the statistics on child well-being to discover the lived experiences of children', using discussions with friendship groups in schools and detailed observations of family life.

Seeing the video made as part of the study was both an exhilarating and depressing experience. Exhilarating because there, on screen, were parents and children whose thoughts and feelings reflected what we had theorized about the effects of inequality: these were the stories behind the statistics we had been working with for so many years. But it was depressing too, because the struggles of the British families were such a poignant contrast to the Spanish and Swedish families. In Sweden, parents talked about children saving their money for special purchases and making and mending toys. In Spain, there were children cherishing books and educational toys and storing them in special boxes to keep them nice. In the UK, the parents appeared universally exhausted and their homes were filled with boxes and piles of discarded toys. As the report stated:

> British families [were] struggling, pushed to find the time their children want.
>
> Many UK children do not refer to material goods when talking about what makes them happy, and also understand the principles of moderation in consumption, but many have parents who feel compelled to purchase, often against their better judgement.
>
> Children [have a] growing awareness of inequality as they approach secondary school, and the role of consumer goods in identifying and

creating status groups within peer groups ... Whilst many UK parents are complicit in purchasing status goods to hide social insecurities, this behaviour is almost totally absent in Spain and Sweden.

Reactions to this second study were mixed. Some media commentators saw the report as blaming parents. As with the prior UNICEF report, there were criticisms of the methods, this time aimed at the fact that the report was based on the experiences of only a small number of families rather than on the timeliness of the statistics. (Unsurprisingly, commentators from marketing and advertising industry bodies opposed the report's call for a ban on advertising to children under the age of twelve, calling the evidence 'weak'.) But taken together, as of course they must be, both the quantitative and qualitative studies show how income inequality increases the strain on family life, and how things replace relationships and time spent together. The stories reinforce the statistics and vice versa. Parental experience of adversity is passed on to children through pathways that include parental mental distress, longer working hours, higher levels of debt and domestic conflict.

The link between materialism and damaged well-being is strong. Tim Kasser, professor of psychology at Knox College in Illinois, developed the Aspiration Index, which places people's values on different continuums. One important axis is the extent to which goals are extrinsic and materialistic (e.g., financial success, image, popularity) versus intrinsic (e.g., personal growth, affiliation, community feeling). Over many years of study, Kasser has found that materialism is related to anxiety and depression, to substance abuse, lack of empathy, higher scores on the Social Dominance Orientation scale, more prejudice, 'Machiavellianism', antisocial behaviour, and competitive versus collaborative strategies. Materialism makes us unhappy, but being unhappy also makes us materialistic.[193] Looking at different countries, he has found that those that value egalitarianism over hierarchy, and harmony over mastery, have better child well-being.[194] Working with Jean Twenge, Kasser found that American children have become more materialistic over the generations since 1976, placing more importance on money and owning expensive things.[195]

Over the decade 2000–2009 some rich countries, such as Ireland

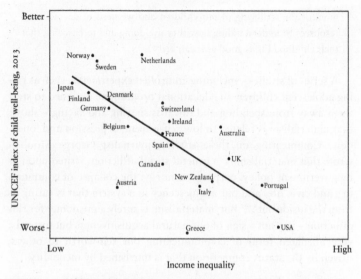

Figure 4.3: Child well-being is worse in more unequal rich countries.[190]

and Sweden, became more unequal, while others, such as Italy and Belgium, became a bit more equal and many, such as Denmark, the Netherlands and Japan, didn't change much. When we looked at these changes in income inequality in relation to changes in child well-being over roughly the same period, we found that countries that had become more unequal tended to have declines in well-being, whereas those that had become a little more equal tended to have improvements. This was a significant link, not due to chance.[190]

On the publication of a 2015 report based on 55,000 children in 15 countries, which once again ranked child well-being in the UK below that of many other nations, Jonathan Bradshaw, professor of social policy at the University of York, said:

Their wellbeing matters to us all. As a nation we pay enormous attention to the wellbeing of our economy, the state of the weather, sporting league tables, the City and the stock market. Indicators of these take up pages of the media every day. We need to make more effort to monitor the wellbeing of our children and we need to devote more resources to understanding how they are doing and to ensuring that their childhood is as good as it can be.[196]

A series of studies – including controlled experiments, such as giving adolescent children an educational programme designed to steer them away from spending and towards sharing and saving – shows that materialism is related to low self-esteem, depression and loneliness. Commenting on these studies, journalist George Monbiot wrote that materialism is 'a general social affliction, visited upon us by government policy, corporate strategy, the collapse of communities and civic life, and our acquiescence in a system that is eating us from the inside out'.[197] But 'materialism' is surely a misnomer for this affliction – it is not a sign of our natural acquisitiveness but instead a very alienated form of communicating our self-worth to others, driven by the status competition that is intensified by inequality.

JUST THE RIGHT AMOUNT

As well as pursuing goals that are unlikely to improve our well-being, excessive materialism and consumerism driven by status insecurity and competition has led to increased indebtedness for many families in developed countries. As well as the onerous mortgages needed to buy somewhere to live in today's inflated housing markets, wages have been stagnant over long periods for most workers. The only way to keep up with the Joneses has been through credit.

Before the global financial crisis, levels of household debt were rising rapidly, in line with rising income inequality (Figure 4.4 shows this relationship for the United States). Between 2005 and 2009, household debt levels increased in all EU countries except for Germany, Austria and Ireland. After the crisis, the number of households reporting arrears in housing, credit and utility payments increased, while governments cut welfare spending and public benefits.[198]

Although the relationships between debt and poor health, including poor mental health, are complex, most researchers and commentators trace a vicious circle from debt to increased stress and its effects on

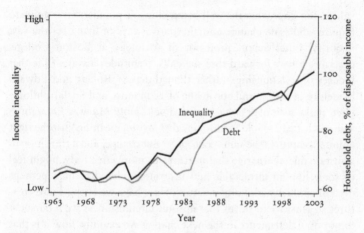

Figure 4.4: Household debt rises with income inequality in the USA, 1963–2003.[199]

health and back again: people with poor health struggle with debt because illness compromises their ability to cope, as well as their ability to increase their income and assets. Household debt also has an impact on children. In debt-stressed families, children and adolescents are acutely aware of the stress being experienced by their parents, raising their vulnerability to mental health problems.

There is a rich literature on the nefarious activities of corporations, especially the big multinationals. Many of them contribute to the hollowing out of societies and communities by paying low wages to their workers and excessively high salaries and bonuses to their senior management, and then aggressively market the message that we can fill that hollowed out space with meaning by buying into their brand lifestyles. Books such as Naomi Klein's best-selling *No Logo* have exposed this strategy to a wide audience.[200] We know corporations play on our desires and fears, and we have the studies to show how empty their promises are. We repeat the old maxim 'money can't buy happiness', and yet still we keep spending.

Whether for religious, ecological or other reasons, there has always been a minority who reject the pursuit of money and materialistic values. But improving the well-being of whole populations is going to require wholesale change and alternative ways of living for the vast majority. Juliet Schor, professor of sociology at Boston College, describes a way forward that she calls 'plenitude': a way of life that focuses on relationships rather than things.[201] Robert and Edward Skidelsky, a father-and-son team of economist and social philosopher, make a similar point in their book, *How Much is Enough?*[202] The newly fashionable Swedish ideal of *lagom*, meaning 'just the right amount', captures the same concept.[203] But change, and a transition to a sustainable alternative that nurtures us more effectively, might feel to some like an intractable and insurmountable difficulty, perhaps even in conflict with human nature. How have we evolved into creatures so sensitive to status that in some circumstances we'll pursue it to our own detriment? In the next chapter we examine how it is that status can matter so much, and why other people's judgements of us affect us so deeply.

PART TWO
Myths of Human Nature, Meritocracy and Class

5

The Human Condition

Larger income gaps make normal social interaction increasingly fraught with anxiety, and, as we have shown, stimulate three kinds of response. Some people are overcome by low self-esteem, lack of confidence and depression; others become increasingly narcissistic and deploy various forms of self-aggrandizement to bolster their position in others' eyes. But, because both are responses to increased anxiety, everyone becomes more likely to self-medicate with drugs and alcohol and falls prey to consumerism to improve their self-presentation. As social life becomes more of an ordeal and a performance, people withdraw from social contact and community life weakens. Crucially, we have seen that the bigger the income differences between rich and poor, the worse all this gets.

So what is the source of this deep-seated anxiety about what others think of us? Why are we so sensitive to each other's judgements? Why do we have this raw nerve which inhibits some of us and almost incapacitates others? Understanding where these sensitivities come from might put us in a better position to combat their dysfunctional effects – not only in ourselves as individuals, but also, through policy, across whole societies. Though modern prosperous societies are particularly plagued by social anxieties, the story of 'The Emperor's New Clothes' suggests they are not a modern invention. Best known through the Hans Christian Andersen version published in 1837, its origins go back at least to the medieval period. It is a cautionary tale about vanity and status in which everyone, including the Emperor, makes a fool of themselves for fear of being thought stupid. Even after a little boy has blurted out the truth, the Emperor prefers to maintain the pretence that he is clothed and continues his parade.

He makes an idiot of himself to avoid the shame of being thought an idiot.

Although we enjoy seeing the Emperor – at the pinnacle of society – humiliated, the reason that the story has attained the status that it has, translated into dozens of languages and with equivalents in numerous cultures, is that he is responding to something common to all of us: embarrassment, and our strong aversion to it. The story also mirrors the widely experienced dream of being naked in public. A common thread in the dream is that we hope other people won't notice our nakedness and we will escape the shame of being exposed for what we are. It clearly reflects our fears and anxieties that people will see through our attempts to present ourselves positively. In his book *The Interpretation of Dreams* Sigmund Freud was unusually naïve about dreams of being naked in public, suggesting that they might be triggered simply by our bedclothes slipping off during sleep, or that they are a memory of being naked as a baby. But Freud was always blinkered when it came to the psychology of class and status, even though his own self-presentation was so accurately tuned to his class and period.

The American sociologist and psychologist Thomas Scheff described shame as 'the primary social emotion'.[204] He included under this heading all the familiar self-conscious emotions running from pride to shame, including embarrassment, humiliation, shyness, awkwardness and feelings of inadequacy and inferiority. Scheff sees shame as arising from the fear of others' negative evaluations, whether real or imagined. He describes how we constantly monitor our actions in each other's eyes to avoid rejection, and cites Charles Cooley, the influential early American sociologist quoted at the beginning of Chapter 1, who taught that: 'The thing that moves us to pride or shame is not the mere mechanical reflection of ourselves, but an imputed sentiment, the imagined effect of this reflection upon another's mind.'[5] We monitor how others react to us for fear of any negative evaluations which might lead to rejection.

Our sensitivities about how we are seen and what might make us feel embarrassed or shamed are clearly not restricted to the more overt markers of status such as income or position within a hierarchy. Beauty, knowledge, attractiveness, intelligence, ability and all their components are also part of the picture. That is because there are dimensions of each which allow us to rank people from positive to negative, from pretty to ugly, from clever to stupid – in short, from better to worse. They contribute to people being valued differently. Status and all the reasons why we may be liked or disliked become entwined.

Our awareness of the power of these valuations drives our fear of falling foul of them, of being perceived negatively by others. Despite this, it is hard to be fully conscious of how important other people's opinions of us really are, and it is worth recalling Cooley's invitation to think about what we would feel if, after some failure or disgrace, people suddenly showed coldness and contempt towards us rather than the kindliness and deference we were used to.[5] Although Cooley suggests that the withdrawal of others' approval would make everyone aware of its importance, he does not go on to consider how difficult it must be for those who live permanently, if not as outcasts, then with few outward signs of success that would gain the respect of others and prevent them experiencing rejection more often than approval.

Like a string of illustrious sociologists before him (including Charles Cooley, Norbert Elias, Erving Goffman, Robert Lynd, Helen Lewis and Richard Sennett), Thomas Scheff considered the way we experience ourselves through each other's eyes as such a normal and fundamental part of social interaction that, barring mishaps and moments of acute embarrassment, we are sometimes as unaware of it as a fish might be of water.[204] It is just part of the social medium in which we exist.

Helen Lewis, who was a psychoanalyst and professor of psychology at Yale University, is credited with being the first person to have identified and drawn scientific attention to the almost continuous behavioural signs that an undercurrent of embarrassment – or anticipation of it – plays an important role in almost all conversations.[205] She painstakingly reviewed, word by word, transcripts of hundreds of her psychoanalytic sessions and found that what her clients said was not only peppered with words indicating underlying shame, but that their speech also had frequent indications of awkwardness, self-consciousness and embarrassment, including uneasy laughter, pauses, disruptions to the flow of speech, changes in manner, tone of voice or saying things almost inaudibly. Lewis provided the evidence of what others had surmised and her work was soon taken up more widely.[206] Once pointed out, our susceptibility to shame and embarrassment can be seen manifesting itself in endless slightly stilted or awkward conversations.

But why is it that we experience ourselves so much through each other's eyes – as what Cooley called a 'looking glass self' – desiring the good opinion of others and fearful of being seen as odd, inadequate, stupid or inferior?

THE SOCIAL BRAIN

To answer this question we need to consider the way social and economic relationships have become intertwined during the course of human evolution. Our evolution has not been driven only by selective forces in the natural environment. Survival has long been about more than our ability to escape predators, endure extreme temperatures, withstand hunger or resist disease. The *social* environment, and our relationships with others, have also been powerful selective forces.

A remarkable example of this is the evidence that coping with the complexity of social life played a key role in the expansion of the human brain. The part of the brain which grew most recently in human evolution is the outer layer called the neocortex. Its greater size in humans is the main reason why our brains are so much larger than those of other primates. Robin Dunbar, director of the Social and Evolutionary Neuroscience Research Group at Oxford University, has shown that the percentage of the brain made up of the neocortex is closely related to the typical size of the social group among primate species. Among solitary species like orangutans the neocortex makes up only a small proportion of the brain, but in more social species it is much larger.[207] Humans not only have the largest neocortex, as a proportion of brain size but, in their prehistoric existence as hunters and gatherers, they also had the largest average group size among primates. The relationship is shown in Figure 5.1.

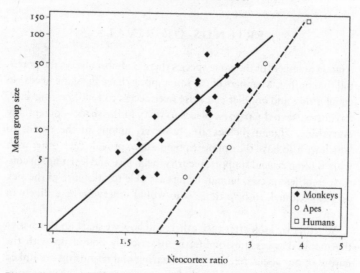

Figure 5.1: The volume of the neocortex as a proportion of the whole brain is related to average group size in different primate species.[208]

The main explanation for this relationship is that social interaction is mentally very demanding, and becomes even more so as group size increases. You not only have to recognize individuals and know everyone's position in the hierarchy, you also have to know who your friends and enemies are and who their friends and enemies are. You have to know who you can trust and who you can't. Above all, you have to be good at reading other people's minds, interpreting facial expressions and body language as clues to their intentions. Since Dunbar first formulated this 'social brain hypothesis', further research has found that among non-human primate species, those with larger group sizes do indeed perform better on tests of social intelligence.[209]

Clearly, the human brain is, in a very real sense, a social organ. Its growth and development have been driven by the requirements of social life. This is the case because the quality of our relationships with each other has always been crucial to survival, well-being and reproductive success.

FRIENDS OR RIVALS

Among members of the same species there is almost always the potential for conflict. Members of the same species have the same needs, so competition and conflict can arise over access to food, nesting sites, territories, sexual partners, places to relax in the shade – potentially everything. Human beings are, however, unique in the extent to which we also have the opposite potential: to provide each other with what is often crucial support, security, help, love and learning. In contrast to other species, human beings are able to take care of the sick or incapacitated, to help those who would otherwise be unlikely to survive.

Whether we look after each other, and how we share and exchange the material necessities of life, is inextricably bound up with the nature of our social relationships. Sharing and friendship are linked because they constitute one end of the spectrum that runs from competition to co-operation and structures our access to resources and other necessities. The word 'companion' – '*compañero*' in Spanish or '*copain*' in French – combines the Latin *com* (with) and *panis* (bread). Companions are people with whom we share food. The connection between social relationships and material life was also summed up by the American social anthropologist Marshall Sahlins. When discussing the use of gifts and systems of gift exchange in hunter-gatherer societies, he said 'gifts make friends and friends make gifts'.[210] He also pointed out that to refuse a gift is, in some societies, tantamount to a declaration of war: it is the rejection of a friendly relationship. Gifts are such powerful symbols of friendship because they show in concrete terms that, rather than fighting over access to material necessities, we recognize each other's needs, and share.

The use of gifts to express or consolidate friendship remains an important part of social life in modern societies. Eating together – whether family meals or with guests – is another indication of the continued psychological and symbolic importance of sharing basic necessities. Many different religious practices attest to the deep roots of this link: food is provided for visitors at all Sikh gurdwaras, and Sikh worshippers share food. Similarly, the sharing of bread and wine in the Christian communion service symbolizes that sharing the necessities of life is the foundation of life. The Prophet Muhammad taught that food should be shared. Likewise, communal eating and food sharing has always been important in Judaism. As well as being enshrined in moral teaching everywhere, the need to co-operate is part of our evolved psychology.

The link between our material interdependence and the nature of social relationships is one of the unconscious givens for human beings everywhere. Exchanging gifts, sharing things or eating together are powerful expressions of close social bonds and friendship. If, instead, people keep what they have to themselves, regardless of each other's needs, it demonstrates a lack of concern for each other's welfare which precludes close social bonds. If they go still further and cheat and steal from each other, that material antagonism leads to conflict. At a macro level, access to resources is a major cause of war between nations. From sharing to preying on one another, material and social relationships speak with one voice. Although the study of economic and social life have tended to be largely separate disciplines, it is clear that rather than being a domain on its own, material life is inextricably bound up with the structure of social relations. We see over the course of this book that different kinds of exchange relationships, and the way goods are distributed across society, have powerful social and psychological implications.

Thomas Hobbes, writing in the seventeenth century, thought that as we all have the same basic needs, life without a strong government to keep the peace would degenerate into a conflict of 'each against all': 'if any two men desire the same thing, which . . . they cannot both enjoy, they become enemies; and . . . endeavour to destroy, or subdue one another'.[211] His view of human beings as natural rivals – no doubt coloured by his experience of the English Civil War – meant that he saw the central problem of politics as one of maintaining a sovereign government capable of keeping the peace between opposed individuals. However, Hobbes largely failed to recognize the depth of our social nature: that as well as the ability to be each other's worst rivals, we also, as a species, have the almost unique capacity to provide support for each other and share the essentials of life. We shall see in the next section that this is not only true of relationships between individuals, but was the prevailing form of social organization among our prehistoric ancestors.

We are so highly sensitized to whether our relationships are friendly or antagonistic because this has been fundamental to individual human well-being throughout our evolution. Whether people share and trust each other, or whether they stand as adversaries in access to necessities, determined the success and survival of our ancestors, shaped our evolutionary journey and the nature and importance of our relationships with others. That is why, even today, friendship and involvement in community life are, as we saw in the first chapter, such powerful determinants of health and happiness, and difficult or antagonistic relationships so damaging.

EQUALITY AND INEQUALITY

To understand the psychological and behavioural effects which equality and inequality have on us, we need only look briefly at some of the main features of social organization during the course of human evolution. At the broadest level, there have been three main periods of social organization in human development: pre-human dominance hierarchies; the egalitarian hunting and gathering societies of human prehistory; and, more recently, the hierarchical agricultural and industrial societies.

Dominance hierarchies are common among animals – baboons, macaque monkeys, chimpanzees, wolves, hyenas, to name but a few. Systems of ranking, from a dominant male at the top to the weakest subordinates at the bottom, determine which members of a group gain access to scarce resources and, as dominant males try to monopolize the females, also to reproductive opportunities. Though there are few clues to social organization in the pre-human fossil record, it is thought that the apes from which we are descended must also have lived in dominance hierarchies, as chimps and many other non-human primates still do. Much later burial evidence – from the Egyptian pyramids to European Bronze Age barrows – leaves no doubt that some people in those societies were of greater importance than others, but evidence about our pre-human ancestors is less plentiful. One of the few important clues as to how these pre-humans lived is the relative size of males and females. Where dominance hierarchies are the norm, the dominant males tend to be the larger and stronger animals. Because dominant males gain more access to females and females tend to prefer them as sexual partners, this selective breeding usually results in males becoming larger than females – so much so that the size differential is reliable evidence that dominance ranking has been a common form of social organization in a species. (The increase in the size of males resulting from male competition for mates doesn't also increase female size because, like horns and canine teeth in animals, their larger size develops as a sex-linked characteristic.) Where males and females are the same size, that usually means something more like pair bonding has been the norm. Enough fossils have been found of at least one of the precursor species of modern humans (*Australopithecus afarensis*) to provide evidence of a size differential between the sexes indicating that 'a strictly monogamous social structure would have been highly unlikely'.[212, 213] Larger males than females indicates that larger males bred disproportionately, and implies that our predecessors probably lived, like chimps and gorillas, with a hierarchical rank ordering within their troops.

The implications for social anxiety of living in a dominance hierarchy are obvious: subordinates have to be careful of more dominant members of the group. As primatologists point out, subordinates who incur the displeasure of higher-ranking animals end up with numerous bite marks to show for it. As a result, most subordinates are constantly vigilant, apprehensive and nervous.[214] But, in contrast to the evidence that our pre-human ancestors lived in dominance hierarchies which are likely to have left some psychological legacy in us, it is clear that throughout most of our specifically *human* prehistory, we lived in extraordinarily egalitarian hunting and gathering societies, in which food was shared and goods were passed between people, not through barter but through systems of reciprocal gift exchange.[210, 215] In such societies social fears would no longer have been about dominance and subordination.

One of the most important but largely unrecognized features of human social organization is that, for about 95 per cent of the last 200,000–250,000 years of human existence, with brains their current size, human societies have been assertively egalitarian. Although generations of anthropologists have recognized, studied and written about the equality of hunter-gatherer societies, our egalitarian past remains virtually unknown to the public at large, and many people imagine that human nature is irredeemably competitive and self-serving.

A study which reviewed over a hundred anthropological accounts of twenty-four relatively recent hunter-gatherer societies from four different continents concludes:

> There is no dominance hierarchy among hunter-gatherers. No individual has priority of access to food which . . . is shared. In spite of the marginal female preference for the more successful hunters as lovers, access to sexual partners is not a right which correlates with rank. In fact, rank is simply not discernible among hunter-gatherers. This is a cross cultural universal, which rings out unmistakably from the ethnographic literature, sometimes in the strongest terms.[216]

People in these societies 'share food, not simply with kin or even just with those who reciprocate, but according to need, even when food is scarce'.[216] This picture of our prehistoric past should be part of general education and taught in all basic courses in economics, politics and the social sciences. The evidence from hunting and gathering societies contains no suggestion of anything like the pattern seen among many other primates – where the dominant individuals eat first and monopolize access to females, and the subordinates eat only if there is enough left over after others have had their fill.

When people are first told of the highly egalitarian nature of prehistoric human societies, there is a widespread tendency to imagine that such statements must be based on a combination of very scant evidence strung together with guesswork and misplaced wishful thinking. Perhaps the most important reason why people find the evidence of an egalitarian human past so hard to accept is that they wrongly assume that it is a denial of a competitive human desire for status and dominance. But that is a fundamental misunderstanding of how these societies worked.[44, 217] The argument is not that people were – or human nature is – naturally egalitarian. The level of equality and co-operation found in these societies did not depend on some

set of genetic characteristics which we have now lost. There is growing agreement among anthropologists that inequality was held in
check because of what have been called 'counter-' or 'reverse-
dominance strategies'. Any single individual's desire for dominance
was effectively opposed by the other members of the group acting
together to safeguard their personal autonomy and protect themselves from being dominated. Rather like the way alliances form
among two or three high-ranking baboons or macaques to depose
the alpha male, these early human societies seem to have worked as
alliances consisting of everyone uniting against anyone who became
too domineering.

This is the conclusion reached by Professor Christopher Boehm,
an anthropologist who put together the most comprehensive collection of accounts of hunter-gatherer societies ever assembled. It
contains all the historical and contemporary accounts he could find,
including those from early explorers, missionaries, colonial adminis-
trators and anthropologists. It now forms an electronically searchable
database with details of social and political behaviour in some 150
such societies all over the world – ranging from Bushmen in the
Kalahari and indigenous Australians, to the Inuit in the Arctic and
Native American societies.

Before this project was completed, Boehm examined data from
forty-eight egalitarian societies to analyse how they maintained their
equality.[217] In all these societies, he found examples of intentional
strategies to prevent anyone from becoming too domineering. He concluded that the equality of these societies arose from a basic dislike of
being dominated and the desire to preserve individual autonomy.
People acted together against any attempt to be domineering.[217]

The change that made egalitarianism possible was not therefore in
human nature itself, but in the effectiveness of social constraints on
domineering and selfish alpha-male tendencies. Whenever individuals
became too domineering or tried to gain more than their share, these
tendencies were strongly opposed. 'Counter-dominance' or 'reverse-
dominance' strategies included every method of curbing antisocial
behaviour – from criticism, ridicule and public expressions of dis-
approval at the milder end, to ostracism, exclusion and death at the
other.

In his survey of how equality was maintained among hunter-gatherer societies, Boehm found numerous accounts of situations in which communities went as far as killing a persistent aggressor or individual who became too domineering or unwilling to share. In some cases, a close relative of the bully would be required to carry out the fatal act, but in several cave paintings there are scenes that look like executions by bow-and-arrow firing squads. In assessing the evidence, Boehm suggests that death rates among hunter-gatherers from these quasi-judicial killings may sometimes have been comparable to homicide rates in modern Chicago – enough to act as a powerful selective force favouring those with more prosocial dispositions.[218]

Anthropologists who have studied recent and surviving hunter-gatherer societies say that rather than just displaying an awareness that if people acted together they could face down any domineering individual, they were consciously and assertively egalitarian.[215] Rather than there being just a neutral absence of inequality, people in these societies regarded equality as a moral principle. James Woodburn, who is a social anthropologist and one of the world's leading theorists of hunter-gatherer societies, wrote:

> People are well aware of the possibility that individuals or groups within their own egalitarian societies may try to acquire more wealth, to assert more power or to claim more status than other people, and are vigilant in seeking to prevent or to limit this. The verbal rhetoric of equality may or may not be elaborated but actions speak loudly: equality is repeatedly acted out, publicly demonstrated, in opposition to possible inequality.[215]

And, because people in these societies consciously subscribed to the idea that all were equal, they tended to make decisions by consensus.

If more helpful and unselfish individuals were, as Boehm suggests, chosen as sexual partners or valued more in co-operative activities, while the more antisocial were shunned, this would have led gradually to the selection of people who were genetically disposed to be more public spirited, less selfish and better at mutual support. Recent research on child development may reflect this process. In a series of experiments, the behavioural and neuro-economist Ernst Fehr and his colleagues have demonstrated that, although the majority of children of around three to four years old tend to behave rather selfishly, an aversion to inequality usually develops in the five years after that. When children reach seven or eight years of age, experiments show that most prefer things to be allocated in ways which reduce inequality – even when that is to their personal disadvantage.[219]

Boehm goes a step further. He regards the systematic use of strategies to oppose dominance and maintain equality in prehistoric hunter-gatherer societies as the precursor of modern historical struggles against arbitrary power, including the fight for the rule of law and the search for democratic structures capable of protecting us from tyranny and dictatorship.

Although there is not yet agreement as to *how* early egalitarian societies replaced the dominance hierarchies of our pre-human forebears, the most convincing explanation is that equality probably started to become widespread when humans developed methods of big game hunting, around 250,000 years ago. Replacing the earlier human reliance on smaller animals for meat probably contributed to egalitarianism in two ways. Most obviously, in societies where people have the know-how and weapons for killing large game, any individual is then also capable of threatening the life of any other – whether dominant or subordinate. Hunting technology dramatically reduced the importance of individual differences in physical strength which, in so many animal species, are the basis of ranking systems and dominance. When anyone can be stabbed in the back or hit over the head in their sleep by almost any other member of the group, the strong can no longer risk incurring the hatred of the weak. The problem for would-be alpha males was not simply whether they could meet challenges from individuals; it was the impossibility of facing down an alliance of well-armed group members. When sheer muscle power was no longer enough to enable an individual to behave with impunity, humanity had reached a fundamental turning point in the nature of social relations.[220]

The second key contribution which big game hunting is thought to have made to this shift in the structure of small-scale societies was that when a large animal was killed, it provided more meat than one person or family could eat before putrefaction made it inedible.

Almost inevitably, the result was that it was shared. But rather than the hunter who made the kill dividing up the meat as if it was his property, with all the dangers of favouritism, the practice in many societies was to allocate the task to someone else. The process has been described as 'vigilant sharing': people kept an eye on the distribution to ensure fair play.[221]

Using first-hand anthropological accounts, Boehm describes the effect which sharing big game has on a group. He says that, apart from occasional superficial squabbling, when meat is shared 'there's obvious community joy in participation – because meat is so deeply appreciated, because no one is left out, and because eating meat together is a splendid way to socialize'. This is in stark contrast to chimps, which kill smaller animals and may for that reason only share with a favoured few – perhaps only enough to ensure that together they can keep the carcass out of the hands of the other chimps standing round begging for pieces. The resulting atmosphere among chimps is described, unsurprisingly, as 'extremely tense'.[218]

There is now a high degree of agreement among anthropologists that the level of inequality we see around us today, which is often – but mistakenly – assumed to be a permanent feature of human social organization, was instead a product of the agricultural way of life. In evolutionary terms, the advent of cultivation is very recent: it dates back around 10,000–12,000 years in places such as the Fertile Crescent in the Middle East, where it started earliest, but it developed independently in other regions as recently as the last 5,000 years.

Most early agriculturalists lived in small communities which practised 'shifting agriculture': an area of forest would be burned off and the ground cultivated for a few years until soil fertility declined, when it would be abandoned and allowed to reforest while a new area would be burned off and cultivated. While these early agricultural communities were often headed by a 'big man', they were still remarkably egalitarian, and, as recent and modern anthropological studies have shown, counter-dominance strategies – including ridicule, ostracism and exclusion – continued to be used.[44] There is less agreement as to why agriculture led to the growth of inequality than that it did so. A number of detailed studies have linked agricultural development and the growth of inequality, some by comparing societies and others by studying the process of change through the archaeological and historical evidence.[222-225] Theories range from the more individual nature of agricultural work and the need to store food, to the establishment of permanent settlements. Societies with fully developed social class hierarchies arose much more recently, and are clearly linked to the development of settled agriculture and much denser populations. Perhaps the most convincing recent explanation for the growth of inequality is that it was linked – as the archaeological evidence suggests – specifically to the cultivation of cereal crops because they facilitated the introduction of systems of taxation in ways which other crops did not.[43]

PSYCHOLOGICAL LEGACIES

Our capacity for social anxiety is likely to be the psychological legacy of the social organization of pre-human and prehistoric human societies. The main features of relationships between animals with hierarchical ranking systems are clear. Subordinate baboons, for example, like subordinates of almost any species, have to avoid incurring the wrath – or usually even the mild displeasure – of the more dominant animals. They must know where they stand in the dominance hierarchy and be constantly aware of where the alpha male is, while at the same time avoiding the perceived challenge of direct eye contact. They need to signal with submission responses that they recognize their own inferiority, that they will surrender anything a more dominant animal might want, and avoid competitive challenges of any kind. Failure to follow these rules could result in serious injury, or even death.

Boehm makes a convincing case for saying that the change from relationships based on position within a dominance hierarchy to relationships based on equality led to the inception of morality as we would recognize it.[218] Rather than having simply to keep on the right side of a dominant individual, the conditions which led to equality almost certainly meant that we all had to keep on the right side of each other. The development of a social morality was underpinned both by the sense of inclusion and security which went with participation in food sharing, gift exchange, co-operation and close community life, and by the counter-dominance strategies that threatened ostracism, exclusion or death to anyone showing persistent antisocial tendencies.

The American anthropologist Marshall Sahlins argues that in the absence of governments capable of enforcing peace between people, it was up to the members of these societies themselves to maintain good relations with each other by avoiding doing things which caused envy or resentment. Food sharing and gift exchange in these societies can be seen as a way of life involving substantial social investments to maintain cohesive relationships and avoid social divisions.[210]

Experimental evidence from modern primate research also suggests that the tendency towards co-operation and fairness reflects the desire to avoid the protests and antagonism which result from the unfair treatment of other members of the troop.[226] Primatologist Frans de Waal suggests that this is why chimps will sometimes do things to help each other, and may prefer to share the food rewards used in experiments.

Perhaps because of the nature of modern market societies, people seem to need little or no evidence to convince themselves of our more antisocial tendencies, such as selfishness, possessiveness, egocentrism and status seeking. We are, however, much more reluctant to believe that we also have characteristics built into us which provide the basis for sharing and co-operation. The evidence on the nature of early human societies and the social behaviour of some non-human primates shows that our view of ourselves is in need of adjustment. Psychologists suggest, for example, that a sense of gratitude and feelings of indebtedness are human universals, occurring in all cultures.[227, 228] These feelings are of course what prompts a return gift and a willingness to share; without them, people would be seen as freeloaders and attract hostility. The desire to reciprocate was the bedrock of systems of gift exchange which, like food sharing, provided the social cement of hunter-gatherer societies.[229] As we saw earlier, Sahlins suggested that the exchange of gifts establishes a basic social compact between people.[210]

Experiments in behavioural economics show not only that we have a deeply ingrained *willingness* to share, but also that we have a *preference* for sharing. Take, for example, evidence that comes from experiments that have used what is called the 'ultimatum game'. After participants have been randomly paired, one of each pair is given some money to split with his or her partner. They can divide it as generously or as meanly as they like – anything from keeping it all to giving it all to their partner and everything in between. The partner's role is only to accept or reject the proposed division. If the partner rejects it, neither of them get any money, but if the division is accepted, they each get the amount proposed in the offer.

According to ideas of economic rationality, it would be rational to accept all offers, however small: you would then at least end up with something rather than nothing. But the most commonly proposed division turns out to be splitting the money 50:50.[230] (Although this was the single most frequent division, the *average* division proposed was 60:40. This was because very few people offered more than a 50:50 split but some offered less.) These findings come from thirty-seven studies which used the ultimatum game in twenty-five different countries, countries at different stages of development and with very different cultures. (Despite this, there was little evidence that results were much influenced by cultural differences.)

One interesting finding was that people are willing to reject offers they think are unfair even when that means turning down the offer of at least some money. You might for instance reject an offer of only 20 per cent of the money from a proposer who wants to keep the remaining 80 per cent. In these experiments, the rejection of an offer like this could not be an attempt to signal that only more generous offers would be accepted in future: participants are told beforehand that they will not be paired with the same partner again. The willingness to suffer a loss in order to reject unfair offers, so denying money to the proposer, has been called 'altruistic punishment'. Our tendency to act in this way, which includes our willingness to take revenge on wrong-doers even at a cost to ourselves, has been shown to be an important way in which co-operation is maintained and high standards of reciprocity upheld.[231, 232]

These and similar experiments are often cited as evidence that human beings don't really act rationally to maximize personal gain in the way that economists often assume. Why we don't is because our motivations are more fundamentally social than that, and have developed to serve social harmony. Through social selection, human psychology has been honed to seek the approval of others.

The results of the ultimatum game seem to suggest that, as well as wanting others to think well of us, we are more comfortable in ourselves when we behave in ways that gain the approval of other people. Robert Frank, an economist at Cornell University, has argued that to present the most convincing impression that we are trustworthy people who others should choose to co-operate with, we need first to convince ourselves that we are.[231] He suggests that it is not enough to simply create an outward appearance of being honest and generous. Because people are, as he shows, very good at detecting whether others are trustworthy, they would see through that. Frank argues that to be really convincing, we must convince *ourselves* that we are trustworthy and unselfish, even in situations where there is no likely benefit to ourselves. That, he suggests, is why people do things like leave tips in restaurants, even when far from home.

THE IMPRINT OF INEQUALITY

The psychological imprint left by the different kinds of social organization in which our early ancestors evolved is not limited to the allocation of material goods. The 'Dominance Behavioural System' discussed in Chapter 2, which we use to deal with aspects of hierarchical social interactions, has its roots in animal ranking systems.[70] As we saw in Chapters 2 and 3, a range of psychological problems involving responses to dominance and subordination increase with greater inequality.

Another particularly telling indication of the same legacy is evidence that bullying is much more common among children in more unequal societies. Although there is no internationally comparable data on bullying among adults, the World Health Organization's Health Behaviour in School-aged Children survey does provide international data on children. As Figure 5.2 shows, there is a strong tendency for bullying to be much more common among children in more unequal societies.[233] The proportion of children involved at least twice a month in bullying incidents is close to ten times as high in the more, compared to the less, unequal societies. Animal dominance hierarchies and bullying hierarchies are structurally similar: both rank individuals by strength, with the strongest at the top and the weakest at the bottom. Figure 5.2 suggests that children in more unequal societies are more likely to adopt similar kinds of behaviour to their dominance-orientated ancestors. Bullying is about competition for dominance, and the fact that it becomes more common in more unequal societies again suggests the involvement of evolved psychological responses to inequality linked directly to dominance strategies.

There are several other indications of responses to greater inequality which also look like evolved adaptations to dominance and subordination. One comes from a study which found that women in more unequal societies prefer more stereotypically masculinized men's faces than women in more equal societies.[234, 235] The study used an online survey to ask nearly five thousand heterosexual women in thirty countries to look at male faces in twenty pairs of photos. They simply had to say which face in each pair they found more attractive.

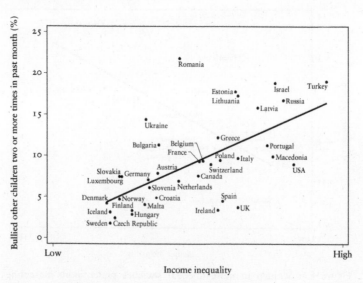

Figure 5.2: Children bully each other more in more unequal countries.[233]

One photo in every pair had been run through a computer program which enhanced the masculinity of the face, for example by strengthening the jaw line. In the more unequal countries women had, as shown in Figure 5.3, a much stronger preference for the more masculine faces. This is particularly interesting because the research report also points out that 'there is compelling evidence that women ascribe antisocial traits and behaviours to more masculine-looking men. They perceive more masculine-looking men as dishonest, uncooperative, and more interested in short-term than long-term relationships.'[234] Women in more unequal societies seem to be biased towards men with the rugged masculine faces and characteristics which might get them nearer the top in a dominance hierarchy – a throwback to an evolved psychology appropriate to the power relations of ranking systems.

Another research finding which looks as if it may originally have been partly an adaptation to the ranking systems of our pre-human past is the tendency for people lower in the status hierarchies of modern societies to have higher levels of a blood clotting factor called

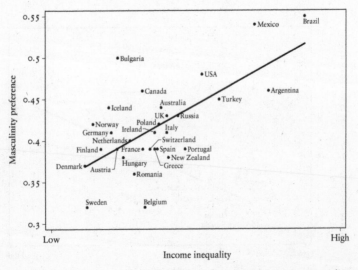

Figure 5.3: Women in more unequal societies prefer more masculine faces.[234, 236]

fibrinogen, which we described in Chapter 2. Fibrinogen makes blood clot faster, and blood concentrations increase when people are stressed. This is beneficial if the stressful situation might lead to injury: wounds stop bleeding faster if fibrinogen levels are higher. Higher fibrinogen levels would have served subordinates well if, in the dominance hierarchies of our pre-human forebears, they risked physical attack from their superiors.

To confirm that fibrinogen concentrations are indeed partly responses to the nature of social relations, more recent research has shown that people with good friendship networks have, as we would expect, lower fibrinogen levels.[237] Fortunately we are no longer at risk of being bitten by those further up the social ladder. But the psychological stress of hierarchical relationships still makes our blood clot faster, just as supportive and unthreatening friendships do the opposite.

GETTING THE STRATEGY RIGHT

The ability to adapt our social strategy to suit different kinds of society became part of our genetic make-up because matching the strategy to the context has always been essential to survival and reproductive success. Individuals who behaved too generously in a dominance hierarchy were likely to be taken advantage of, just as those who were too self-serving in an egalitarian society risked ostracism. In societies with strong ranking systems, the threats to the survival of subordinates came not only from dominants but also from restricted reproductive opportunities and insufficient access to scarce resources. In contrast to the pressures towards self-advancement in dominance hierarchies, egalitarian societies provided both negative selective pressures, such as ostracism for antisocial behaviour, and positive selection for more co-operative characteristics. People who were less selfish and more generous and trustworthy would have been more popular as partners in co-operative activities as well as being preferred as mates.

Through these rewards and sanctions, egalitarian societies created a strong evolutionary pressure towards the development of more sociable characteristics in our evolved psychology. We have already seen a few examples of this inheritance: in the contrasting effects of hierarchy and friendship on blood clotting, in the fact that the social pain of exclusion engages the same parts of our brains as physical pain, in our tendency to eat together, in the religious symbolism of food sharing and in the derivation of words like 'companion'. It is woven into the fabric of our lives. Take, for instance, our need to feel that we have a role or function in relation to others. We like to feel that others appreciate what we do and regard us as helpful. This can amount almost to a sense of self-realization in relation to others' needs, whether as parents satisfying the needs of children or as individuals performing tasks which others value. Although modern wage-labour means that many employees feel unappreciated or exploited, unemployment is nevertheless still experienced partly as an assault on people's sense of self-worth. Having no useful role in society can leave people feeling worthless. The desire to feel that we have a valued and appreciated role in relation to the needs of others would once have been our best guarantee against the risks of exclusion. By being useful to others, we maximized our security as members of the co-operative group.

It is often thought that values such as honesty, generosity and kindness were almost invented by, and remain dependent on, religion. But although religious convictions and teachings may help to sustain standards of kindness and generosity (despite sometimes also creating problems of intolerance), we can now see that prosocial characteristics were instilled in us during human prehistory by the evolutionary power of social selection in egalitarian societies. As anthropological accounts of recent hunter-gatherer societies suggest, the tendency to value unselfishness, generosity and kindness dates back into the distant mists of time. Although religious belief can add emphasis to these instincts, prosocial values are etched more deeply into our evolved psychology and are much older than any religious ideology that has arisen in the last few thousand years.

There is clear evidence from a number of animal species that apparently altruistic behaviour can become genetically encoded,[238,239] and evolutionary psychologists have given much thought to trying to understand the selective processes likely to be involved. Why do people risk their lives to help a total stranger who seems to be drowning? Why do so many people give anonymously to charities, or leave tips in restaurants in towns they will never visit again? This used to be considered a theoretical problem because if you have a genetic tendency to put yourself at risk to help others, or to share your food when it is scarce, then your genes are less likely to spread through the population. Group selection can only help spread characteristics that are already common in the group. But a tendency to be brave and put yourself at risk for others does not look likely to help your genes become more common than others in the local population. The individuals whose genes do best after war or conflict are, inevitably, the survivors, not those who died. Although some argued that these altruistic tendencies favour the survival of the group as a whole, group selection can only spread these characteristics once a substantial proportion of people in the population have them.

The power of Christopher Boehm's work, described earlier in this chapter, lies in his recognition that it is the social rather than the natural environment that would have selected individuals with more prosocial behaviour. The positive selective pressure coming (particularly when choosing a mate) from the preferences of other members of the group for people who were more unselfish, combined with the negative pressure created by people discriminating against those who were antisocial, made a powerful selective combination. This fits with the conclusions of researchers who have identified an aversion to unfairness and a willingness to behave co-operatively even among some *non*-human primates. The evidence suggests that species which do show some apparently unselfish behaviour traits came to do so to avoid angry reprisals from members of their troop whom they failed to treat fairly or co-operatively.[226]

THE SOCIAL ENVIRONMENT AND EPIGENETICS

We have shown a number of indications of what look like built-in behavioural responses to more and less equal societies. The rapidly developing field of epigenetics shows just how fundamentally we are programmed to adapt to the kind of society in which we find ourselves.

Epigenetics is the study of the way in which the environment affects what genes do. Without altering the basic genetic code passed from generation to generation, a wide range of environmental stimuli have, nevertheless, been found to change gene expression – switching genes on or off – in ways which affect development and behaviour. In many different species, including humans, epigenetic changes enable organisms to develop differently in different circumstances. For example, worker bees and queen bees have exactly the same genes, but what those genes do is affected by whether larvae are provided with more or less 'royal jelly'. The jelly changes gene expression in larvae so that instead of becoming a short-lived, sterile worker, the bee develops into a much larger, egg-laying queen with a longer life-span. In effect, development can be adjusted to experience.

In humans and other primates, experience in early life, including during foetal development before birth, fine tunes responses to stress. A dramatic illustration of the influences which stress during pregnancy can have on children's development came from a study that showed it could do more damage to their emotional and intellectual development than exposure to potentially dangerous levels of radiation. Researchers studying a group of Belarusian children whose mothers had been exposed during pregnancy to radiation from the 1986 Chernobyl nuclear reactor disaster, found significant increases in developmental and cognitive impairment compared with children whose mothers had not been exposed to radiation.[240] But the researchers were surprised to see that radiation exposure had less of an impact on intellectual functioning, speech, language and emotional disorders than the worries about exposure and the stress and disruption of the evacuation itself.

Although the important effects of early childhood experience on the course of a person's later psychological development have long been recognized, research has only recently shown that the processes involved are substantially underpinned by epigenetic changes. Children who experience a lot of stress are likely to become more reactive to it, more anxious, and more vulnerable to depression later on.[241]

A review of research concluded that social stress, particularly stress between parents and children, changes the expression of a wide range of genes that regulate stress responses.[242] As a result, the dice are loaded very differently according to whether you are brought up with the benefit of secure loving relationships, or whether you are among the 10–15 per cent of the population who have suffered psychological or physical abuse, been neglected or witnessed parental conflict and violence, or whether your experience was somewhere between these two poles.[243]

Many species have sensitive periods in early life that enable development to be informed by experience. Even plants seem to have an epigenetic capacity to change their developmental trajectory in response to an early experience of drought or salt, so they are better equipped to deal with any similar experiences in the future.[244] Epigenetic changes are not triggered just by exposure to aspects of the physical environment. What makes them relevant to the ways people adjust to the different quality of life and social relationships associated with more or less hierarchical societies is that they are also triggered by *subjective* perceptions of our circumstances – including more stressful family relationships.[245, 246] Our perceptions and feelings about our social situation and circumstances can alter the expression of hundreds of genes.[245]

The discovery that our early social experiences trigger changes in gene expression affecting how we develop indicates that we have, throughout our evolution, needed to adapt flexibly to very different kinds of social environment and the different demands they entail. Over the course of evolution, humans have experienced societies based on everything from 'might is right' dominance hierarchies at one extreme, to caring, sharing reciprocity at the other. Rather than being adapted to one environment once and for all, epigenetics and our evolved psychology have equipped us with what amounts almost to two human natures, each triggered by the demands of the prevailing social system. It is rather as if babies were actors coming on to the stage and having to discover which of the plays in the human repertoire they need to perform.

What matters is the quality of social relationships. Early development is shaped by whether we find ourselves growing up in a world where we must be ready to fight for what we can (except when deferring to dominants), learning not to trust each other because we are all rivals for scarce resources, or whether we find ourselves living in a society where we depend on co-operation and reciprocity, where empathy and trust are important. Each system requires a different social orientation, a different kind of emotional and cognitive development. People who have had stressful childhoods are not damaged in any simple sense of the word, but may be better adapted to function in a stressful social world. They may be more streetwise, less willing to trust others, less likely to have a false sense of security and more prepared to fight their corner.

These epigenetic processes would have been beneficial in our prehistoric past when children were not separated off from the rest of the group in detached nuclear families. The childhood experience of social relationships among a group of nomadic hunter-gatherers would have been a good indication of the kind of society a child was born into and would have to deal with in adulthood. Now that family life is partly separated from the rest of society by the privacy of the home, childhood experience may often be a poor guide to relationships in society more widely. Some families are loving, while others are riven by conflict – a child's early experience will set them off on a particular developmental trajectory regardless of whether that experience remains a useful indication of the nature of relationships in the wider society. But of course the modern nuclear family is far from impervious to the stresses of the wider society. Financial stress and debt, a difficult work–life balance, unemployment, mental health or addiction problems, or feelings of inferiority – all associated with inequality – take their toll on family relationships. Indeed, there is evidence that rates of child maltreatment are higher in the more unequal states of the USA (see Chapter 6).[247]

While some epigenetic changes are fairly short lived, others can be carried between generations, even though they are not changes in DNA itself. For example, epigenetic changes identified in Holocaust survivors were also found in their adult children, showing that maternal stress even before conception can affect the next generation.[248]

SOCIAL STATUS

As well as the radical differences in the general quality of relationships from one society to another, there are also different adaptive challenges of living nearer the top or the bottom of the social ladder. In more unequal societies, the quality of social relations and the experience of adversity can vary dramatically according to where you are on the social ladder. As a result, there is evidence of epigenetic differences between people living in richer and poorer areas of our cities. A study carried out in Glasgow in Scotland compared the DNA of people in manual and non-manual jobs, as well as of people living in more or less deprived areas. Both comparisons showed that there were large epigenetic differences between socio-economic groups. Although the effects of most of these epigenetic changes are still unknown and more research is needed, there can be little doubt that they involve the insidious effects of inequality.[249]

Fortunately, many changes in gene expression are likely to be reversible if and when an individual's experience changes. A study in which the social rank of macaque monkeys was changed by moving them into different groups found that their epigenetic profile changed with their rank.[250]

Although it might be assumed that these changes helped individuals to adapt their behaviour to their new status, little is yet known about the effects of specific changes in gene expression. They are thought to underlie many of the effects of stress in early life, including heightened responses to worries and anxieties, and are likely to have long-term health consequences. At Stanford University, the neuro-endocrinologist and primatologist Robert Sapolsky has described how stress changes our body's physiological priorities.[246, 251] The 'fight or flight' responses, which help us deal with an emergency or threatened attack – for example by mobilizing energy for muscular activity and increasing reaction speeds – are prioritized at the expense of things like tissue maintenance and repair, growth, digestion and reproductive functions. Although this does no real harm when triggered briefly by a threat which is soon over, if worries and anxieties continue for weeks or years, health is likely to suffer.

INEQUALITY AND POVERTY

The effects of low social status are often confused with the effects of poverty. It is often assumed that deprivation and poverty affect people primarily through the direct effects of exposure to poor material circumstances, such as damp or overcrowded housing, low quality food and so on. However, even though material standards become less important for their own sake as societies become richer, they remain important as indicators of people's ability to take part in the normal life of society and avoid 'social exclusion'. This is why poverty in developed countries is now almost always measured in relative terms. For instance, the European Union defines poverty as living on less than 60 per cent of the median income in each country. This is a recognition that what matters is how your material standards compare with others – your *relative* deprivation. Although the predominant view focuses on 'social exclusion', what is actually most demeaning about the experience of poverty is living in circumstances that define you – in most people's eyes – as inferior to others. Marshall Sahlins went as far as to say that 'Poverty is not a certain small amount of goods, nor is it just a relation between means and ends; above all it is a relation between people. Poverty is a social status.'[210] In a similar vein, the Nobel Prize-winning economist Amartya Sen suggested that shame was the 'irreducible absolutist core' of the experience of poverty.[252]

Research that demonstrates the truth of these statements particularly clearly was provided by an international team which arranged for poor people – adults and children – to be interviewed about the experience of poverty in seven developed and developing countries: rural Uganda and India, urban China, Pakistan, South Korea, the United Kingdom and Norway.[253] The material living standards of the people interviewed differed radically from one country to another. The poor in India typically lived in one- or two-roomed huts with an earth floor, corrugated iron roof, an outside cooking space, a communal tap and usually no access to lavatories. Respondents in Uganda were subsistence farmers living in earth-floored thatched huts which were not properly weatherproof; they cooked outside and many lacked access to clean water. In contrast, those interviewed in Britain and Norway usually lived in three-bedroom houses or flats, they had hot and cold water, electricity, heating, kitchens and bathrooms. Because most of the British and Norwegian respondents were unemployed, they lived on social security. However, despite these differences, and the corresponding differences in access to adequate food and clothing, the subjective experience of being poorer than others in each society was found to be remarkably similar. In order not to introduce bias, the researchers avoided using words like 'shame' and 'poverty' in the interviews, but they nonetheless concluded that:

> Respondents universally despised poverty and frequently despised themselves for being poor. Parents were often despised by their children, women despised their men-folk and some men were reported to take out their self-loathing on their partners and children. Despite respondents generally believing that they had done their best against all odds, they mostly considered that they had both failed themselves by being poor and that others saw them as failures. This internalisation of shame was further externally reinforced in the family, the workplace and in their dealings with officialdom. Even children could not escape this shaming for, with the possible exception of Pakistan, school was an engine of social grading, a place of humiliation for those without the possessions that guaranteed social acceptance . . . No parent was able to escape the shame of failing to provide for their children even when children were prepared to stop asking for things – the latter itself being a further source of shame.[253]

As well as self-loathing, the sense of shame also led to 'withdrawal . . . despair, depression, thoughts of suicide and generally to reductions in personal efficacy'. For respondents, the most telling symbol of failure was 'the inability to provide appropriate food and shelter for oneself and one's family'. 'For men, relying on others or on welfare benefits was perceived as a challenge to their sense of masculinity: a British father to two children admitted that he felt "like shit . . . I'm the man in this relationship. I am meant to be the man . . . to take care of the missus and my kids. And I don't." '

As well as this internalized sense of shame, the researchers found that the poor also experienced explicit shaming by the wider society in each of the seven countries. It was noted that in Britain the mass media added particularly to this shaming by reinforcing the view that poverty was the result of personal failures.

The effects of poverty and inequality cannot be properly understood without regard to our inherited aversion to low social status.

As part of our evolved psychology it must date back to pre-human dominance hierarchies, but its grip is still felt strongly in relation to modern inequality. Those who fail to acknowledge its power often continue to imagine that economic growth can deal with what are actually status effects of inequality and relative poverty. Given the power of subjective experience, being substantially poorer than others will, as we have seen, have powerful epigenetic effects.

TWO SOURCES OF SOCIAL ANXIETY

We can now see that there are likely to have been two main sources of the human vulnerability to social anxiety which have etched themselves into our psychology. The first is the legacy of pre-human dominance ranking systems, and the second comes from the egalitarian period of our prehistory.

Competition for status is predicated on being highly aware of rank, and is likely to be the source of much of the downward prejudice seen in human societies towards those lower on the social ladder. Among non-human primates it is clear that each individual can treat those of lower rank with impunity – that is part of what superior status is about. But to compete for status without offending superiors in a dominance hierarchy is difficult: you have to be able to recognize your own inferiority in relation to a dominant to ensure you back off from unwinnable conflicts and potential injury, while also attempting to maintain and improve your position relative to near equals.

The psychological impact of dominance hierarchies is evident in the amount of time that subordinates of almost all the strongly rank-ordered monkey species spend checking on the location and disposition of dominants – so much so that the dominant members of a group can be identified just by seeing which are most watched by others.[254] That this vigilance reflects fear and the need to avoid conflict has been confirmed by observations that subordinates look most frequently at the most aggressive members of their troop.[255]

Human beings still show a remarkable ability to judge dominance characteristics in each other. One study observed interactions among small groups of students meeting each other in experimental conditions for the first time. It found that even 'at first glance' – actually within one minute of meeting and before they had spoken to each other – they had made subliminal assessments of each other's tendency to dominant behaviour as expressed in body language. These assessments were then borne out in observations of subsequent interactions.[256] The study was designed to exclude the influence of external signs of status such as clothing. The researchers concluded that the clues to dominance behaviour which were most likely to have been influential from the start were things like whether people looked confident, how active they were, and whether or not they looked away when they met each other's eyes. Particularly interesting in this context is that the researchers who conducted the study said that their findings were 'consistent with primate literature which shows that dominant animals receive many short gazes' from subordinates.[256]

Pre-human ranking systems have left us with an overwhelming concern for, and sensitivity to, social status.[257-259] Our tendency to compare ourselves with others is presumably as old as the face-offs between animals competing for dominance as they assess each other's strength and decide whether to fight or concede rank. Few things are as important as your position in the pecking order. And as we saw in Chapter 4, our concern with status drives consumerism in modern societies. Because we are attuned to even subtle markers of status, consumerism becomes a fight for status by other means.

A difficulty we faced when studying the effects of income inequality across whole societies was the question of who people compared themselves to. The consistent finding from research on relative deprivation suggested that people have a strong tendency to compare themselves with others like themselves, with near equals – such as neighbours or work colleagues – rather than with those much further up or down the social ladder.[260] This appeared to suggest that the very rich and very poor don't make much difference to the vast bulk of the population in the middle; it seemed to run counter to the copious evidence that income inequality, measured from richest to poorest across the whole spectrum of inequality, does matter and leads to many different forms of social dysfunction. Looking again at this puzzle from an evolutionary perspective, we can see how the two can be reconciled. Robert Sapolsky, who made annual trips for some twenty-five years to study troops of wild baboons in the Serengeti, found that fights for dominance tend to be between near neighbours in the ranking system.[261] Hence, number seven in rank order will contend for position with numbers six and eight and not with numbers one or twenty. Seven gives way to one because it knows it would lose; similarly, number twenty won't fight number seven because it knows that it would be defeated. However, if an animal might gain or lose position in the rank hierarchy, that animal must watch that it isn't bettered by its nearest neighbours. If there is any chance of a change in rank, seven has to watch numbers six and eight. This does not mean that much higher or lower ranking animals are unimportant. Recognizing the superiority of dominants is crucial to survival – hence the constant glances towards dominants among non-human primates and, presumably, the higher levels of blood clotting factors among junior civil servants in London offices described above.

Perhaps this is why it is when our friends and near equals start to talk or behave as if they think they are better than us that it elicits the angry response: 'Who the hell do you think you are?' It surely is also the reason why the increased violence found in more unequal societies is not the result of the poor attacking the rich, but primarily an increase in violence among those at the bottom of the ladder.[1, 262] Violence is more common in more unequal societies because the heightened importance of status makes it even more necessary to defend our position when we feel disrespected or suffer real (or imagined) slights from near equals. Concern with social status is inevitably about how others see us, about respect, about being thought well of, being looked up to rather than down on. Equally inevitably, it brings with it the obsessive concern with self-presentation and our vulnerability to advertisers' promises that the right purchases will enhance our image and status.

It is likely that one of the epigenetic changes caused by exposure to greater inequality as status becomes more important, is that we become more vigilant towards social comparisons with those around us. But whether or not epigenetic processes are involved, it is clear that increased inequality makes everyone more attentive to status, touchier about how they are seen and more watchful for possible slights.

The second source of our vulnerability to social anxiety, and our tendency to see – to know and experience – ourselves through the eyes of others, comes from our egalitarian prehistory. It is from our pre-agrarian ancestors that our worry about social exclusion and our need to feel liked and appreciated by others stems. Unlike animals, among which vulnerability is very largely a matter of differences in physical strength, human egalitarianism had its origins in our mutual vulnerability to each other – including the strongest to the weakest – which developed with our capacity for big game hunting. It became essential for all members of a group to maintain good – or at least tolerant – relations with everyone. As important as avoiding conflict was the need to avoid exclusion from the co-operative, mutually protective, food-sharing group.

This history may be the origin of what psychologists call our 'inequality aversion'. There is now a substantial body of research (including findings from the 'ultimatum game' discussed earlier) showing that, alongside (and despite) our concern for status, human beings also have a dislike of inequality. For example, in one carefully designed experimental game reported in the scientific journal *Nature*, people interacted anonymously on computer terminals in groups of four.[263] The computer then randomly allocated different sums of money to each of them. They could either keep what they had been given or spend some of it to buy tokens that could be used to reduce or increase the incomes of others. A token costing $1 could be used to raise or lower someone else's income by $3. These interactions were repeated many times with different combinations of participants. Participants also had the following points explained to them: they could keep the money they ended up with; anonymity would be maintained throughout the game; they would only interact with each person once; and they would have no knowledge of each other's performance in previous rounds. The result was that a large majority of the tokens bought by participants were used to reduce the incomes of people who received a high initial allocation, and a large majority of the tokens bought to increase people's incomes were given to people who got a lower than average initial allocation. People who got a high initial allocation were accordingly heavily penalized, and those who got less than other group members had their allocations substantially increased. Those with the bigger initial allocations spent more money to raise the lower incomes of others, and those with the smaller initial allocations spent more on tokens to lower the higher incomes. These patterns of behaviour, and the emotions (including anger) shown by some of the subjects while they played these experimental games, suggest that at least in some contexts people have an aversion to inequality.[263]

The large body of work, mainly from behavioural economists, using these and other experimental 'games' to explore human social motivations, has led to broadly similar conclusions.[232] We saw earlier that the ethos of people in hunter-gatherer societies was consciously and 'assertively' egalitarian. The advantage for them of avoiding inequality was that it was a precondition (albeit not necessarily a sufficient condition) for maintaining harmonious relations between people.[210] Egalitarianism reinforced reciprocity and co-operation. An aversion to inequality was essential to gaining the benefits of friendship and sharing, and was foundational to social life among our hunter-gatherer predecessors. Both our preference for fairness and sense of indebtedness, which may prompt us to reciprocate kindnesses, can, of course, be eclipsed, but they are characteristics which contrast sharply with the 'each against all' self-serving principle of dominance hierarchies. Above all, these prosocial values depend on our desire for the good will of others and to be regarded as co-operative and an asset to the well-being of the group. The experimental evidence strongly suggests that high levels of inequality aversion are sustained only if there are possibilities (such as forms of 'altruistic punishment' discussed earlier) for sanctioning those who abuse the generosity of others.

LEARNED CULTURE AND SOCIAL ANXIETY

Our sensitivity to the judgements of others is likely to have made a major contribution to the development of our species' unique dependence on *culture* – that is to say, on a learned way of life rather than simply on instinctive behaviour. Other primates have been found to have a few learned forms of behaviour – washing the earth off edible tubers before eating them, or using sticks to pick up termites to eat – but none have developed learned forms of behaviour much further. Only among humans does learned behaviour accumulate sufficiently to add up to an entire learned way of life. The transition from a rather inflexible lifestyle dependent on instinctive behaviour to our almost infinitely adaptable way of life is what has enabled us to respond to different circumstances and live as anything from early nomadic hunter-gatherers to modern wage-labouring city-dwellers.

From the point of view of each child as it grows up, other people are the bearers of culture. They are the carriers, the exemplars and guardians of a way of life. Growing up is a matter of learning to behave and live in ways which other people find acceptable or 'proper'. So whether it is a matter of acquiring particular skills, accumulating knowledge, or pronouncing words in ways that don't attract laughter or derision, learning has depended substantially on our desire for the good opinion of those around us. We become adept practitioners of a certain way of life because we want to be seen as proficient, or at least as competent, people.

Thomas Scheff regarded our desire to avoid shame and embarrassment as underpinning our tendency to conformity: we don't want to look odd or stupid in front of others. From there it is only a short step to the idea that our desire for approval and to avoid derision may be what enabled human beings to develop a way of life so overwhelmingly dependent on learning. It looks as if a learned way of life must have arisen on the basis of a conformist tendency to imitate and learn the behaviour and practices of others. (In contrast, innovation or taking a new approach is a risky strategy; but even those who break with convention in one area of life tend still to depend on a learned culture in almost everything else.)

Our desire for respect is likely to have been a powerful motivation for all kinds of learning, whether of specific skills or broader aspects of behaviour. And effective learning and self-development would have brought powerful selective advantages to those who excelled in particular skills and abilities. They would have been admired and highly valued partners and members of the community. Presumably as important, however, was the rejection of the incompetent and those who appeared inadequate.

It is because of the evolutionary importance of passing on our genes to the next generation that these kinds of selective pressures, and the worries about other people's judgements of us, seem to be at their height among people in their teens and twenties, when sexual selection is most intense. The desire to make as good a match as possible dramatically increases anxieties about looks, competence and status among young people.

REDUCING SOCIAL ANXIETY

Although we have emphasized the evolutionary roots of major features of our psychology affecting social relations, this does not mean they are fixed by our genes. Instead, there is an immensely complex interaction between genes and environment. Sapolsky provides a simple example of how many of our genetic characteristics, rather than determining behaviour regardless of our environment, instead provide us with more sophisticated ways of responding to different circumstances. He points out that a rat's sense of smell enables it to distinguish between males and females, between close relatives and strangers, between different kinds of food and non-food, and to respond differently to each. As human beings, we know intuitively how to behave towards friends and in relationships between equals. We also know about the importance of social status and power. Modern societies include situations that bring out our prosocial tendencies, our desires to be liked and valued as equals. However, in other situations the striving for self-advancement and our preoccupation with status comes to the fore, and people tend to value – or devalue – each other and themselves according to status. Often the respect we want from others seems to depend on gaining higher status (or at least some outward appearances of it), but at the same time we want to be treated as equals. Contradictions abound.

The evolutionary roots of the contrasting sets of strategies we use cannot be understood in isolation: our varying circumstances influence which strategy comes to the fore. Because these different patterns of behaviour have such divergent implications for well-being, it is crucial to recognize the powerful influence that the scale of inequality has on social behaviour across whole societies.

WELL-BEING

Both sources of social anxiety we have highlighted concern our desire for the good opinions of others and are rooted in our evolutionary history, but they are nonetheless radically different. One is about building friendship and good social relations, about mutual support and contributing to each other's well-being. The other is much more antisocial. It is about being seen as better than others, looking down on one's inferiors, kowtowing to superiors, and being vulnerable to feelings of inadequacy when we are outdone by others. Though we will always live with a mix of the two, we need more of the first of these two social strategies and less of the second.

Although humans have lived with – and adapted to – extremely different levels of inequality and hierarchy, they have sharply contrasting implications for well-being. Social relations based on status competition foster needless opposition and so are more stressful than those based on greater equality and reciprocity. The evolutionary thread that runs all the way from the bullying structure of animal ranking systems to the ten-fold higher rates of bullying in schools in more unequal societies (Figure 5.2), illustrates what is at stake for us all. Bullying relationships are a source of profound misery. Some children are so badly affected that they vomit with fear at having to go to school each morning and suffer serious depression. People who were bullied at school often carry life-long psychological scars as a result. What goes for the effects of greater inequality among children also goes for the quality of relationships among all of us in more unequal societies. We know in our bones that status competition is a zero-sum game: we cannot all improve our status relative to each other. If some gain, others lose.

The research outlined above that uses experimental 'games' to explore human social behaviour demonstrates how flawed the idea really is of ourselves as fundamentally self-interested and possessive. As we saw in the first chapter, the evidence that good social relationships are the key to improved health and happiness is underpinned by studies of wound healing, vulnerability to infections and longevity.[28-30, 33, 264, 265]

By reducing the material differences between us we can improve well-being and the quality of social relationships across whole populations. As the data show, the more equal a society is, the stronger its community life becomes and the more we feel we can trust each other. Status anxiety, consumerism and violence all decrease, and social relationships become less stressful.

Unless we understand these links, we will go on wishing for a better society and that people would treat each other better, but to no avail. Exhortation alone will not stop people judging each other by outward appearances, or treating wealth as an indication of personal worth. Responses to hierarchy are too deeply ingrained to make it possible to switch them off while ignoring the scale of inequality. Similarly, we could wish that people would pull their self-confidence up by their own boot straps, make friends and contribute to community life, but again, for many the feelings of inferiority will be overpowering. We can wish that large income differences would not lead to feelings of superiority and inferiority, or for people not to be snobbish or look down on people lower on the social ladder, but to make any real difference we have to take account of the factors that provoke these reactions in us.

Because there are no perfectly equal societies, it is impossible to know whether there is a point at which reducing income differences stops being beneficial. There is no data from more equal societies to tell us whether we would benefit from becoming even more equal than the most equal of the developed countries. It is hard to imagine an egalitarian world without the highs and lows of status, a world in which that simple polarization of how we see and value people is absent. If the real differences in people's endlessly varied skills, interests, abilities, knowledge and personality characteristics were no longer so hidden behind the masks of status, their true individuality might be more freely and clearly expressed.

6

The Misconception of Meritocracy*

Boris Johnson, the former Mayor of London who became Foreign Secretary in Theresa May's Conservative government in 2016, was educated at Eton and Oxford. Giving 'The Margaret Thatcher Lecture' to a think tank in 2013, he articulated the view that economic equality will never be possible because some people are simply too stupid to catch up with the rest of society: 'Whatever you may think of the value of IQ tests it is surely relevant to a conversation about equality that as many as 16 per cent of our species have an IQ below 85.' Comparing society to a box of cornflakes, he praised inequality for creating the conditions under which the brightest triumph: 'the harder you shake the pack, the easier it will be for some cornflakes to get to the top'. Inequality 'is essential for the spirit of envy and keeping up with the Joneses that is, like greed, a valuable spur to economic activity'.[266]

Whether or not Johnson is quite as clever a cornflake as he presumably likes to think, he certainly isn't in command of the facts. Nobel Prize-winning economists,[267, 268] as well as the OECD and IMF,[269, 270] have shown how inequality, far from spurring on economic growth, leads to stagnation and instability. Social mobility is reduced where income inequality is greatest and, far from inspiring innovation, it turns out that there are actually slightly more patents granted per head of population in more equal countries. And, as we've seen in the previous chapters, there is also the undeniable

---

* This chapter includes material from: K. Pickett and L. Vanderbloemen, *Mind the Gap: Tackling Social and Educational Inequality*, York: Cambridge Primary Review Trust, 2015.

human cost of our fixation with keeping up with the Joneses. But Boris is far from alone in his misconceptions about the relationships between inequality and ability.

The idea that people are naturally endowed with differences in ability, intelligence or talent, and that those differences then determine how far up the social ladder they reach, is a powerful popular justification for social hierarchy. The presumption is that we live in a 'meritocracy', in which the key to status is ability. We think of society as shaped like a pyramid: the supposition is that most people are near the bottom or only a little above it because the bulk of the population lack the special talents that we imagine get people to the top. The belief that differences in ability are the main influence on where people end up on the social ladder is so strong that we tend to judge everyone's personal worth, ability and intelligence from their position in society. Nor is this confined simply to how we judge others: it also affects how people see themselves. Those at the top often believe that they are there because they were naturally endowed with plenty of 'the right stuff', just as those near the bottom often think that their low status reflects a lack of ability.

That picture is not, however, supported by the latest scientific evidence. First, research now shows that a very major part of what happens to people and where they end up is the result of totally unpredictable influences and occurrences amounting to pure luck. Second, aside from luck, the most important links that exist between ability and status operate in the opposite direction to that imagined by most people. Rather than different endowments of talents determining position in the hierarchy, it is much nearer the truth to say that position in the hierarchy determines abilities, interests and talents. Let's address luck first.

Whether or not we consider ourselves successful, most of us can probably look back across our own life histories and recognize the roles that luck and chance have played getting us to where we are today. We were perhaps lucky with schools or teachers, with the questions in an important exam, with some nameless person dealing with university applications, or we got on well with an interviewer when applying for a job. Perhaps a chance meeting was important, or perhaps an opportunity for promotion came up unexpectedly. Finding a life partner is just as important for our quality of life as our career or income, but we are far happier to acknowledge that chance and luck played a key role in meeting that person than we are in acknowledging luck's role in our career. No one minds mentioning the chance meeting, the circumstances that put you both at ease with each other, or the shared interest that might easily have gone unrecognized.

The role of chance makes people's lives highly unpredictable. Although there are huge social class biases in social mobility, there are at the same time vast numbers of people moving up or down the social ladder in ways that even the most detailed analysis of parenting and ability fail to predict. Similarly, although there are differences of perhaps ten years in the average life expectancy of upper and lower social classes, that explains very little of the individual differences in how long people live: inevitably some rich people die young and some people live in poverty to a great age. And, as some public health mavericks used to say, even if you exercised, ate healthily and didn't smoke, your most likely cause of death was still heart disease. In addition to all this, there may be a large element of chance in whether our experiences – including subjective experiences – trigger the kind of epigenetic changes affecting subsequent development that we discussed in the last chapter.

Just as the development of weather systems is sometimes said to be so chaotic that it can be changed by the flapping of a butterfly's wings, so what amount to chance events at the social or the cellular level are now thought to play a very substantial part in our lives. So much so that scientists have worried that if random chance and luck are such important determinants of whether or not an individual becomes sick, gets good exam results or has a good marriage, it becomes difficult to understand causal pathways at all, and to do anything about preventing or remedying bad outcomes. In the social sciences this has become known as the 'Gloomy Prospect' – the notion that scientific inquiry will bump up against Lady Luck and be of no further explanatory or practical use.[271] But although the role of luck shows us the unpredictability of individual lives, it impinges little on our understanding of average or *group* differences among large populations. It is a bit as if life was played using dice weighted according to the social class in which we grow up. Outcomes of each roll of the dice are still very much a matter of chance, but when you look at a large number of throws the biases in favour of some and against others become clear. So to attribute an individual's success in life largely to luck is not incompatible with our ability to demonstrate that, on average, people from poorer backgrounds do worse and have shorter lives, or that the majority fare worse in a more unequal society.

This is not to deny that there are differences in ability, skills and interests, or that those nearer the top often score better on at least some of the most highly regarded measures of ability. The distribution of ability in society would, however, look rather different if – for instance – people were rated on the various kinds of technical ability used in manual occupations, or on driving skills, DIY know-how, or the skills involved in living on a small income. Even though some kinds of ability are privileged over others, our argument is not with the measures of ability but, instead, concerns where those differences in abilities come from.

Boris Johnson's crediting differences in intelligence to biology, and his belief that people have a 'natural' endowment of talent, mainly determined by the genes they inherit from their parents, are not new. At least since classical times, there has been a tendency for the rich and powerful to believe – and encourage others to believe – that members of each class in society are made of different stuff. Plato imagined that members of the ruling class had souls made of gold. In the class below them were people with souls of silver and, below them, of bronze or iron.[272] Class and racial prejudices have always been bolstered by beliefs that there are innate differences in ability between groups that explained social position – from philosopher kings at the top to slaves at the bottom. As we now know, however, social classes are not based on genetic differences.[273]

SHARED INHERITANCE

Any genetically determined characteristic that confers a substantial survival advantage will tend to become universal among members of a species. We all have two eyes because binocular vision is so useful.

Whole populations have lighter or darker skin to provide the appropriate level of protection from sunlight needed at the latitudes where their forebears lived. Of several hundred primate species, we are almost the only one to have whites to our eyes; in the others the sclera is brown. As we are a highly social species the ability to follow each other's gaze and see what anyone is looking at is advantageous and has therefore become a universal human characteristic. It is therefore hard to imagine that if any specific genes for intelligence conferred significant survival advantages that they would not have become universal among human beings. Nevertheless, the improbable idea that some groups of humans have particularly advanced 'intelligence', which substantially enhances their ability to solve almost any kind of problem, while others are persistently poorly endowed, has until relatively recently appeared to have scientific support, and remains widely held.

WE'RE GETTING SMARTER . . .

The belief that there are major genetic differences in intelligence has been struggling to survive evidence that the intelligence of whole populations has been increasing rapidly over time. In the 1980s, Professor James Flynn, a psychologist in New Zealand, first began to publish studies showing that in many different countries – indeed wherever he could find data allowing him to make accurate comparisons over time – populations had made huge gains on IQ tests across the twentieth century. This fact has now become so well established, and has been observed so widely, that it is known as the 'Flynn effect'. Among developed countries, measurements have been made in the USA, fifteen European countries, four Asian countries, Australia, Canada and New Zealand. All show the 'Flynn effect'. Developing and emerging economies, including Kenya, Dominica, Brazil, Turkey and Saudi Arabia, are now also making explosive gains.[274] The typical rate of increase in IQ is close to three points per decade. By the IQ standards of the year 2000, that means people living in 1930 would have had an average IQ of about 80, regarded as the point below which 'dullness' becomes 'borderline deficiency'.

Clearly, if people today are massively more intelligent than their own parents and grandparents, then IQ tests are not measures of anything we can regard as innate intelligence.

Flynn points out that IQ tests measure 'habits of mind' that are cultural and learned, rather than innate. He describes modern, Western habits of mind as being like wearing 'scientific spectacles' – we see the world through the prism of scientific learning, rather than from a purely practical point of view. Thus, the 'correct' answer to a question on an IQ test that asks, 'What do dogs and rabbits have in common?' is that both are mammals (scientific classification), rather than that dogs can be used to hunt rabbits (a practical view, more likely to be offered by someone not raised with Western culture and education). IQ tests are geared towards measuring hypothetical logical thinking, as well as symbolic thinking, and their consequences. It seems likely that through differences in work and life circumstances, some sections of the population get their 'scientific spectacles' before others.

Flynn suggests that there have been substantial changes in the cognitive skills valued by society, taught by educators and rewarded in IQ tests, rather than a gain in innate intelligence. He says 'the ultimate cause of IQ gains is the Industrial Revolution. The intermediate causes are probably its social consequences, such as more formal schooling, more cognitively demanding jobs, cognitively challenging leisure, a better ratio of adults to children, richer interaction between parent and child.' In other words, the enormous gains in IQ over the twentieth century are socially constructed, not genetic. He also reminds us that few developing nations now have average IQ scores as low – for example – as the USA had in 1900.

WHAT ABOUT THE TWIN STUDIES?

Scientists seeking to understand inheritance and whether it is genes (nature), or environment (nurture), which primarily affect human characteristics, traits and behaviours, have for a long time studied people who are genetically related to one another. Studies of twins have been particularly useful, and most useful of all have been studies of identical twins raised apart. Identical twins share 100 per cent of their genetic make-up, and even when they are brought up separately, they score much more like each other on an IQ test than two people randomly selected from the population. It was this evidence that led scientists to conclude that intelligence is highly heritable, predominantly genetic, and that the environment plays a much smaller role.

With hindsight, we can see that this finding has actually been misleading, not because the results are incorrect in themselves but because of the way they have been interpreted. In fact, twins reared apart tend to have been brought up in much more similar environments than two people chosen at random from the population. Imagine identical twins adopted at birth into two different families – they may well be adopted within a restricted geographical area, for example by adoptive families in the same local authority, perhaps by families with quite similar socio-economic status, from the same ethnic and cultural background, and so on. Despite being reared apart, their environments might not differ very much.

Still more important is the fact that small genetic differences tend to become dramatically amplified by the environment. Imagine, for example, someone who, perhaps for genetic reasons, is marginally better at sport than others. As a result, they are more likely to enjoy it and to practise more. They may then be picked for the school team and given more coaching, further improving their performance. In this kind of way, small innate differences in ability are magnified by being nurtured through the way people are set off on different developmental trajectories of behaviour and environmental choices. The same is true of almost any slight advantage or predisposition we might start off with, whether it is learning to read at a young age, being musical, having an aptitude for mathematics, or a curiosity about how things work. Having any such aptitude tends to mean people do more of that activity, they enjoy it more, get better at it, are rewarded for doing it well and develop it further – in effect, we choose activities and circumstances which amplify our ability to do things we were initially good at. As a result, small biologically based differences in our aptitudes nudge us a little in one direction or another so that small initial differences get magnified and developed by what we choose to do. Similarly in twin studies: differences or similarities between twins or non-twins, whether reared together or apart, which may in these studies be attributed to genetics, are actually reflections of small genetic differences or similarities that have been amplified by the activities and environmental choices people make.

There are a number of concrete examples demonstrating almost exactly these processes in action. Rather than genetic advantages, we shall look at examples of how random differences in children's ages confer small biological advantages, which are then amplified in ways closely analogous to those in which genetic advantages are amplified.

Entry into school systems is almost always determined by an annual cut-off date. If, for example, children must be aged five years by 1 September in any year to start school, then children born just after that date will enter school almost a full year older than children in the same classroom with birthdays just before 1 September. The children who are among the oldest in their class have a small but significant developmental advantage over their classmates. Studies show that, as a result, they do better in many ways: their educational attainment is better, they have more friends, take on more leadership roles, and are more likely to succeed throughout life.[275] In an international study, relative age when entering primary school was found to have a positive effect on long-term test scores in ten out of the sixteen studied countries.[276]

People used to think that this might be because summer-born children were more exposed during early foetal development in the womb to maternal infections during the previous winter months. But we now know that the lasting benefits of being one of the older children in a class holds true whatever the cut-off date for entry. A small developmental advantage becomes magnified through classroom interactions in just the same way as small genetic differences in one or other skill or ability can become magnified by practice as people select and are selected by their environment.

The same mechanism explains why more than twice as many professional hockey players are born in the first three months of the year than in the last three months.[277] Figure 6.1 shows the data for American and Canadian players selected to play in the National Hockey League. The cut-off birth date for youth hockey leagues (and

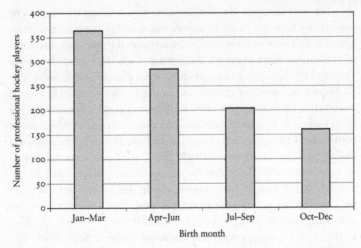

Figure 6.1: Players born earlier in the year are more likely to play in National Hockey League teams.[277]

therefore access to training, practice and other opportunities) is 1 January, so those born in the early months of the year are, on average, bigger, stronger, faster and more developed than their team-mates born later in the same calendar year. Their chances of being recruited into elite training programmes, travelling teams, scholarships and so on are therefore higher from the start, resulting in significantly different trajectories for those born earlier in the year. A large number of studies have now identified these processes in at least fourteen other sports including football.[278, 279]

Sporting ability may be a better guide to forms of ability relevant to social mobility than some would expect. It would be easy to imagine that physical and mental abilities are quite separate. But a recent study found that sporting prowess depends not only on physical ability but also on very rapid information processing in quickly changing contexts.[280] Tests found that a group of cognitive abilities known as 'executive functions' (including working memory, mental flexibility and self-control) were not only much higher in male and female footballers playing in league teams, but were higher in first- compared to second-league players. The same study also found that the results of executive function tests were predictive of the numbers of goals scored by players. This should caution us from saying someone is simply 'good with their hands' as if that did not depend on the brain guiding their hands (or feet!). We would not, after all, say that a good novelist is simply good with a pen – or perhaps keyboard.

Just as minor initial differences in ability arising from any source – including the way birth dates can affect selection – are amplified by what people choose to do, so the differences in ability from other sources, including those attributed to genetics, are also amplified. The other side of that coin is that the importance of all the things we do which develop our skills and abilities have generally been underestimated. A pianist might have a small genetic aptitude which contributed to taking up or persevering with the piano, but the overwhelming determinant of ability is, in the end, practice.

It is likely that small genetic advantages in one or other activity have such an influence on individual development because we get pleasure from doing what we are best at relative to others. That nudges us to specialize in areas where we have the greatest comparative advantage – a principle fundamental to economics and perhaps to evolution. It is probably particularly important in relationships between siblings. If your elder sibling is the sporty one, then maybe you have to be the bookish one, the practical one, or the funny one. A mechanism of this kind, which pushes siblings to differentiate themselves from each other, would explain why some research suggests that siblings are no more alike than random pairs of the population.[281] In effect, the important environment is sometimes less a matter of the bricks and mortar as of the subjective niche we create for ourselves.

THE PLASTIC BRAIN

The past several decades of research have transformed our knowledge of the extent to which our brains (and so minds) are flexible and capable of development. There are now numerous studies using brain scans that show that when we exercise the 'muscles' of our mind, through different kinds of learning and practice, we shape the very structure and functioning of our brains. There is a celebrated and well-known study of the brains of London taxi drivers that shows that their hippocampi – the area of the brain used (among other things) for navigating through three-dimensional space – are enlarged after (and not before) acquiring 'The Knowledge'.[282] (To get their licence, taxi drivers have to pass a stringent test that involves memorizing the location of 25,000 streets and 320 main routes across London without looking at maps, using satellite navigation or asking for help via radio.) The brains of professional musicians (when compared to those of amateurs and non-musicians) similarly show changes that are particularly closely related to the intensity of practice.[283] In another study, volunteers who learned to juggle were found to undergo structural changes in brain areas involved in the processing and storage of complex visual motion.[284] Other studies have shown changes in the brains of people who learned a second language or were given golf lessons, in dancers and tightrope walkers, and in volunteers who practised mirror reading for fifteen minutes a day for two weeks. And a study of medical students revising for exams showed that learning so much abstract information led to structural changes in particular areas of their grey matter.[284]

There can now be no doubt that with practice and training our brains adapt to make us better at whatever it is we do. The brains of architects, footballers, lawyers, psychologists, musicians, cabinet makers, policemen, accountants, motor mechanics and artists will each develop to give them particular abilities, sometimes amplifying earlier predispositions that led to an initial interest in a field. Nor are these effects confined to the young. Similar processes have been shown in middle age and beyond. Though brain plasticity declines in old age, studies indicate that even the brains of the elderly respond to enriched environments and training.[285–287] Lives can change course and our brains respond. The limitations of childhood circumstances or poor schooling need not be permanent.

The evidence suggests, then, that what is measured by IQ tests and rewarded with financial and social advantages develops in much the same way as the expertise of a taxi driver, musician or bricklayer. What we now know about the plasticity of the human brain means that these issues are basically the same whether the skills and abilities are social, artistic, mathematical, spatial, linguistic, practical, musical or kinaesthetic. Nor should we forget that brain development is also affected by stress in pregnancy, by conditions in early childhood, by nurturing, teaching and schooling, by family circumstances, and by respect and love.

DIFFERENT CIRCUMSTANCES

Rather than innate ability determining where people end up in a supposedly meritocratic hierarchy, the apparent abilities of children and their subsequent social status are instead heavily influenced by their family's position in that hierarchy. Vast numbers of studies have now demonstrated the cognitive damage that living in poverty does to children. They also provide strong evidence that lower levels of ability among children in poorer families reflect the less stimulating and more stressful family circumstances that poverty produces. The cognitive deficits found in studies of children from poorer families show clearly that they are created, rather than being innate and unalterable givens.

A recent study in the USA used MRI scanners to scan children's brains up to seven times each between the ages of five months and four years. Comparing children from high- , medium- and low-income families, it found that children in lower-income families had lower volumes of grey matter (containing neural cells, dendrites and synapses), which is essential for cognition, information processing and behavioural regulation. Although there were not clear ordered differences at five months, by four years of age the volume of grey matter was around 10 per cent lower among children from less well-off families compared to the most well-off group. These differences were not accounted for by infant birth weight, early health, or by differences in head size at birth. Nor were the differences explained by maternal smoking, excessive drinking in pregnancy, birth complication, significant language or learning disorders and a number of other risk factors – children with risk factors such as these were excluded at the start of the study. Differences in brain volume between the income groups emerged and widened as children grew up and were exposed to their contrasting home environments for longer.[288]

Other studies have also shown that the harmful effects of relative poverty on children's cognitive development become more severe when their families remain in poverty for longer periods. Data from the Millennium Cohort Study in the UK showed not only that children in poverty had lower cognitive development scores at three, five and seven years old, but that the longer they lived in poverty, the more marked the effects were.[289] The evidence that the more time families spend in relative poverty, the worse the effects on the cognitive development of children has been clear from numerous studies for well over twenty years.[290, 291] Family income has been found to be a more powerful determinant of children's level of cognitive development at age three than either maternal depression or whether children are brought up by single parents, married or cohabiting parents.[292]

The ways in which poverty damages development seem to be mediated by stress and lack of mental stimulation. A study which measured levels of the stress hormone cortisol in the saliva of infants of seven months, fifteen months and two years old, found that the cognitive deficit of poor children was closely related to their cortisol levels, indicating that the effects of poverty were transmitted by stress.[293] In another study, researchers measured the mental stimulation children received, their parents' parenting style, the quality of the physical environment and the child's health. They found that these factors *completely* accounted for the effects of poverty on cognitive development.[294] Confirming the role of stimulation, it has been shown repeatedly that if children from poor families are enrolled in parental and child support services such as Early Head Start in the US, children's performance improves and some of the effects of poverty are offset.[295]

When parents' ability to provide a nurturing and stimulating environment for development is compromised by their experiences of inequality, then children miss out on some of the essential building blocks for development and later educational attainment. Figure 6.2 shows that children growing up in professional families in the USA

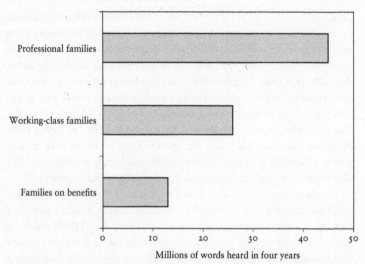

Millions of words heard in four years

Figure 6.2: Children from families receiving welfare benefits and in working-class families hear fewer words than children in professional families.[296, 297]

hear a vastly richer vocabulary during their early years than children in working-class families or families receiving benefits.

Perhaps the most striking illustration of how educational inequalities are a consequence of socio-economic inequalities, rather than a cause, comes from a series of studies of UK children that tracks educational performance over time, comparing high and low achievers from different social backgrounds. The most recent of these studies is shown in Figure 6.3.[298] It compares the educational performance of children from more and less deprived backgrounds over time. Their progress is charted from their initial test results at age seven (shown as high, average and low on the left), and, moving rightwards, tracking their subsequent performance at ages eleven, fourteen, sixteen, eighteen and then at university.

Regardless of whether their initial scores are high, medium or low, the gap between the performance of children from the most and the least deprived backgrounds (the gap between the continuous and the dashed lines) widens as they get older. Children from the least deprived families either maintain their initial high relative position, or improve their average or low scores. Education enhances their performance. In contrast, the relative performance of children from deprived backgrounds who initially achieved a high or average score, declines over time. Deprivation makes so much difference that children from the least deprived backgrounds whose performance at age seven was only average or low, overtake – or at least catch up with – children who initially performed better than them but came from deprived backgrounds. And we should keep in mind that by age seven, when the graph in Figure 6.3 starts, family background has already had major effects on children's cognitive development.[289]

In summary, Figure 6.3 shows that family background trumps what people continue to regard as 'natural' ability in accounting for children's educational performance over time. An OECD study of resilience showed that in some countries, up to 70 per cent of poor children are educationally resilient, whereas in the UK less than a quarter of children manage to exceed expectations based on family

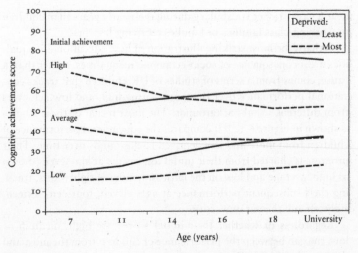

Figure 6.3: How family background shapes educational performance over time.[298]

socio-economic circumstances.[299] Taken together with Figure 6.3, it is clear that differences in cognitive development and intelligence are the consequence of inequality rather than its cause.

INEQUALITY AFFECTS TEACHERS TOO

The evidence that family poverty affects children's intellectual development is incontrovertible, and refutes the notion that some people are born bright and others stupid and there is not much that can be done about it. Although we know that everyone's cognitive performance can be increased, schools often become instruments of social sorting as differences in infant ability are widened further until they become the basis for the occupational and class differences of adulthood.

Researchers at the University of Bristol compared the marks given by classroom teachers with those given in national tests marked remotely by people unaware of who they were marking.[300] They found that children from poor neighbourhoods were consistently given worse grades by their teachers, compared to children from more affluent neighbourhoods. Black children were also systematically marked down by their teachers, while children of Indian and Chinese origin tended to be marked upwards. The researchers interpreted these findings as an indication of unconscious stereotyping by ethnicity and class, and found that discriminatory marking was most pronounced in the areas with fewer black or poor children. This phenomenon, where children do better or worse depending on their teachers' expectations of them, is known as the 'Pygmalion effect' and has been consistently reported in studies from the late 1960s onwards.[301, 302] Nor is it confined to rich countries like the USA and the UK; a recent study in India found that teachers gave lower scores to exam papers they believed to come from lower-caste children.[303] The point is not to criticize teachers, but to highlight our subconscious perceptions.

Social class has been called the 'zombie stalking English schools' by Professor Diane Reay of the University of Cambridge, who argues that social class issues have never been adequately addressed within education.[304] Efforts to widen participation in higher education have benefitted the middle class more than poorer children,[305] who were too often seen as 'inadequate learners with inadequate cultural backgrounds'. In the study examining the experience of poverty in different countries mentioned in Chapter 5, interviewees often experienced school as 'an instrument of social grading'.[253] In numerous papers, and in her recent book, *Miseducation*,[306] Reay describes how many working-class children have a sense of educational worthlessness, and feel that they are not valued or respected within their schools. They feel that teachers look down on them, make them look stupid and treat them as dumb. Too often teacher-training courses are not geared towards enabling trainees to think about social class, socio-economic position and inequality in relation to education. Schools, classrooms and overstretched teachers are expected to overcome educational inequalities in spite of the social context of poverty and inequality, which they are powerless to address. As Reay concludes: 'We cannot rely on serendipity, the fortuitous chance that teachers will educate themselves about the importance of social class in schooling, that they will have knowledge and understanding of the different class cultures of the children in their classes.'[304]

Decades of research show that low socio-economic status predicts a 'wide array of health, cognitive and socio-emotional outcomes in children'.[307] Researchers have shown that if children are already behind in terms of school readiness and cognitive development when they start school, then unfavourable educational outcomes are much more likely, in spite of good schooling.[308-313] And the challenge for individual life trajectories and well-being is compounded by the fact that when children are not ready for school, this puts the school and all its pupils, as well as each deprived child, at a disadvantage.

STEREOTYPE THREAT

Children's development is not affected just by what the outside world does to them, whether through poverty or the social grading they might experience in school. There are also signs of processes that look almost like self-stigmatization. We described in Chapter 1 how status differentiation – the awareness of how other people perceive your status – affects the body, mind and emotions. We also saw how tasks that involve 'social evaluative threat' (threats to self-esteem or social status) are especially stressful.[58] *The Spirit Level* included a study showing how children's aptitude for solving puzzles was affected by status differentiation. In an experiment published by the World Bank, a group of eleven- to twelve-year-old Indian boys from high and low castes were able to solve mazes equally well before they knew each other's caste. But as soon as the caste of the participants was made known, the lower-caste children did much less well and a large gap opened up between the performance of the groups.[314] There are now several hundred, mostly experimental, studies of this process.[315, 316] They show that people perform less well on tests when they are made even subtly more aware that they belong to a group stereotypically regarded as performing poorly in the test area, or when the task is made to appear more challenging to their abilities in an area in which they are typically regarded as less able. For example, low socio-economic status children performed less well when told that tests were a measure of intelligence rather than just a 'general test'.[317] Similar processes have been shown to affect the performance of African American schoolchildren and college students.[318] When black and white students were given tests that they were told were measures of intelligence, the black students did much less well than when they were told it was a questionnaire designed to identify psychological factors involved in problem solving. The belief that their intelligence was being tested provoked their awareness of stereotyped perceptions of African Americans.

Gender stereotyping has also been shown to affect the performance of women. After women were 'primed' by being shown TV commercials selected for their gender stereotyping, they were more likely to prefer the verbal options to the maths questions in an aptitude test, and were less likely to favour quantitative educational and career options.[319] Other studies have found that old people perform less well on memory tests when they are made more concerned about the effects of ageing on memory.[320]

To see if similar effects could be induced even when there was no general stereotype, an experiment compared maths-test scores of two groups of white men, all of whom were particularly good at maths. One group was told that the test was to help understand why whites tended to do less well than Asians on particular test questions. Despite the lack of a prior stigmatizing stereotype, this was enough of a threat to lead to poorer performance.[321]

Much of the effect of stereotype threat seems to result from additional anxiety, which reduces attention and mental capacity for the task at hand. This seems to be stronger among people who are more self-conscious about their stigmatized status and among those for whom the area being tested is important to their identity.[322] African Americans, for example, were found to have higher blood pressure than European Americans in response to a stereotype threat involving intelligence tests.[323] Studies have found that the working memory capacity of people under stereotype threat is reduced by factors such as increased physiological stress, monitoring their performance more and trying to suppress negative thoughts – all of which impair task performance.[324, 325]

Studies like these reveal our sensitivity to status differences and show why they are so powerful and so damaging – actually increasing people's conformity with the stereotypes. They help to explain why the early effects of family income on children's cognitive development are so difficult to eradicate during their school life and careers.

The evidence in this chapter shows how mistaken it is to see the social hierarchy as a reflection of natural differences in people's abilities. There are differences in ability between people at different levels in the social hierarchy, but those differences are more the product of that hierarchy than the source of it. The idea that the success of a society depends on identifying natural talents early, and hot-housing those who possess them as if they were a rare natural resource, is almost the opposite of the truth. Educational systems that separate out the more and less talented children as if the differences between them were set in stone, do so on the basis of a fundamental misunderstanding. We should instead be removing the causes of underperformance to maximize the talents and abilities of the whole population.

The research papers on the effects of poverty discussed earlier in this chapter are concerned with the effects of relative poverty, defined in terms of the incomes elsewhere in society and usually measured as below 60 per cent of the national median income. The effects those papers showed were not confined just to the poor. Typically the poor do least well, but each layer in the income hierarchy tends to do less well than those above it. So the study which showed that the volume of grey matter grew more slowly among children from poor families, also showed that the gap between children in high- and middle-income families was just as big as that between children from poor and middle-income families. Similarly, in Figure 6.2 we saw not only that children in families receiving state income support hear fewer words – less conversation – than those in working-class families, but also that those in working-class families hear less than children in professional families. The issue is not simply how the poor do compared to everyone else, but that people do less well at each step down the social hierarchy from top to bottom.

The underlying issue is, as we saw in the last chapter, our human sensitivity to social status and rank. The central issue in this chapter has been whether the differences in ability, talent and intelligence, which people see as giving rise to the social pyramid, are innate or whether they come from the differences in class and income that influence our circumstances: the evidence points strongly to the latter. In the following section we will see the evidence that a range of outcomes, crucial to child development and education, are worse in countries where bigger income differences increase the influence of status on all.

'AND WORSE WITH MORE INEQUALITY . . .'

Figure 6.4 shows that countries with bigger income differences have, as we would expect, bigger differences in educational performance, as measured by literacy scores (the same relationship is shown for twenty countries in an OECD report of 2014[326]). This is powerful evidence of the effect of social status differences on educational performance. The larger the income differences, the more strongly educational performance is marked by status differences.

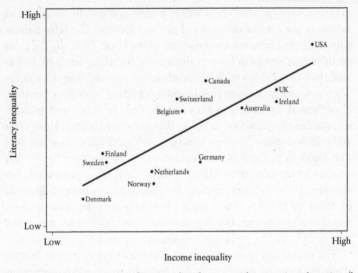

Figure 6.4: Income inequality is related to a wider gap in educational attainment among adults.[327]

Bigger income differences in a society not only make inequalities in educational performance larger, they also lower the average levels of educational attainment for children across the whole society. We showed in a paper published in the *Lancet* in 2006 that the national average performance of countries on the 2003 Programme for International Student Assessment (PISA) tests of maths and reading literacy was significantly related to a measure of income inequality among rich nations (Figure 6.5).[328] And in *The Spirit Level*, we showed the same thing for educational attainment of eighth graders (thirteen- to fourteen-year-olds) in relation to income inequality among the fifty states of the USA.

Income inequality affects the educational standards of whole societies because bigger income differences depress performance at each step down the social ladder. The data show that the relationship between income inequality and educational outcomes spans the economic spectrum, worsening the performance of a large majority of

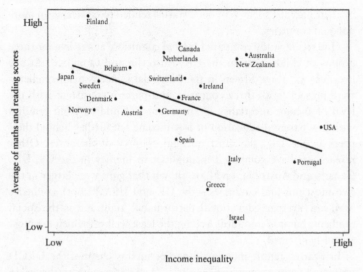

Figure 6.5: Maths and literacy scores tend to be higher in more equal rich countries.[328]

children. The differences in educational attainment are, however, most marked at the bottom of the social ladder: that is where inequality does most damage. A crucial influence on average performance – on national levels of achievement – is the steepness of the social gradient, and it is this which is increased by bigger income differences.

This pattern has been demonstrated for a set of developed countries by the OECD and Statistics Canada.[327] When countries were grouped by income inequality, literacy scores of fifteen-year-olds not only tended to be higher in the more equal countries, but nearly all socio-economic groups in those countries had scores above the international average: the social gradient in literacy was shallower in the more equal countries. A 2013 report from the Programme for the International Assessment of Adult Competencies (PIAAC) showed a similar pattern of social gradients in adult literacy.[329] And a 2010 OECD analysis of PISA literacy scores in sixty-five countries again showed that the gradients in performance among children (classified by their parents' socio-economic status) tended to be steeper in more unequal countries.[330]

One recent study compared 'verbal cognition' at age five for three groups of children, from the UK, Australia and Canada.[331] At age five, just as at age fifteen in the PISA data, steep social gradients were present in all three countries in a pattern consistent with the level of income inequality in the country. Children from families with low parental education or low income fell further behind their peers in the UK, the most unequal country of the three. Other researchers have compared inequalities in literacy in the US, UK, Canada and Australia, and have shown that gaps were larger in the two most unequal countries – the UK and USA.[332] Both countries have low average educational performance right across the social gradient, but it is standards among the least well-off which are most seriously affected.

In a 2012 report mentioned earlier in this chapter, the OECD presented findings on which countries seem to promote 'resilience' in children and families, in other words the ability of children to achieve better educational outcomes than would be expected given their family socio-economic position.[299] The UK performs worse than average in the OECD on the proportion of disadvantaged students who are resilient to their socio-economic background. Conversely, countries with less economic inequality, such as Canada, Finland and Japan, perform well overall and their children do well regardless of their socio-economic background. In China more than 70 per cent of poor children are educationally resilient in this way, whereas in the UK less than a quarter of poor children manage to exceed expectations based on family background.

The USA and UK are also falling behind other countries in further education outcomes. As well as considering PISA scores, a UNICEF report looked at the proportion of children aged between fifteen and nineteen who had left full-time education and who were classed as Not in Education, Employment or Training (NEET) in 2009/2010. Young people in the USA and UK are NEET more often than young people in many other rich countries, ranking twenty-fifth and twenty-seventh out of thirty-three countries, respectively.[333]

Among many other factors linking inequality to poor educational performance, two stand out. Being bullied is an experience singularly corrosive to the self-esteem and educational performance of those who suffer it. In Chapter 5, we described the study by Canadian psychologist Frank Elgar and his colleagues, who found that inequality was significantly related to large differences in the frequency both of bullying others and of being a victim of bullying.[233] We have also found that the proportion of children who say their peers are not kind and helpful is much higher in more unequal rich countries.[189] The relationship between inequality and bullying is much like that between inequality and homicide, presumably because children are immersed in the same social milieu of status differentiation and interpersonal violence as adults and are similarly affected.[334] Juvenile homicides rates are, like adult homicide rates, correlated with income inequality.[335]

Another factor contributing to the link between inequality and educational performance is the rate at which children from less well-off backgrounds drop out of high school before graduating. In *The Spirit Level* we showed a strong relationship among the fifty states of the USA between high school dropout rates and inequality.[1]

The most fundamental effect of inequality on children's physical and cognitive development can be seen in measures of child well-being. As we described in Chapter 4, UNICEF compiles an index specifically to measure child well-being in rich countries. The data bring together some forty different aspects of child well-being including, for example, whether children feel they can talk to their parents, whether they have books at home, rates of child immunization, drinking, smoking and teenage birth rates. In a paper in the *British Medical Journal* we showed that the 2007 UNICEF index and most of its components were much more strongly related to income inequality than to measures of average income.[189] Figure 4.3 (page 107) shows the same relationship using data from the 2013 UNICEF report,[190] and we described how, using the twenty indicators that were measured in both reports, which included reading, mathematics and science literacy, participation in further education and the proportion of young people not in employment, education or training (NEETs), we were also able to compare changes in child well-being between the 2007 and 2013 reports.[190] We found a statistically significant tendency for changes in

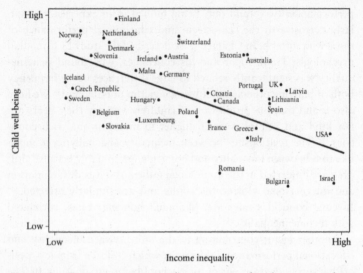

Figure 6.6: Greater income inequality is associated with poorer performance on the 2016 UNICEF Index of Child Well-being in wealthy countries (Turkey, with very low child well-being and high inequality, not shown).[336]

a country's income inequality between 2000 and 2009 to be mirrored in the changes in child well-being soon afterwards. Figure 6.6, using data from the 2016 UNICEF report, shows how consistent this relationship remains.

CLIMBING THE LADDER

We now have a clearer understanding of where individual differences in ability come from and how children's differing circumstances affect the subsequent development of their cognitive capacity. Income and status differences are, as we have seen, at the heart of these processes at the level of the individual, but bigger income differences also reduce educational outcomes across whole societies. We have seen something of the mechanisms behind these processes, how they affect the vast majority of the population, and why they damage those at the bottom most. The evidence presented in this chapter shows not only that it is mistaken to think that the social hierarchy is a reflection of innate differences in intelligence, but also that much the greater part of the differences in ability reflect rather than determine position in the hierarchy. In short, in any relation between ability and social position, the causality goes in the opposite direction from the view used to justify privilege.

Perhaps the final proof lies in the strong tendency shown in Figure 6.7 for more unequal countries to have less social mobility; or, to put it another way, in the countries where income differences are larger, children are even further away from enjoying equal opportunities. Inequalities in outcome cannot easily be combined with equal opportunities. The data in Figure 6.7 show intergenerational income mobility – the income of parents when a child is born compared to the income of the child when it reaches thirty years of age. The correlation between the incomes of parents and their adult children shows the

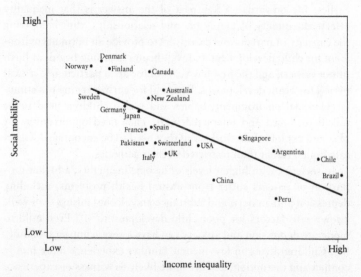

Figure 6.7: There is less social mobility in countries with bigger income differences.[337]

extent to which rich parents have children who grow up to be rich and poor parents have children who grow up to be poor. The USA and UK do particularly badly, and much has been written on the scale of their declining or stagnating social mobility over the past half century and the reasons behind it.[337-341] The graph is a testament to the cumulative weight of disadvantage and inferior status bearing down on the opportunities and development of less well-off children.

INEQUALITY PENETRATES FAMILY LIFE

We saw earlier that schools, instead of offering opportunities for poorer children to develop, may compound the damage already done to them by inequality. But how does inequality take root before these children have started their education and become integrated into society? How does societal inequality get so deep into family life that it affects children's developing capabilities and attainment from their earliest life onwards? A key part of the answer is that inequality affects the quality of family life and relationships, thus hampering the capacity of parents and caregivers to provide an optimal environment for child development and well-being. Learning begins at birth (if not earlier), and the first few years of life are a particularly critical period for brain development. Essential for early learning is a stimulating social environment; babies and young children need to be talked to, loved and interacted with. They need opportunities to play and explore their world, and they need to be encouraged within safe limits, rather than restricted in their activities.

In societies with higher levels of income inequality, a higher proportion of parents suffer from mental health problems, including depression and anxiety, and substance and alcohol misuse – all well-known risk factors for poor child development.[59, 189] Even mild to moderate depression and anxiety can have a severe impact on family life. Children living in low-income families experience more family conflict and disruption, and are more likely to witness or experience violence, as well as to be living in more crowded, noisy and substandard housing.[342] An American study found higher levels of child maltreatment in counties with higher levels of income inequality, even after adjusting for parents' level of education, levels of welfare and benefits, child poverty rates and state-level variations in rates of maltreatment.[247] Some families react to deprivation with more punitive and unresponsive parenting, even to the extent of becoming neglectful or abusive.[343, 344] Income inevitably affects the quality of family life, the difficulties faced by families and their ability to deal with them.[345] Showing the toll of inequality on marriage, another American study linked rising divorce rates to increases in income inequality in counties over time.[346]

The effects of inequality cannot, however, be explained by family breakdown, as is sometimes asserted by politicians and media commentators. Although children raised in single-parent households in some of the more unequal developed countries, like the UK, are indeed at a disadvantage, we found no international association between the UNICEF measures of child well-being and the prevalence of single-parent households.[1] In more equal developed countries, such as the Scandinavian countries, poverty among single parents is dramatically reduced by both generous universal and targeted provision of family support and services. And, as Professor Kathleen Kiernan and others have found, it is the poverty in which most single parents live, rather than single parenthood itself, which does the damage.[292]

As we have seen, income inequality heightens the importance of status, and consequently of income and status competition. Consumption increasingly becomes a measure of personal worth and, consequently, people in more unequal societies work longer hours, and accumulate more household debt.[199, 347] Lack of time for family life and the stress of debt that result were powerfully illustrated in the report (quoted in Chapter 4) on a qualitative UNICEF project looking at family life and child well-being in three countries with contrasting levels of inequality.[192]

It is important to emphasize here that difficulties in family relationships and parenting are not, of course, confined to the less well-off. Within a large study of children born in 2000 and 2001, even mothers in the second from the top social class group are more likely to report feeling incompetent as parents or having poor relationships with their children, compared to those in the topmost group.[1]

We saw in earlier chapters the evidence that inequality increases status anxiety among adults,[57] reduces solidarity,[39] and agreeableness,[105] and leads to a greater tendency to 'self-enhancement', i.e., claiming you are better than others.[112] We can expect that children will detect all of these and become aware of status differences in the wider society, and so – inevitably – become affected by the unequal context in which they grow up. The age at which children become consciously aware of class and status differences varies, but research has found that by the time they leave primary school, children are able to rank occupations hierarchically and place people into social classes by indicators such as clothing, houses and cars.[348, 349]

PICKING UP THE PIECES?

In November 2014, Professor Danny Dorling, from the University of Oxford, commented on income inequality and educational attainment in the *Times Higher Education*:

> Numeracy levels in . . . six wealthy countries . . . as assessed by the OECD, display an almost perfect inverse relationship to the countries' levels of economic inequality. So in places where the rich take far more, young people find it harder to understand why there can be such large differences in income between the median and the mean.[350]

The point is both ironic and rather poignant. To understand economic inequality – inequality of income and/or wealth – requires an understanding of the statistics of distribution. In nations where inequality is more of a problem, fewer young people will understand how it is measured.

Among health researchers, there is a popular analogy used to teach students about different approaches to population health. Students are asked to imagine a cliff that people keep falling off. If there is an ambulance waiting at the bottom of the cliff, a person who falls can be quickly taken to hospital for treatment, but this is a costly business and many lives will still be lost. Alternatively, we can also imagine that a safety net is provided halfway down the cliff so that most people are less injured than they would otherwise have been. This is analogous to the use of medicines to manage chronic conditions such as high blood pressure and diabetes – known in medical care as secondary prevention. Primary prevention is like putting a barrier at the top of the cliff to stop people falling down in the first place, for example reducing pulmonary disease by getting people to stop smoking and to take up exercise. But none of these strategies stop people running towards the cliff edge in the first place. If we could stop people doing that, none of the later, partially effective preventive and treatment strategies would be needed.

The educational parallel to the ambulance and the cliff analogy is that educational policies and interventions cannot themselves address the issues of poverty and inequality that are the root causes of poor educational performance. Primary prevention consists of early childhood interventions, like Sure Start in the UK and Head Start in the USA. Secondary prevention consists of policies like the pupil premium in the UK (extra funding given to schools with more pupils from poor backgrounds), and intensive remedial education interventions might be used to help children who are failing in the system. These strategies and programmes are expensive and never more than partially effective, but, unless the root causes of educational inequality are addressed, they will continue to be necessary.

While the idea that poverty negatively affects an individual child's ability to learn and to perform well in school is relatively uncontroversial,[307] the impact of societal inequality is less well known, although it too reduces average educational attainment and increases inequality of educational outcomes. There are low levels of absolute poverty in rich countries, although some children still lack sufficient nutritious food or adequate shelter. (In some countries, including the UK, these numbers are increasing.) Relative poverty, in contrast, is widespread.[351] According to government statistics, in the UK in 2015/16, 4 million children, or 30 per cent, were living in relative poverty (on less than 60 per cent of the median household income), and in some areas the proportion rose to 50–70 per cent.[352] Two-thirds of these children lived in a family where at least one adult was working. As a higher proportion of single parents were employed and benefits paid to low-income families increased, child poverty fell dramatically between 1998 and 2012. But since then absolute and relative poverty have risen. It is projected that 4.7 million children will be living in relative poverty by 2020.[353] The USA measures poverty against a threshold set by the Federal government, which is intended to provide an absolute standard. When established in 1964 it was equal to about half the US median income, but is now around 30 per cent.[354] Nevertheless, more than 20 per cent of Americans report that there are times when they cannot afford food for themselves or their family, and 20 per cent of children live below that Federal poverty line.[355] Measures of relative poverty suggest that about 30 per cent of all American children live in relative poverty.

Low rates of relative poverty are accepted internationally as a benchmark of well-being. In 2015, the UK government sought to pass new legislation relieving itself from the obligation to report on family income as a measure of child poverty, and to substitute measures of worklessness, levels of educational attainment, family breakdown, debt, and drug and alcohol dependency. It was decried at the time as an attempt to redefine the consequences of poverty as the causes of it, and after a battle with the House of Lords, the government retreated and agreed to continue to report measures of material deprivation. Had the government succeeded in changing the definition of poverty, it would have made it impossible to say whether its policies were increasing or decreasing child poverty.

It might seem sensible to assume that spending more money on education would help overcome the disadvantages of poverty, deprivation and inequality. To test this, researchers examined national income, income inequality and government spending on education in relation to educational achievement among adolescents.[356] They used OECD data on almost 120,000 students from over 5,000 schools in 24 countries. After controlling for individual pupil and school differences, they found that higher Gross Domestic Product per person – a measure of average income and living standards – had only a small beneficial effect on educational achievement. In contrast, income inequality turned out to have a large and damaging effect on literacy among these adolescents, while spending specifically on education had no effect. Neither economic growth nor the allocation of the proceeds of growth to public education appear to be panaceas for poor educational outcomes.

A case study that exemplifies how countries can transform and improve education and children's life chances is offered by Finland. It has a wholly non-selective school system from early childhood to age sixteen, and pupils score consistently highly on the international PISA tests.[357] Finland made a wholesale reform of its educational system about forty years ago and moved to an entirely comprehensive school system. It also improved the quality of teacher training and raised the status of the teaching profession: all teachers now have a Master's degree and a great deal of autonomy in what and how they teach within the framework of the national curriculum. Children start school at a later age than in many other countries, are subject to less standardized testing, and have more break-time during the school day. After rapid improvement in its education attainment, Finland topped the PISA league tables in 2000, 2003 and 2006, came third in 2009 and, although it moved down the rankings slightly in 2012, it has remained the best-performing country in Europe. It also has a higher proportion of resilient students (who do better than expected given their family background) than any other European country.

Sweden, which used to be seen as a model for high-quality education, has in contrast seen a steep decline in its PISA rankings and an increase in educational inequality. In the 1990s, it started to experience rapidly increasing income inequality and, despite strong international evidence that comprehensive schooling narrows educational inequality gaps,[299] began to allow private ('free') schools to compete with public schools for government funds. A 2015 report from the OECD urged the Swedes to undergo 'a comprehensive education reform', limiting parental and pupil choice, to restore their previously high educational standards.[358] The report called for higher teacher salaries, better training, more rigorous inspection of schools and a focus on integrating immigrants into the educational system. Sweden has also seen a decline in child well-being significantly related to its increasing income inequality.[190]

At best, educational institutions can only partly offset the damage caused to children by wider inequalities in society, but they can avoid adding to it. Schools need to be based on a much broader concept of ability than they have been in the past. They should aim to introduce children to such a wide range of activities that they can all discover something they are particularly good at and are therefore likely to enjoy. Despite the advantages of developing an area of ability that coincides with some natural aptitude, the biggest constraint on almost any form of ability is a culture in which children come to see themselves as failures in almost every area of education and, so often, learn that they are socially inferior as well.

FLAKES AND CORNFLAKES

It is now widely accepted that lower family social class, education and income are important predictors of lower levels of educational achievement at all ages.[307] In their report, *A Comprehensive Future*, Melissa Benn and Fiona Miller conclude that 'one of the biggest problems facing British schools is the gap between rich and poor, and the enormous disparity in children's home backgrounds and the social and cultural capital they bring to the educational table'.[357] The same is true of US schools, or schools in any highly unequal society. Benn and Miller write: 'The comprehensive ideal is a powerful one, challenging as it does deep and often unconsciously held notions about class background, motivation, innate ability and those who are considered to "deserve" or merit a good education and those who are not.' Of course, on top of the effects of different school systems and educational policies comes the dead weight of inequality. The greater that weight, the more class and status matter, and the greater are the inequalities in children's opportunities, educational performance and outcomes.

As we come to understand how the health, development and happiness of children are compromised by forces beyond their or their families' control, jokes about the cleverest cornflakes rising to the top when we shake the cereal box of society seem inappropriate as well as inaccurate. Privilege begets privilege, ever more forcefully in more unequal societies. Inequality, like poverty, creates intergenerational cycles of disadvantage, and wastes vast swathes of human capabilities, talents and potential.

7

Class Acts

To understand why differences in income and wealth matter, we must understand how they are used divisively to express social distinctions which foster feelings of superiority and inferiority. That is the subject of this chapter. To see how the cultural processes of social division work, it is often easier if we are not too close to the issues to see them dispassionately. We will therefore begin by looking at processes of class distinction in previous centuries, where we have the benefits both of detachment and hindsight.

MANNERS AND CIVILIZATION

Though they have changed beyond all recognition over the centuries, differences in personal styles, conduct and behaviour are often taken as markers of class differences. In the thirteenth century, Bonvicino da Riva wrote an etiquette book – *Fifty Table Courtesies* – to provide advice on 'proper' behaviour. He thought it necessary to warn his readers that blowing your nose on the tablecloth during meals was a sign that you were ill-bred. In the mid-sixteenth century, when handkerchiefs had started to gain popularity, Giovanni della Casa felt the need to point out that it was unseemly 'after wiping your nose, to spread out your handkerchief and peer into it as if pearls and rubies might have fallen out of your head'. In 1530, Erasmus instructed people to 'Turn away when spitting, lest your saliva fall on someone. If anything purulent falls to the ground, it should be trodden upon, lest it nauseate someone. If you are not at liberty to do this, catch the sputum in a small cloth. It is unmannerly to suck back saliva.'

'That man is not our superior – he's just our boss'

These examples are all cited in Norbert Elias's classic book *The Civilizing Process*, published in 1939.[359] Elias was a sociologist, a refugee from Germany, who worked in England. He made a careful analysis of books on etiquette and other sources of advice on manners published over many centuries, to identify the forces behind what he called 'the civilizing process'. The picture which emerged is far from being a continuous process of improvement as the lower orders sought to imitate their betters. At many points in history, those at the top of society behaved at least as disgustingly as everyone else. For example, Horace Walpole, the eighteenth-century English aristocrat and man of letters, described the Palace of Versailles as:

> a vast cesspool, reeking of filth and befouled with ordure ... The odour clung to clothes, wigs, even undergarments. Worst of all, beggars, servants, and aristocratic visitors alike used the stairs, the corridors, any out-of-the-way place to relieve themselves. The passages, the courtyards, the wings and the corridors were full of urine and faecal matter. The park, the gardens and the chateau made one retch with their bad smell.[360]

This was despite an earlier ordinance, issued shortly before Louis XIV's death in 1715, that had decreed that faeces left in the corridors of Versailles would be removed once a week.[361]

We might have expected hygiene considerations to have been a powerful driver of behavioural change, but Elias argues that there was little or no rational basis for changing manners and customs. Instead, he emphasizes that notions of 'acceptable behaviour' were shaped by class distinctions, social aspirations, shame and embarrassment.

When explaining why 'the civilizing process' progressed more rapidly and consistently from the sixteenth century onwards, Elias points to the growing involvement of the upper classes in the court, which, he says, intensified social comparisons and led to a shift in what he calls 'the frontier of shame and embarrassment'. Self-control became more important as people were drawn closer together and saw more of each other. Courtly life heightened interpersonal sensibilities, their corresponding social prohibitions and the reasons for shame and embarrassment.

Elias suggests that a decline in interpersonal violence was part of these changes and came about as a result of the gradual transformation of the warrior nobility into a courtly aristocracy. The feasting, dancing and 'noisy pleasures' in which the former had indulged were often dangerously disruptive because they frequently gave way to 'rage, blows and murder'. As a result, people had to develop more self-restraint. The nobility's respect for each other's strength had to be replaced, and some other basis of merit found; self-control and the ability to avoid touching on each other's vulnerabilities and causing offence became increasingly encoded into aristocratic behaviour. In Elias's words: people became 'sensitive to distinctions which previously scarcely entered consciousness . . . The direct fear inspired in people by people has diminished, and the inner fear mediated through the eye and through the super-ego is rising proportionately.' He goes on to say:

> The very gesture of attack touches the danger zone; it becomes distressing to see a person passing someone else a knife with the point towards him. And from the most highly sensitized small circles of high court society, for whom this sensitivity also represents a prestige value, a means of distinction cultivated for that very reason, this prohibition gradually spreads throughout the whole of civilized society.

Social dominance and subordination came to depend less on overtly resorting to force and more on cultural expressions of the superiority of one class over another. During the sixteenth century the concepts of 'civility', and being 'courtois', were repeatedly used by those writing about the distinction between good and bad manners. The nobility of the Middle Ages had not regarded the gestures, or the depiction in art, of lower-class people as objectionable; however, as they developed a distinct culture of superiority themselves, they began to feel – or at least claimed to feel – repulsed by anything 'vulgar'. Maintaining the cultural barricades between themselves and the social ranks immediately below required 'affect-laden gestures of revulsion from anything that "smells bourgeois"'. It was in the fifteenth century that noble families began to establish their own private quarters, and stopped sleeping in the great hall with everyone else. The nobility became more sensitive to any markers of the lesser sensibility of lower-ranking classes. Elias describes the constant aristocratic attempts to remain distinct from the bourgeoisie as a 'tug of war' motivated by a

> permanently smouldering social fear . . . [which] constituted one of the most powerful driving forces of the social control that every member of this court upper class exerts over himself and other people in his circle. It is expressed in the intense vigilance with which members of court aristocratic society observe and polish everything that distinguishes them from people of lower rank: not only the external signs of status, but also their speech, their gestures, their social amusements and manners.

But, again and again, manners and behaviour that initially served to distinguish the aristocracy from their inferiors became useless as they were adopted by the bourgeoisie. Customs that were once 'refined' became 'vulgar', forcing new elaborations as the 'embarrassment-threshold' advanced. Elias suggests that this process only lost its force with the French Revolution and the downfall of the absolutist court society of the *Ancien Régime*. The general pattern is, however, clear: the refined self-presentation of a superior class, despite appearing as second nature, is driven by continual pressure from below.

The constant shifts in what was acceptable, and the deep-seated revulsion at practices which had once been accepted as normal, seem to amount almost to a change in human sensibilities. Against the belief that class behavioural codes are merely an expression of superior aesthetic standards, Elias argues that 'many of the rules of conduct and sentiment implanted in us as an integral part of our conscience, of our super-ego, are remnants of the power and status aspirations of established groups, and have no other function than that of reinforcing their . . . status superiority'. This is true of the observance of many of the most trivial markers of social position in speech and manners.

A core component of the changes in what was previously deemed acceptable behaviour was what Elias refers to as 'the weeding out of natural functions from public life'. A gradual 'intimization of bodily functions' and the 'concealment of drives and impulses' seems to have coincided with long-term economic and social development over the centuries. As a result, people were 'increasingly split between an intimate and a public sphere, between private and public behaviour'. People hid aspects of their nature because it became shameful not to do so and, to this day, people in 'polite society' continue to demarcate themselves from the rest of society partly by concealing their sexuality and other bodily functions more completely than others. One of the inevitable consequences of the requirement that adults hide bodily functions more strictly than people once did is that children have to undergo a more comprehensive social transformation – involving repression, shame and embarrassment – in order to become adults able to behave in ways acceptable to society.

The historical changes that have produced modern social norms and lengthened the psychological journey which children have to make to become acceptable adults indicate the extraordinary power status inequalities have over us. They shape our being and self-presentation in such detail that denying their importance begins to look like the wilful repression of how far we are subject to social pressures. We should not, however, forget that the desire to create a good impression and enjoy the approval of others pushes us in different directions in different kinds of society. We saw in Chapter 5 that in a highly egalitarian society it might serve primarily to push us towards being less selfish, more considerate of others and keener to be seen as helpful. But in societies marked by large status differences, the same desire for approval becomes muddied by the quite contrary desire for self-advancement, for superiority and to avoid the shame of lower status: we become more attentive to our own and other people's use of status indicators. To quote Elias once more, 'The feeling of shame is . . . a kind of anxiety . . . [a] fear of social degradation or . . . of other people's gestures of superiority.'

Looking back on the transformation of our sense of disgust and need for privacy over the generations, it seems plausible that, alongside the various behavioural affectations driven by status aspirations, there were changes driven by practical hygienic considerations that represented real, objective progress. It is easy to imagine that we would have continued without washing, without lavatories, still spitting indoors and blowing our noses on tablecloths until hygiene began to be understood in the middle of the nineteenth century.

Insofar as real progress often depended on greater wealth, the rich would usually have been able to afford improvements before the poor. But we should note that the imitation of our superiors was not the source of piped water supplies, flush lavatories and sewerage systems. The sanitary reforms of the second half of the nineteenth century were instead responses to the appalling squalor, health and hygiene problems that resulted from rapid urbanization. The absence of plumbing does, after all, have very different implications in rural and urban settings. The provision of sewers and water supplies depended not on private provision driven by emulation, but on public infrastructure and expenditure, which, because it tended to be opposed by the better-off, was not forthcoming until after the franchise had been extended and more democratic local government brought to big cities. Change depended on technological advance, on social reform, on the growing understanding of the relationship between health and hygiene and, above all, on public expenditure.[362]

MANNERS AND SOCIAL DISTINCTION

Different layers of society continue to be so strongly marked by differences in manners, style and aesthetic taste that people who move up the social ladder – for instance, from working-class backgrounds to professional occupations – usually feel they have to change their social identity, and often feel themselves to be imposters, constantly at risk of being found out. In her memoir, *Respectable: Crossing the Class Divide*,[363] Lynsey Hanley describes how, after going to university, having someone correct a malapropism was such an embarrassment that she wished the ground would swallow her whole, yet using words that had become normal from mixing with members of the middle classes led former friends and family to ask if she had 'swallowed a fucking dictionary?' She explains that when she fluffed exams, it was not because of any lack of ability but instead because she felt that anyone marking her work would see it as she did – as 'a half-baked, cringeworthy, autodidact's attempt to pass as someone who'd always known the stuff'.

For people taking a different path into the upper echelons of society there are still a couple of dozen guides to modern etiquette in print today. They include several general guides to etiquette and 'modern manners' from Debrett's, guides for the 'modern girl' or 'gentleman', as well as specialist guides to etiquette for entertaining, for weddings, for business and golf. Along with Bluffer's Guides to wine, management, opera, poetry, etc., there is also a *Bluffer's Guide to Etiquette*.[364] The title is apt, acknowledging as it does the status-driven motives for learning the mores of a different class. It offers advice on the right choice of words, table manners, pronunciation, dress codes, 'good' manners and social graces – all to help people pass as if they were naturally 'well spoken', 'from a good family' and long-term members of the social class they aspire to. It begins by stating that good manners and etiquette are almost the same thing. But the practices the book recommends are never justified as kindnesses or as ways of putting people at ease, of making them feel welcome and appreciated or showing that you care about them. Instead, the underlying justification for the recommended behaviour is almost exclusively unalloyed snobbery. Practices are recommended because they are 'an easy way to identify good breeding'. At various points readers are told that the 'wrong' behaviour will show you up as 'an imposter', or that it amounts to 'social suicide'. This or that practice is said to be 'beyond the pale' or 'a clear sign to everyone that you are parvenu and not to be trusted'. Various things are described simply as 'ghastly', 'to be avoided at all costs' or because the upper classes 'abhor and shun them'. The book ends by claiming to have offered 'a code of behaviour with which you will need to be very familiar if you seek to join the upper echelons of high society'.

What is 'ghastly', however, is the extent to which these behavioural trivialities remain the basis of social judgements and rankings of personal worth – matters as insignificant as which of several words with the same meaning you use (toilet, loo, lavatory, ladies'/men's room, convenience, bathroom, WC, etc.), or how you hold your knife when eating. These gain their power simply as signifiers of class. And even while most people profess to hate snobbishness and the idea that some people are worth more than others, many are still highly attentive to these markers of social superiority and inferiority, knowing that they serve to trip up the unwary. Even if we regard ourselves merely as creatures with fixed habits, unable to change our own use of many of these class signifiers, or imagine that they are aesthetic rather than social choices, few people are unaware of the class prejudices which might be aroused in others towards ourselves if we were to make different choices of words or behaviour. Worries about showing yourself up through aspects of self-presentation make a central contribution to the social evaluation anxieties that are a focus of this book. Though we might credit ourselves with being egalitarian and unprejudiced, we are often unwilling to risk others' judgements of us.

The widespread belief that the behaviour of the upper classes epitomizes good manners does not stand up against the research findings of Paul Piff, which we discussed in Chapter 3. He showed that, at least in more unequal societies, the higher people's status the more antisocial their behaviour becomes: they are more likely to cut-off other drivers at road junctions or to help themselves to sweets intended for children. And if, as you would expect, there is an inbuilt tendency to be more attentive to our social superiors than to our inferiors (think baboons), then perhaps the behaviour of those nearer the top is simply a reflection of the fact that more of us are their social inferiors.

Just as we saw in Chapter 2 that levels of status anxiety are higher – across all income levels – in societies with bigger differences in income between rich and poor, so the power of all the markers of class and status tends to increase or decrease depending on the scale of inequalities in income and wealth in society. In Chapter 4 we saw how conspicuous consumption and consumerism increase with inequality as people spend on prestige items to express status. However, in the 1930s, when Norbert Elias was writing, he noticed that the endless ratcheting up of symbols of refinement and class superiority, which he had tracked historically over the centuries, seemed in decline. The tendency to ape the behaviour of the upper classes was becoming less pronounced. The most obvious examples can be seen in new styles of popular music and dance (which later led to the flowering of rock 'n' roll from the 1950s). What Elias didn't know was that income differences peaked in the 1920s, and that what he was witnessing was the result of the rapid beginning of the long decline of income inequality that lasted until the late 1970s (see Figure 9.1, page 237).

A glimpse of how the downward trend in inequality before, during and after the Second World War percolated through popular culture can be seen in a 1943 Sherlock Holmes film. Once justice has been served, the beautiful heroine chooses to pass up her inheritance for the benefit of her tenant farmers. Holmes, hardly a radical in Conan Doyle's books, explains to Watson:

HOLMES: 'There's a new spirit abroad in the land. The old days of grab and greed are on their way out. We're beginning to think what we owe the other fellow – not just what we are compelled to give him. The time is coming, Watson, when we shan't be able to fill our bellies in comfort while other folk go hungry, or sleep in warm beds while others shiver in the cold. And we shan't be able to kneel and thank God for blessings before shining altars while men anywhere are kneeling in either physical or spiritual subjection.'

WATSON: 'You may be right Holmes – I hope you are.'

HOLMES: 'And God willing, we will live to see that day, Watson.'

As the reduction of income – and so of status – differences continued through the 1950s and '60s, the direction of cultural transmission also changed. New styles of music, dance and fashion started to permeate upwards from lower down the social ladder, reversing the top–down movement which had been dominant historically. Rock music and the dance styles which replaced traditional ballroom dancing invaded upper classes from below, as did many of the popular clothing fashions of the 1960s and '70s. Noticing these changes, many academic sociologists began to think that social class divisions had transformed into something less to do with occupation and more to do with a sense of identity, constructed and expressed through consumer choices.[365, 366]

CLASS RENEWAL

As income differences in many countries began to rise from about 1980 onwards (see Figure 9.1), the importance of class and status has grown again. The decline in intergenerational mobility in Britain (the difference between people's own social status and that of their parents) suggests that the class hierarchy has become more rigid – or the social ladder steeper – than it was a generation ago. The same pattern can also be seen in the proportion of marriages between people who come from different social classes. Among women reaching the age of twenty-five in the early 1980s who married, 61 per cent married men with different class backgrounds from their own. But twenty years later, among women who reached the age of twenty-five just into the new century, this proportion had shrunk to 44 per cent.[367] The decline in the proportion marrying either up or down, and the decline in social mobility, suggest that class differences have strengthened their grip on us as income differences have widened again.

We saw in Chapter 6 how problems of class and status penetrate and damage family life. Although the proportion of interclass marriages declined as wider income differences strengthened social divisions, differences in class backgrounds have remained a difficulty in a large minority of marriages. How often do the parents on one side of a marriage harbour the view that their son or daughter has married 'down' and 'could have done better', that their offspring's husband or wife is 'not good enough' for them? Even when nothing is said, the partner from the lower-status background will often fear that he or she is not really accepted by their in-laws and will interpret any potential criticisms in this light. Because women continue to be more involved in domesticity and child-rearing than men, conflicts over domestic standards and how grandchildren are brought up contribute to making mothers-in-law the traditional butt of jokes. For daughters-in-law who feel at a social disadvantage, it is hard not to be particularly sensitive to criticism.

In a Mumsnet poll of nearly 2,000 people, almost a third of them said they were made to feel they were not good enough for their partner. Some families even moved house to escape these tensions. Others said the conflict had been bad enough to have caused the breakdown of their marriage. A more detailed study of problems between in-laws found that class differences were one of the most common causes of difficulties and created more problems than either ethnic or religious differences.[368] Rather than implying that these latter differences are easier to overcome, this may simply reflect that there are fewer marriages across these divides.

The power of class differences in family life is also seen in the way middle-class parents attempt to 'correct' their children's speech or behaviour to avoid habits that might have inferior social connotations. As a result, many teenagers have to develop different class codes depending on whether they are at home or with school friends. Children become aware of social differences early on. Interviews show that children from poorer backgrounds feel ashamed when friends who live in posher houses come to their homes. An eight-year-old girl living in a poor area of Bradford said: 'What I hate about the flats is you feel that you want to be sick when you have visitors. I don't like having pals in my house, in case they bully me.' A friend of hers chipped in: 'Some people bully you because your house is not all fancy.'[369]

Research we looked at in Chapter 5 shows that bullying between children may be as much as ten times as common in countries with bigger income differences (and so steeper social gradients) between rich and poor.[233] The divide between the bullies and the bullied is, as you might expect, often a matter of whether children see each other as coming from richer or poorer families. One study combined data from 28 separate pieces of research that looked at bullying among a total of almost 350,000 children in North America, Europe and Australia.[370] It found that while bullies came from all classes, their victims were more likely to be poor. But whether it is rich attacking poor or the other way round, it seems clear that the struggle for status is again heightened in societies with larger income differences.

Another indication of the personal costs of inequality and the recent escalation in status consciousness associated with its increase comes from a study of 1,600 British children. It found that if boys (but not girls) from poor families lived in better-off areas, they were more likely to engage in antisocial behaviour, including lying, cheating and fighting.[371] Behaviour was significantly worse if they lived in middle-income areas, and worse still if they lived in affluent areas where the inequalities were most apparent.

These examples all show how intimately we are affected by class differences and inequality: our personal lives and homes cannot be insulated from them. Family life, marital relationships, relationships between parents and children, as well as children's relationships with each other are all damaged by them. The same divisions are also damaging to people's sense of themselves. People who have moved into professional occupations from backgrounds in manual occupations often say that they feel as if they are not the genuine article and will at some point be exposed as fakes. We asked supporters of The Equality Trust to tell us about their experiences of class and status anxiety. One informant told us that the more academic qualifications he gained, the more he felt that he was an imposter and would one day be found out. In much the same way, a former teacher said that when he was made redundant, he couldn't shake off the feeling that he had been discovered to be a fraud and was not a real teacher. Another who attributed his low self-esteem, sense of inferiority and feeling that he was a charlatan, all to his working-class upbringing, no doubt spoke for many others when he said that he had always felt 'less than' because of his social origins.

If these are the feelings of people whose upward social mobility would normally be regarded as evidence of success, what must it feel like to experience either downward mobility or a failure to rise from the bottom of the social ladder? Economic growth sometimes softens the experience. One of the effects of periods when inequality isn't rising and the proceeds of growth are shared across all income groups making everyone richer, is a reduction in the sense of failure felt by those whose aspirations to climb the social ladder are thwarted. Even if you are not 'moving up' relative to others, you can still feel that you are making progress and live better than your parents did.

However, in the USA, increases in inequality have meant that poorer people have gained very little from economic growth for several decades. And among middle-aged (forty-five- to fifty-five-year-old) white Americans in lower income groups – the group we would expect to feel most acutely that they had failed to live up to their aspirations – death rates have been rising since the late 1990s.[66] Increasing numbers of deaths (particularly among women) from alcohol and drug poisoning, cirrhosis and suicide – which are all reflections of stress – account for the bulk of the adverse trend. In contrast to these trends among whites, health among middle-aged Hispanics and African Americans has continued to improve, and these same causes of death have declined among them.[67] Perhaps they never developed the same unrealistic aspirations as poorer white Americans. If there has recently been any lessening of the ethnic discrimination that blocked black and Hispanic aspirations in previous generations, it is possible that poor whites could have experienced it as a loss of superior status.

ART AND CULTURE

Appreciation and knowledge of the arts, classical music and literature have not escaped the divisive processes that have made trivial aspects of aesthetic taste, accents and word choice into markers of class and status. As we shall see, the use of 'high' culture as an indicator of social position narrows its following and alters the way it is made and appreciated. Artistic sensitivity is sometimes deployed as a sign that someone possesses refined sensibilities and the ability to enjoy more sophisticated cultural forms than those enjoyed by the masses. That is presumably part of the reason why the super-rich pay astronomical sums for original paintings, which, when hung on their walls, serve to testify – to themselves and others – that they are more refined than most people and possess aesthetic sensibilities profound enough to justify the price they pay.

This refinement is, of course, what the story of 'The Princess and the Pea' is about. The unknown young woman who claims to be a princess does eventually win her prince, but only after having been tested to see if she notices a pea placed secretly on her bed under a vast pile of mattresses. When asked how she slept she replies (in the 1835 Hans Christian Andersen version) by saying, 'Oh, very badly! I have scarcely closed my eyes all night. Heaven only knows what was in the bed, but I was lying on something hard, so that I am black and blue all over my body. It's horrible!' As Andersen says, 'Nobody but a real princess could be as sensitive as that.'

Needless to say, in the real world claims to such elevated sensitivities are often more imagined than real. If the test had instead been whether someone could distinguish more expensive wines from cheaper ones, a trial involving 6,000 blind tastings found that most people would fail. No doubt because we are not princes or princesses, the bulk of the population were found (presumably to the consternation of wine sellers) to have a slight preference for wines that turned out to be the cheaper ones.[372] The strong links between class culture and the arts act rather like the varnish often applied to old masters which has to be removed before a picture can be fully appreciated. As so many of the greatest artists have recognized, the best art, whether painting, music, theatre or literature, touches on aspects of our deepest humanity that are often obscured behind the social forms which divide people.

Aesthetic taste is an arena which gives almost unfettered expression to issues of class prejudice and distinction. Popular taste is often labelled 'poor taste', tacky, kitsch, obvious, crass, gaudy or sentimental. People will sometimes claim that the aesthetic tastes of elites really are better, and that they are guided by an appreciation of an objective aesthetic rather than a conditioned snobbery. Accents are sometimes dismissed as 'ugly', just as particular choices of words or a way of holding a table knife are thought to be 'nicer' than others. The deception is that these trivial distinctions are a matter of aesthetics rather than of social discrimination. Wherever there are class differences, we tend to regard the characteristics associated with people lower on the social ladder as inferior. That applies not only to behavioural characteristics but also to skin colour, religious affiliation and linguistic group, wherever they become associated with social status.

Several recent pieces of survey research have shown that liking or not liking classical music and opera continues to be highly correlated with social status.[373] It was found, on further questioning, that even interviewees who initially said they liked most kinds of music tended to conform to class stereotypes. The desire to do what is associated with a higher status can, however, boost people's interest in the arts. Mike Savage, professor of sociology at the London School of Economics, describes how, during one week in 2013, there was a sudden and surprising surge in demand for London theatre tickets.[374] It turned out to coincide with the launch of a BBC online poll called 'Class Calculator', which had been completed by 161,000 people. Among the questions used to categorize people socially was one asking whether you go to the theatre, and how often. Savage suggests that the desire to tick 'yes' and thereby affirm cultural status led to an actual increase in ticket sales.

What is classified as 'high' culture in music is in danger of becoming confined to an ossified traditional repertoire. When first making this point, the historian Eric Hobsbawm pointed out that in a season in which the Vienna State Opera performed sixty different works, only one was by a composer born in the twentieth century.[375] The classical music that is performed most frequently was composed between 100 and 250 years ago. No modern composers have achieved any really substantial popular following. Hobsbawm contrasts this with the continuing creativity in rock and pop music. For example, the Glastonbury Festival attracts 175,000 people over 5 days, has 100 or so music venues on site, and an official line-up of over 2,000 performances by live bands of every conceivable variety, usually playing their own music. We will never know how far the development of classical music may have been affected by its use as a marker of class differences.

Some classical musicians, such as the violinist Nigel Kennedy, choir master Gareth Malone and Gustavo Dudamel, former conductor of the Venezuelan Simón Bolívar Youth Orchestra, have made successful attempts to break classical music out of its class mould. The Simón Bolívar Orchestra is linked to El Sistema, an educational programme that is believed to have encouraged hundreds of thousands of young Venezuelans, many from poorer areas, to learn an instrument. Its adherents argue that playing together provides a model and experience of co-operation, while others – as if trying to protect the cultural position of classical music – claim to be disturbed by the impression that 'art is being used to civilise the lower orders'.[376] But when a woman, living in a deprived inner-city area of

Britain, showed one of us photos of her granddaughter learning the violin as part of the spread of El Sistema, she was moved to tears. Explaining her emotion, and apparently fully aware of the class symbolism of classical music, she said it was just so wonderful that people 'like us' could have the chance to do something like that.

Research has shown that the popularity of, and participation in, the arts is substantially reduced in societies with bigger income differences.[377] Using data for twenty-two European countries, researchers found that the frequency with which people visited museums and galleries, read books or went to the theatre was two or three times higher in the countries with smaller income differences (Figure 7.1). Similar results were found using different measures of cultural participation and different measures of income distribution. These findings, particularly the large differences in attendances, suggest that there are major contrasts in the position of the arts in different cultures and that these are related to inequality.

There are several possible causal processes that might account for

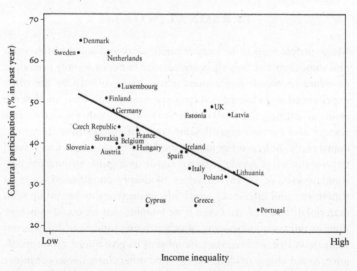

Figure 7.1: Museums and art galleries are much more popular in more equal countries.[377]

this finding. Perhaps, in more unequal societies, the arts are more likely to be regarded as the exclusive domain of the better off; or maybe encouraging broader access to the arts is regarded as less important in more unequal societies. Because inequality makes status differences more important, people will more often feel out of place and want to avoid more socially exclusive contexts – just as many people feel more at ease eating in pubs than in up-market restaurants (even when someone else is paying the bill). It is nevertheless clear that the research findings illustrated in Figure 7.1 show that inequality leads to the cultural impoverishment of whole societies.

It is hard to imagine how the arts would develop if freed from the burden of having to serve as markers of status and class. Perhaps the expressions of joy at some of the performances of people like Kennedy, Dudamel and Malone are indicative. In a much more equal society, the arts might enjoy an increase in participation and popularity which would spread their creative roots and stimulate development in new directions.

PERSONAL WORTH

Many people tend to be evasive about class and status differences, and some deny not only their importance but occasionally even their existence. Personal interactions across class differences are often experienced as awkward and embarrassing. People imagine that the solution is simply for us all to learn to treat each other with the same respect and dignity, regardless of large differences in material circumstances. But even the most considerate of us would find it hard to stop ourselves seeing external status as a guide to internal personal worth, or to rid ourselves of deeply conditioned ideas of superiority and inferiority which are so inextricably bound up with material differences. And even if we imagine that we could somehow prevent our own judgements of others being influenced by external signs of wealth or class, the care most of us give to our own appearance, to our choice of clothing, cars and other conspicuous consumer goods, suggests that we do not trust others to be free of similar biases in their estimation of us.

We assume that appearances do matter, and not without reason: many studies have shown how strongly social class and ethnicity bias our judgements of people, consciously or unconsciously. Research has shown that this is true whether we consider teachers' assessments of schoolchildren, employers' judgements of job applicants, or the evaluation of criminal suspects by the police and courts.[378] In each case, there is a tendency to assume that those who appear to be from lower classes are less capable and less trustworthy. Paul Piff's research – see Chapter 3 and above – demonstrated the tendency among the better-off to show less respect to the majority who are less well-off than them. Our assumption that others will judge us by what we can afford becomes a powerful additional driver of status consumption.

Our awkwardness when faced with social inequalities leads people to choose their friends from among their near equals. That tendency is so strong and reliable that some sociologists have used friendship networks as a basis for classifying occupations into social class categories, reflecting people's 'similarity of lifestyle and of generalised advantage/disadvantage'.[379] People are asked about their own occupations and those of their friends, and occupations linked by many ties of friendship and marriage are then classified as being of a similar social standing; for example, solicitors, doctors and similar professionals are much more likely to socialize with each other than they are with unskilled manual workers.

In his book *The Moral Significance of Class*, Andrew Sayer, professor of sociology at the University of Lancaster, points out that, when people are asked in interviews what class they belong to, their replies are

> often awkward, defensive and evasive, treating the question as if it were ... about whether they deserve their class position or whether they consider themselves inferior or superior to others ... Class remains a highly charged issue because of the associations of injustice and moral evaluation. To ask someone what class they are is not simply to ask them to classify their socio-economic position, for it also carries the suggestion of a further unspoken and offensive question: what are you worth?[380]

Sensitivity to these issues is clearer still if we imagine having to say what we think we are worth.

Sayer has done an extraordinarily good job of exposing how morally awkward people find class differences. Most fundamentally, friendship means treating each other as equals, but where that friendship is across class differences, both sides have to pretend the class inequality is either non-existent or irrelevant. They are caught between the equality of friendship and its denial by the class difference that positions one as superior and the other as inferior. In a context where superiority is embarrassing and inferiority shaming, anything which shows up the social superiority of one over the other has to be avoided. As a result, people in conversations across a class divide often attempt to minimize differences in accent, grammar and word choice, and to talk about things which avoid displaying the differences. They must avoid conversation that brings differences in circumstances, incomes, education and status to the fore. If they were to talk – for instance – about rising food prices in the shops, they can only pretend that it means the same to each of them. In a friendship across classes each person has to give an impression of helplessness towards the system which has allocated them different positions in the hierarchy, as if the fact that they come together as employer and employee, richer and poorer, better or worse educated, was natural and inevitable. Any sense that one person is looked down on, pitied or disrespected by the other is offensive and totally inimical to continued friendship.

The awkwardness of social class divisions shows just how fundamental the opposition – discussed in Chapter 5 – is between the behavioural strategy appropriate to a dominance hierarchy and the strategy of reciprocity and sharing, which is appropriate to friendship and equality. That the two don't easily mix, and often cause embarrassment when we try, shows how deeply embedded these contradictory social strategies are in our psychology. A human relationship of equality and reciprocity is fundamentally contradicted by the implied inequalities in 'worth' that are part of a class hierarchy.

Alexis de Tocqueville, a French aristocrat, writing about his visit to the USA in 1831, argued that people could not empathize with each other across stark differences in their material circumstances.

He gave two examples. The first was the French aristocracy, who, he said, would show enormous sympathy for each other when faced with difficulties but appeared to be completely indifferent to the much greater suffering of the peasantry. The second was the contrast between the remarkable willingness of white Americans to help each other out and identify with each other, and their inability to recognize the suffering of slaves.[381] What stands out in the record of human callousness and cruelty is the ease with which we can disregard the suffering of any group we regard as inferior, just as we tend to portray as inferior any group we are opposed to.

An example of the effects of inequality on the relationship between different social groups can be seen in the extraordinarily close correlation between a society's level of income inequality and the proportion of its population who are imprisoned. In *The Spirit Level* we showed that in the more equal of the developed countries, only about 4 people in every 10,000 are in prison at any point in time, but this rises to ten times that level – around 40 per 10,000 – in the more unequal countries. As we showed, only a small part of this difference can be explained by the higher crime rates in more unequal societies. Much the most important factor seems to be harsher and more punitive sentencing. More unequal societies create a tougher and less forgiving climate of opinion, so people are sent to prison for less serious offences and given longer prison sentences. The same process can also be seen in the tendency for more unequal countries to hold children criminally responsible at younger ages. We used data from Child Rights International Network and found a statistically significant relationship between inequality and a lower age of criminal responsibility.[382] Among more equal rich countries, children younger than fourteen are rarely considered to be responsible for criminal actions, but in Singapore and some US states, children only have to be seven years old (Figure 7.2).

This more punitive sentencing reflects some combination of increased fear and less empathy towards people who are convicted. This fits the evidence we saw in Chapter 3, showing that people in more unequal societies are much less likely to trust each other.

The long decline in income inequality from the 1930s to the 1970s in most of the developed countries was accompanied by a slow change

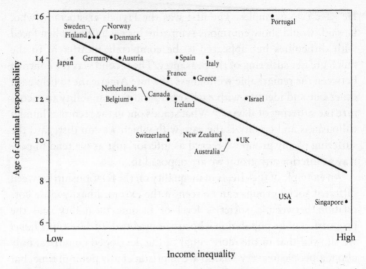

Figure 7.2: The age of criminal responsibility is younger in more unequal countries.[382]

in class relations. While class barriers to empathy are still clearly evident, they weakened while income differences were diminishing. This has sometimes been interpreted as an inexorable historical increase in human empathy.[383] Gradually, the argument goes, the boundaries of our 'moral universe', which once hardly extended beyond the family or local community, have widened to include the nation state, and were beginning to become globalized – at least until the modern rise (from around 1980 onwards) in inequality and xenophobia. The forces of social exclusion – whether organized around divisions of gender, sexuality or race – had weakened. Political campaigns to protect health and safety at work, the rights of employees, the improvement of housing conditions and the rights of tenants transformed living and working conditions. As a result, the systemic insensitivity of the upper classes to the lower became less stark.

But following the general growth of income differences from the end of the 1970s, much of this progress has been undone. Although discrimination by race, gender, disability and sexuality has continued to decline, other forms have been reinvigorated. The position of people renting their homes has become more precarious and homelessness has grown; employees have been pushed into nominal self-employment and on to zero-hours contracts; social security systems have been weakened and the proportion of the population – including the proportion of children – living in relative poverty has increased. All this has coincided with a growing consensus that the influence of money in politics has increased and the democratic process been subverted. With large business corporations and rich individuals escaping much of their tax liability, the public sector is increasingly underfunded. The tendency for inhumanity to march under the banner of inequality is also evident in the rise in more punitive prison sentences, and the younger age at which children are treated as criminally responsible in more unequal countries.

A CLASSLESS SOCIETY?

Karl Marx and John Major, the British Conservative Prime Minister who succeeded Margaret Thatcher, are unlikely bedfellows but, in his victory speech after winning the party leadership and the premiership, John Major announced that his government would 'continue to make changes which will make the whole of this country a genuinely classless society'.[384] Almost all politicians in modern democracies at least claim to want to reduce class differences. Major failed in that aspiration because he failed to recognize that larger differences in income and wealth increase both the social distances between people and the importance of markers of class and status. In contrast, the Swedish Social Democratic Prime Minister Per Albin Hansson, who was in office from 1932 to 1946, made real progress towards his objective of making Sweden a 'classless society' and 'the people's home'. But what made most difference was that these objectives were maintained over a period of forty-four years while the Social Democratic Party remained in power almost continuously, from 1932 until 1976. During that period, the share of income going to the richest 1 per cent of the population was reduced from around 13 per cent to 5 per cent of all taxable income. That the scale of the material differences in a society provides the framework which makes the class hierarchy steeper and more important – or shallower and less important – should now be beyond dispute.

What makes it difficult for many people to recognize the effects of the material differences between us is that any of the markers of status difference or of a person's social class are perceived as though they reflected much more fundamental differences between people than they really do. The human tendency to explain other people's (but not our own) behaviour in terms of their inherent personal characteristics, rather than their circumstances, has been labelled 'the fundamental attribution error' by social psychologists.[385] You might make that error if, for instance, you regard an example of aggressive driving as a reflection of the driver's aggressive personality rather than thinking that he or she might have a reason for rushing which would have led most people to hurry. And if you think that you jumped to this conclusion simply because you had no way of knowing what was making them rushed, note that a willingness to put it down to their personality was not deterred by a similar lack of knowledge of the driver.

These attribution errors play a powerful role in our perceptions of people lower in the social hierarchy. There has always been an unedifying tendency to ignore the force of circumstances and to assume that the poor are poor because they are lazy and stupid – indeed, that is almost the definition of prejudice. This is why the devastating effects of the treatment and marginalization of the indigenous populations of Australia, New Zealand and North America have, in each case, been interpreted as reflections of the inherent characteristics of those minority ethnic populations. Rather than recognizing the consequences of what these communities have been through, the dominant European-origin populations have preferred to believe that the high rates of alcoholism and violence are 'just the way these people are'.

GENETIC DIFFERENCES?

To ascribe the problems that disproportionately affect these communities to their inherent characteristics is to pass the blame from their situation to their genetics. The history of colonialism is full of such assumptions of superiority and inferiority. Wherever colonizers encountered less technologically sophisticated cultures, they assumed that the populations in those societies were inherently less intelligent. The same pattern of prejudice can be identified within all hierarchical societies. Nowhere are these processes as powerful as when they are focused on explanations of inferior social status. The same pattern runs all the way from the history of slavery to Owen Jones's *Chavs*, which documents how any marker of low social status, however trivial, invites a deluge of prejudiced assumptions about people's inferior personal characteristics.[386]

Even though we are slowly becoming more aware of these processes, we are still very far from being free of them. Surveys have asked people how important they think genes, the environment and choice are in explaining individual differences in the drive to succeed, in mathematical ability and in tendencies towards violence. They show that European Americans put more emphasis on genetics than African Americans do.[387] Despite the racist implications of ascribing ability to ethnicity, if people had been asked about the causes of any ethnic group (rather than individual) differences in these characteristics, it seems likely that white Americans would have shown an even stronger preference for genetic explanations.

We saw in Chapter 6 that there is a widespread but largely false belief that people's social status reflects their individual genetic endowments of cognitive ability: the idea that the naturally clever move up and others don't. Associated with that is the tendency to imagine that racial differences in social status reflect basic racial differences in ability: the idea that some groups are inherently more intelligent than others. Skin colour is assumed to be a marker for a wide range of genetic differences, which somehow explain group differences in social status. Although there is no shortage of evidence that this is what people think, we shall see that modern genetic analysis shows it is not true.

In a survey of 1,200 Americans designed to explore people's understanding of genetics and ethnicity, the majority agreed with the (false) statement that: 'Two people from the same race will always be more genetically similar to each other than two people from different races.'[388] A much larger majority also believed (wrongly) that: 'Our genes tell us which race we belong to.' Since the international collaborative project to sequence the human genome was completed in 2003, we have learned a great deal about our genetic similarities and differences as a species. One of the basic truths to emerge is that, of all the genetic differences between individuals across the world, the vast majority are found *within* any population or ethnic group rather than *between* groups. Between 85 and 90 per cent of the small amount of genetic variation which exists between human beings is found within each continent. Differences between ethnic groups account for only the remaining 10–15 per cent of variation.[389] Hence, most of the genetic similarities and differences between, for example, a Masai from East Africa and an Englishman, are likely to be individual differences rather than differences between those two populations.

Skin colour is one of the few genetic exceptions. The main differences in skin colour of the world's populations are adaptations to climatic differences. But, despite widespread misunderstandings, skin colour is a very poor guide to other genetic characteristics. If all genetic characteristics were as visible as skin colour, we would see that 80–90 per cent of all human genetic variations occur in all geographical populations. That was true even before the massive mixing of populations that has taken place over the last generation or so with the advent of modern travel.

The reason why skin colour is such a poor guide to other genetic characteristics is likely to be that lighter skin colours may be very recent developments. The genetic analysis of a prehistoric human skeleton found in Spain suggests that as recently as 7,000 years ago its owner had dark skin but blue eyes. The authors of the research report say: 'Our results indicate that the adaptive spread of light skin pigmentation ... was not complete in some European populations by the Mesolithic' period, implying that it has become complete only during the last 7,000 years – the briefest moment in genetic terms.[390] Because skin colour cannot be regarded as a predictor of other genetic characteristics, there will be multitudes of people of a different skin colour from you with whom you nonetheless share many other genetic similarities, and many people with the same skin colour with whom you share relatively few. What matters then, are not any insurmountable biological differences, but the social prejudices which lead us to burden anything associated with low social status with a raft of imagined inferior characteristics. It is as if we believed any visible difference was like the tip of an iceberg, indicative of its submerged 90 per cent. But for the vast majority of individual genetic or cultural differences this view is simply mistaken.

The Holocaust, which led to the deaths of more than 80 per cent of Jews in Germany, was based in part on the false belief that people who were culturally Jewish were a distinct genetic race.[391] The same goes for the genetically very similar Hutu and Tutsi, resulting in mass slaughter in Rwanda in 1994. Once any characteristic, whether physical or cultural, becomes a social status marker, it becomes overloaded with scientifically untenable inferences about inherent differences. The 'fundamental attribution' error leads us constantly to imagine that problems arise from people's inherent characteristics rather than from their circumstances, and the racializing of class or cultural characteristics is a prime example of this process at work.

Rich and poor attribute quite different inherent personality characteristics to each other. By seeing these issues as if, for instance, they reflected heightened inbuilt levels of greediness or laziness, we fail to see how most of us would respond much like the rich and poor do to the experience of living in wealth or poverty.

Although there is a strong tendency to imagine that the social class hierarchy is a meritocracy which reflects innate differences in people's abilities, we saw in Chapter 6 that the truth is the other way round: one's starting position in the social hierarchy is the primary cause of the differences in ability that ensue. In this chapter we have also seen that the unthinking tendency to explain people's class position in terms of innate characteristics, rather than in terms of their circumstances, is a widespread psychological error. Social prejudice exacts an appalling human price in terms of stunted lives and unrealized potential; as prejudices are internalized and transmitted from one generation to the next, the harm is magnified and perpetuated. But the most important cost for most people in everyday life comes from the creation and maintenance of the divisions which are at its core – from the social awkwardness they create, from the damage they do to friendship, conviviality and community life, as well as from the fear of being seen as inferior which makes so many people shun the social contact we need.

Modern societies are in a position to counter these hierarchies and make the next great leap in human social development. The necessary background conditions – not only of affluence but also of the interdependent and co-operative nature of modern production and consumption – are in place. Equally important is the conceptual background: the evidence that shows beyond doubt that the importance of class and status can be reduced by making the material differences between us smaller. In *The Spirit Level*, we showed that the many problems associated with low social status become much less common throughout society when income differences are smaller. We have also seen that how people treat each other is negatively affected by larger income differences: people trust each other less, they are less likely to be helpful to others, violence is more common, and community life atrophies. At the same time, we see unmistakable signs of class and status once again becoming increasingly important in more unequal societies: social mobility slows, people are less likely to marry across social classes, and measures of status anxiety are higher at all income levels. Responding to these raised status anxieties, people in more unequal societies spend more on status goods; they work longer hours and get into debt more as they try to appear successful.

Envisioning a future in which these problems are dramatically reduced is difficult. It will involve a great transition, changing how we live with each other and enabling us to live within the environmental limits of the planet. A better world is not only possible but essential. We shall discuss its outlines in the next two chapters.

PART THREE
The Road Ahead

8

A Sustainable Future?*

The final chapter of this book will set out practical policies for increasing equality, but it would be wrong to do so without first thinking about how greater equality can be integrated with the need to move towards environmental sustainability. The long-term well-being of populations requires that we take an integrated view of the direction in which our societies should be moving. Fortunately, as we shall show in this chapter, greater equality not only contributes to the well-being of entire populations, but also eases the path to sustainability by lessening the environmental impact of those populations.

LIMITS TO GROWTH

We should start with the relationship between economic growth and well-being. Although economic development in rich countries has transformed people's real quality of life during the last couple of centuries, a large and growing body of evidence suggests that when societies have reached current levels of prosperity, growth has largely finished its work. Measures of the quality of life show that higher average material standards in the rich countries no longer improve well-being.[392] Given that throughout human history 'more' has almost always meant 'better', this marks a fundamental turning point in human development.

---

* Chapters 8 and 9 include material from R. Wilkinson and K. Pickett, *A Convenient Truth: A Better Society for Us and the Planet*, London: Fabian Society and Friedrich Ebert Stiftung, 2014.

The changing relation between life expectancy and national income per head (shown for countries at all stages in economic development in Figure 8.1) illustrates this pattern. Life expectancy rises rapidly in the early stages of economic growth and then gradually levels out until, among the richest countries, the relationship becomes horizontal and the connection disappears: as growth continues it is no longer associated with increases in life expectancy. Indeed, some countries – such as Cuba and Costa Rica – achieve levels of life expectancy comparable with the richest countries despite being only one-third as wealthy in terms of their GDP per head.

This plateau is not a 'ceiling effect' caused by nudging up against the limits of human life expectancy. Even in societies where longevity is greatest, life expectancy continues to rise just as fast as it has done in other periods during the last century: we continue to gain two to three years' longer life expectancy with every decade that passes (except under conditions of austerity, as in the UK in recent years). The difference is that these gains now take place regardless of the

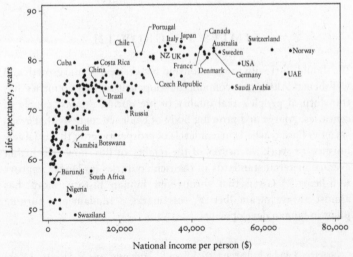

Figure 8.1: Life expectancy levels off at higher levels of economic development.

pace of economic growth. Even over periods of ten, twenty or forty years, there is little or no correlation in these countries between rising national income per head and changes in life expectancy.[393]

Similar patterns can be seen if, instead of life expectancy, we look at measures of happiness and well-being. Rapid rises in the early stages of economic development are followed by a levelling out, even though countries continue to get richer. What the data are telling us is a simple but fundamental truth: for people in less developed countries, where many do not have access to basic necessities, economic development and rising material standards remain important drivers of well-being. But, for people in rich countries, having more and more of everything makes less and less difference. After our most urgent needs have been satisfied, there are only diminishing returns to further increases in income. It is a pattern that is almost bound to emerge at some point as countries get richer over the long course of economic development. Although higher material standards continue to be needed in low-income countries, in rich societies they have ceased to make important contributions to well-being: having more clearly makes least difference to those who have most. Rather than there being a well-defined threshold level of income or standard of material adequacy, it appears from Figure 8.1 that there is a long, slow transition as economic growth makes a gradually diminishing contribution.

The Genuine Progress Indicator (GPI) was designed to provide a better measure of economic well-being than Gross Domestic Product (GDP). Unlike measures of subjective well-being, which reflect our experience of the totality of emotional, social and economic life, it is (like GDP) a measure only of the value of economic transactions, but with some major adjustments. It is calculated by subtracting from GDP the many harmful things which nevertheless generate economic activity (such as car crashes and air pollution, environmental damage and loss of leisure) and then adding in the value of unpaid work (including caring and volunteering). The aim is to provide an estimate of the economic activity which we value positively. GPI has now been measured in at least seventeen different developed countries and the results confirm that economic well-being has ceased to increase with economic growth.[392] Averaging the data across these countries shows that despite continuing huge rises in GDP per head, measures of economic well-being peaked in the later 1970s. Figure 8.2 shows the data for the USA. Note that even if economic growth had fewer negative consequences and the calculation of the GPI continued to produce a positive balance, this would not necessarily – as the USA life satisfaction data in Figure 8.2 shows – translate into an increase in human subjective well-being. The process of diminishing returns to well-being from increased production is more fundamental than that. The problem is not just a matter of subtracting the 'bads' from economic activity, it is also that the more we already have, the less difference additions to consumption make to well-being. In short, you *can* have enough – even of a good thing.

As soon as economic growth parts company from increases in well-being for society as a whole, continued economic growth loses its

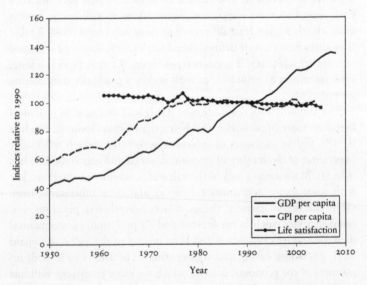

Figure 8.2: GDP per head continues upwards, but Life Satisfaction and the Genuine Progress Indicator no longer rise with it. Figures for the USA 1950–2008.[392]

rational basis. But everyone's desire for a higher income continues to be driven by status competition, although it no longer serves the overall well-being of the population and causes significant damage to the environment (see below).

A common argument marshalled against attempts to redirect economic policy away from growth is that doing so will diminish innovation. Clearly, however, if we are going to reduce carbon emissions, cut our use of non-renewable resources and develop a high and sustainable quality of life, technical change must be made to serve new objectives. New technologies must be harnessed to the development of cleaner and more resource-efficient ways of living. Rather than growing the economy, we need to 'grow' sustainable well-being. As Tim Jackson, an ecological economist and professor of sustainable development at the University of Surrey, has argued, our task now is to improve well-being without growth.[394] And, as continued innovation raises productivity, we must use it to increase time devoted to leisure rather than consumption. Leisure, as time freed from the demands of necessity, to be spent with friends, family and community, or doing whatever we enjoy, makes a major contribution to well-being. And as automation and artificial intelligence replace many forms of employment, it is crucial that this change is used to increase leisure for everyone, rather than increase unemployment for a growing minority.[202]

CLIMATE CHANGE NEEDS A NEW ECONOMY

It is a remarkable coincidence that, in the period in which it has become clear that economic growth in the rich countries has largely finished its work in transforming the quality of human life, we have also become aware of the environmental limits to growth. Though ignored by sceptics, the scientific evidence on the consequences of carbon emissions is incontrovertible. In May 2013, carbon dioxide concentrations in the atmosphere (measured at Mauna Loa in Hawaii in the middle of the Pacific – far away from any local sources of pollution) surpassed 400 parts per million (ppm) for the first time. That is 40 per cent higher than before industrialization – and higher than humans have ever breathed before.

For those who find it hard to imagine how human activity can change the climate, it may help to imagine that, if you were to take a desktop model of the globe, about 30 centimetres in diameter, 95 per cent of our atmosphere would lie within a very thin layer round it, only about a quarter of the thickness of a credit card. Now imagine pumping world emissions of 36 gigatonnes of carbon dioxide into that layer each year.

Global warming is an inescapable consequence of rising levels of carbon dioxide and other greenhouse gases, which allow the sun's rays in through our atmosphere but prevent some of the heat they generate from escaping back into space. The separate contributions to the increased CO_2 levels in the atmosphere from each of the main sources – the burning of oil, coal and natural gas, from forest clearance and cement production – are well-known. Measurements by key institutions such as NASA in the USA and the Intergovernmental Panel on Climate Change, show how CO_2 concentrations and global average temperatures have been rising almost in lockstep. Others show the rapid shrinking of the polar ice-caps and the rise in sea levels.

As long ago as 2007, James Hansen (head of NASA's Goddard Institute of Space Studies), working with an international scientific team, estimated that 350 ppm was the upper limit for atmospheric CO_2 concentrations if we were to keep the rise in global temperatures below 2°C – the level once regarded as relatively safe.[395]

A decade on, it now appears that the consequences of the 1°C rise in global temperatures that has already taken place are closer to those originally predicted for a 2°C rise, and that there is probably no such thing as a 'safe' rise in global temperatures. In 2009, the Geneva-based Global Humanitarian Forum, presided over by Kofi Annan, former Secretary-General of the United Nations, estimated that, through heatwaves, drought, water shortages and flooding, climate change was already causing 300,000 deaths a year and that it had already displaced 26 million people; the number of deaths is thought likely to triple by the 2020s. Ninety per cent of these deaths occurred in developing countries, rather than in the rich countries which produce the highest carbon emissions per head. The World Health Organization has estimated that, through floods, drought and crop failure, global warming will, between 2030 and 2050, cause 250,000 additional deaths each year just from heat exposure, diarrhoea, malaria and childhood undernutrition.[396]

Global warming is proceeding more rapidly than previous estimates had suggested. The US government's National Oceanic and Atmospheric Administration reported that global average temperatures for 2016 were the highest recorded; in addition, the sixteen warmest years ever recorded were all in the period 1998–2015. Because some of the effects already set in train by higher CO_2 levels take long periods of time to work their way through, even if we stopped further increases in CO_2 concentrations in the atmosphere immediately, sea level rises (currently around 3mm per year) and climate change will continue into the distant future.[397] It is estimated that to stabilize atmospheric concentrations of CO_2, the carbon emissions caused by global human activity would have to be reduced by 80 per cent on 1990 levels.[398]

The environmental crisis caused by human activity is, however, greater and more pervasive than climate change. It extends to soil erosion, deforestation, water salinization, the systemic effects of insecticides and pesticides, toxic chemical waste, species loss, acidification of the oceans, decline of fish stocks, hormone discharges into the water supply and a multitude of other forms of devastation.[399]

Many climate scientists believe that without sufficiently rapid and drastic reductions in world greenhouse gas emissions we could soon be locked into the devastating consequences of 4°C of global warming by 2060 – when present-day schoolchildren reach middle age. Carbon emissions have been cut substantially in a number of developed countries in recent years. Some of this is simply a result of the decline in their manufacturing sectors and growing dependence on imports from countries like China, but the replacement of coal – one of the most polluting sources of energy – by oil and gas has been a significant factor. Once coal use has been eliminated altogether, further reductions in emissions may be substantially more difficult. And the development of cleaner sources of power to fuel the economic development of poorer countries is particularly urgent.

Even as the costs of climate change and environmental devastation become frighteningly tangible, the kind of urgent political action that might address this crisis has not been forthcoming. Why? Climate change denial aside, an important reason is that reducing carbon emissions is perceived as an unwelcome belt-tightening exercise. People assume it would mean policies such as carbon taxes, which would reduce real incomes and material living standards, thereby lowering the 'quality of life' as it is usually understood. New technologies such as low-emission car engines and environmentally friendly light bulbs are adopted only when, by saving costly energy, they serve to increase rather than reduce our real incomes. A car that uses less petrol means you can afford to travel further or have some spare cash to spend on other consumables. In short, sustainability is welcome when it is presented as a matter of preserving our lifestyles and way of life as far as possible in the face of the threatening implications of climate science. The truth, however, is almost the opposite: sustainability will remain beyond our reach unless we make fundamental changes in social organization.

SHIFTING FOUNDATIONS

Life on our planet is changing more rapidly than ever before, and we are on the verge of one of the great transitions in human history. There are at least five major elements to this. The first, as we have seen, is the uncoupling of well-being from economic growth. Second is the environmental crisis, which means that if we fail to change the way we fuel our economies and way of life we face disaster. 'Business as usual' is not an option. Third is the process of 'globalization', which, rather than being an entirely modern process, is really part of the long-term transition: from the self-sufficiency of peasant farmers producing for their own consumption, to a system of international interdependence in which we rely on, and contribute to, a worldwide network of production and consumption aided by electronic communication. This process, linking all humanity into one vast system, looks rather like the formation of a global organism analogous to the transition from single-celled organisms to the formation of multicellular organisms.[400]

Linked to that, the fourth component is the unprecedented and accelerating scale of migration and mixing. Humans originally emerged from Africa and, as we spread across the world, we diversified both culturally and biologically. We are now coming together again. Through international travel, migration and intermarriage, what we are now seeing amounts to nothing less than the reunification of the human race. The process has caused friction, and rapid migrations are often resisted, but as a step in human development, the reunification of humanity is both inspiring and, in the long term, completely unstoppable. Fifth and last, the pace of technological change continues to accelerate. The seemingly endless innovations coming from areas such as electronics, artificial intelligence, bioengineering and nanotechnology are reconfiguring the landscape on which our way of life is built. Used wisely, technical innovation should make us more adaptable and give us more choice in the way our societies develop and how we move towards sustainability.

As the human way of life has developed – from foraging and hunting, through agriculture to industrialization – the foundations of social organization have shifted under us. We saw in Chapter 5 that the egalitarianism of early human societies was based substantially on co-operative hunting. Hunting was not only a co-operative activity, in which individual contributions could not be separately assessed, but, when an animal was killed, sharing made sense because there was more meat available than one family could eat. With the development of agriculture, however, that basis for egalitarianism was lost. Production became individualized: people grew food by their own efforts for their own family on their own patches of land. Just as hunting is inherently egalitarian, so pre-industrial agriculture is individualistic and potentially unequal.

The complexity of modern industrial production has, however, returned us to an inherently interdependent, and so potentially co-operative, way of life. We now make almost nothing for our own use but work instead in highly co-ordinated groups to produce goods and services almost entirely for the benefit of others. When such highly integrated and co-ordinated behaviour is essential, building it on systematic inequality looks like an irrational hangover from a past era.

The periods of scarcity common to pre-industrial agricultural societies were also conducive to inequality. Hierarchies among animals and humans alike are, like pecking orders, about privileged access to scarce resources; and they only make much sense if there is – genuinely – not enough for everyone. Agricultural societies have always suffered at least occasional years of hunger when harvests are poor. But an important precondition for the remarkable equality among hunter-gatherers was, as a great deal of anthropological evidence suggests, that they were remarkably well-off.[401-403] These societies have been dubbed 'the original affluent societies', primarily because our forebears had few needs and those they had could be easily satisfied. Far from a constant struggle to survive, anthropological studies of hunters and gatherers show that people in these societies preferred leisure to higher levels of consumption and could commonly get all the food they needed in just two to four hours a day.[404] They knew of a very large number of edible species of animals and plants which could provide a kind of emergency reserve, but most of the time they could choose to eat only their preferred species. Having little was not a matter of poverty, but of having few needs. Skeletal evidence suggests that hunter-gatherers were often as tall as people in modern societies. Declines in human height and health came with the beginnings of agriculture.[405, 406] The deterioration has been attributed to nutritional diseases resulting from seasonal hunger, reliance on single crops deficient in essential nutrients, crop blights and harvest failures.

Though agriculture is often perceived as a liberating discovery which replaced the uncertainties of foraging and increased production, it was in fact born of necessity. The reason why hunters and gatherers didn't cultivate crops was not any lack of comprehension, but rather that they could acquire all the food they needed from what grew naturally, without having to engage in the back-breaking labour of seed collection, soil preparation, planting, weeding, harvesting and threshing. Agriculture only came about when population densities increased beyond the level at which people could subsist comfortably on what grew wild.[403] They were pushed into it by force of circumstances.

In Britain, the first industrial revolution was also born of necessity.[403] Pressures on the land for food, for woollen clothing, firewood and animal fodder (the basis of horse transport) needed to support a growing population had intensified. With the industrial revolution the pressures began to be eased, with cotton imports, coal and canals, but it took almost a hundred years before there were clear signs of improvements in living standards. The result today is that living standards in rich countries have risen well beyond the point where poverty or a scarcity of necessities is unavoidable. Although inequality and recent austerity policies have driven a growing minority to homelessness, foodbanks or soup kitchens, the vast majority of people living in rich countries have heated homes, comfortable beds and plenty of food. The scarcities associated with conspicuous consumption and the desire for fashionable brands of goods are driven by status competition and intensified by inequality, as we saw in Chapter 4.

By transforming us into an interdependent species and ending any necessary scarcity, modern economic development has recreated the two crucial conditions for equality. The co-operative nature of production and high living standards mean that current levels of inequality are now an anachronism. Taking the long view, history is on the side of egalitarians. Modern living standards mean that we no longer need to remain imprisoned within outmoded forms of society based on genuine scarcity and the necessity of guarding our consumption from the needs of others.

As our societies are tossed about by changes which will, if left to themselves, threaten human survival, it becomes crucial to have a clear idea both of the conditions that need to be met to ensure human well-being and of the kind of society we should be moving towards.

INEQUALITY AND SUSTAINABILITY

There are powerful links between inequality, the threat to the environment, and the failure to achieve genuinely higher levels of well-being. Most obviously, greater inequality intensifies consumerism and status consumption. Starker material differences magnify status differences and make us more prone to worries about the impression we create in the minds of others and, as we cloak ourselves in the symbols of status and success to communicate our 'worth' to each other, money becomes even more important. As a result, we work longer hours, save less, get into debt more and spend more on status goods.

Instead of being a source of well-being and fulfilment, as advertisers would have us believe, psychological studies confirm that consumerism is driven by status insecurity. A recent review of the findings of over 250 studies of the relationship between aspects of well-being and having a 'materialistic' and consumerist orientation, found 'a clear, consistent, negative association between a broad array of types of personal well-being and people's belief in, and prioritization of, materialistic pursuits in life'.[407] The connection between materialism and lower levels of well-being seemed to involve 'negative self-appraisals' and 'low levels of satisfaction of needs for autonomy, competence, and relatedness'. Insecurities and self-doubts lead people to seek solace in acquisitiveness. The review also showed that those who get into serious personal debt, particularly those who use pawnbrokers and moneylenders, suffer higher rates of common mental disorders.[408] Shopping is 'retail therapy' because it speaks comfortingly to status insecurities. Indeed, the marketing and fashion industries exploit these links expertly and relentlessly.

But status competition is a zero-sum game. In a hierarchical ranking system, one person's gain is another's loss: we cannot all improve our status in relation to each other. Although increases in someone's income relative to others moves them up the social ladder and so tends to improve their well-being, we cannot all enjoy the benefits of increased status in relation to each other. And, as we have seen, even if 'trickle down' really happened and economic growth managed to make everyone better off, it would no longer improve overall well-being. In the rich countries, it is therefore no longer legitimate to think that individual desires for higher incomes amount to a societal demand for economic growth. To reduce consumerism, and the damage it does to our wallets and world, the inequality which intensifies status competition must be reduced. If it is not, then the same energy which we saw in the last chapter powering social class differentiation will continue to drive an insatiable torrent of consumption as we try to keep up with, or gain advantage over, each other.

It is hard to tell how much higher consumption is in rich countries than levels which might be enough to support similar standards of well-being. If we take life expectancy as a central measure of well-being, it is related to CO_2 emissions in much the same way as it is related to GDP per head, as shown in Figure 8.1. Just as some countries achieve levels of life expectancy comparable with the richest countries despite much lower income levels, so some countries achieve high life expectancy while emitting less than a third of the carbon emissions per head typical of the richest countries.

Having reached the end of what rising material standards can do for well-being, it is important to recognize that improvements in our social environment and relationships can now provide very major advances in the quality of life, consistent with sustainability. In more unequal societies, where community life is threadbare and the desire for status is intensified, the consequences for people with little chance of gaining recognition and respect are profound. At the extreme – and even after taking into account gun control, poverty and other factors – mass shootings (those with three or more victims) have been shown in a study using data for the 3,144 counties of the USA, to be responsive to increased inequality.[409] How many of these angry, suicidal shootings express a desperate desire to show the world that the perpetrator cannot be ignored? To die killing others has often been a protest against feeling you have been cast as a loser, and to kill in the name of a cause, of a supposedly greater good, can transform the gesture (at least in the mind of the perpetrator) into an honourable act. Although these acts involve only a tiny minority, they surely speak volumes about the experience of vast numbers of people who do not try to punish others for their suffering.

Much the most important increases in levels of well-being in the future will come from improvements in social relationships and the quality of the social environment and, as such, they are entirely compatible with environmental sustainability. We have seen already that people in more equal societies are more inclined to help others – the elderly, those with disabilities, or anyone else.[39] We have seen too that community life is stronger in those societies, and that people are much more likely to feel they can trust others. With increasing levels of inequality, the data show that this all declines, social life atrophies and violence – as measured by homicide rates – increases.[38, 410] In countries with the highest levels of inequality, such as South Africa and Mexico, signs that trust and reciprocity have been replaced by fear can be seen everywhere. Houses are surrounded by high walls topped with razor wire or electric fences, and windows and doors are reinforced with iron bars. Guide books instruct tourists not to go out at night. This transition from sociability to fear goes to the heart of what inequality does to human societies. Another very different kind of evidence that inequality does indeed bring exactly this catastrophic change in social relationships comes from research showing that the proportion of the labour force employed in what has been called 'guard' labour (such as security staff, police and prison officers) increases as income differences get larger.[411, 412] These are jobs concerned with protecting people from each other. Few things are as damaging to the real quality of our lives as the effect of high levels of inequality on social relationships.

The stronger community life and better social integration that lower levels of inequality foster make people more public-spirited and less out for themselves; that strengthens our sense of mutuality and co-operation. If the world is to move towards an environmentally sustainable way of life, it means acting on the basis of the common good as never before, indeed acting for the good of humanity as a whole. But the status insecurity and individualism promoted by inequality distance us from both the means and the will to take action on problems that threaten us all. The nature of the environmental calamity now unfolding, and the means by which we might avert its severest effects, demand that we act for the common good.

An international survey of the opinions of business leaders included a question about how important they thought international environmental protection agreements were.[413] As Figure 8.3 shows, business leaders in the more equal countries rated environmental agreements as much more important than their counterparts in more unequal countries.[414] A similar pattern has been found for recycling: more equal societies recycle a higher proportion of different waste materials.[1] Both these indicators show that people in more equal societies are less self-centred and more willing to act for the greater good.

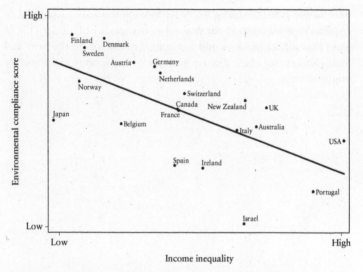

Figure 8.3: Business leaders in more equal countries regard it as more important to comply with international environmental agreements.[414]

The processes which affect our willingness to act for the common good determine whether societies are able to adapt to new circumstances and problems. Researchers using a mathematical model called 'Human and Natural Dynamics' showed that when societies were faced with environmental resource scarcities, those divided by large economic inequalities were much more at risk of collapse than more equal societies.[415] The fact that no strategy proportionate to the environmental crisis we face has so far found broad support suggests that levels of inequality are too high – and so self-interest too strong – to enable populations and politicians in many societies to focus effectively on the transition to sustainability.

Greater equality is not only consistent with moving towards sustainability, but a precondition for doing so. It is the key to moving societies from the pursuit of false, and environmentally damaging, sources of well-being to genuine social ones. Rather than being an unwelcome belt-tightening exercise, moving towards sustainability requires that we improve the real subjective quality of modern life in ways that higher incomes and consumerism cannot. In the next and final chapter, we shall discuss how major reductions in inequality might be won.

9

A Better World

The choice which confronts us is whether we expand the vertical and hierarchical or the horizontal and egalitarian dimension of our societies, whether we increase inequality and the status divisions between us, or reduce them; whether we increase appearances of superiority and inferiority, or whether we decrease them and improve the quality of social relations and well-being throughout society. The evidence we have seen shows that higher levels of inequality raise levels of social anxiety and heighten its psychological and social costs among the vast majority of the population.

There will always be people who, while claiming to deplore class and status divisions, nevertheless imagine that large income differences do not matter. Across the political spectrum, many politicians and policy makers express a desire to minimize class divisions: they want to give children more equal opportunities, reduce differences in their educational performances and increase social mobility. Others say they would like a more cohesive society, with a stronger sense of community. But despite these aims and values, many continue to dismiss the popular demand to reduce income differences as just 'the politics of envy'. Let us therefore briefly summarize the evidence that bigger income differences really do make class and status divisions more powerful.

THE FIVE LINKS

1. Inequality makes problems with social gradients worse

International comparisons show that bigger income differences increase the prevalence of almost all socially graded problems (i.e.

'I believe the president is very concerned about minorities.
We rich are a minority, you know.'

those which become more common lower down the social ladder). For example, health deteriorates lower down the social scale and is less good for most people in more unequal societies. The same is true of a host of other issues, including violence (as measured by homicide rates), teenage birth rates, poor educational performance of school-children, drug abuse, mental illness, child well-being, rates of imprisonment and obesity. In *The Spirit Level* we showed that all these problems are between twice and ten times as common in the more unequal of the developed countries (such as the USA and the UK) than they are in more equal societies such as the Scandinavian countries or Japan. The effects of inequality are greatest among the least well-off, but also affect – to a lesser extent – the better-off, including those with good educations, jobs and incomes. The result is that in more unequal societies, health and social problems develop steeper social gradients and so bigger differences in outcomes between rich and poor.

Our hypothesis in *The Spirit Level* (summarized in the Prologue to this book) was that it is not just any or all problems that were related to inequality, but specifically those with social gradients. We tested this by looking at different death rates.[416] As predicted, we found that death rates and causes of death that are more common among the least well-off (like heart disease, respiratory disease and infant mortality) were much more common in more unequal societies; those with no social gradient, like breast and prostate cancer, seemed unrelated to inequality. This tendency for bigger income differences to increase the health inequalities between social groups has since been confirmed by other researchers.[417] If problems related to social status get worse where income differences are bigger, that strongly suggests that the processes responsible for social gradients are made more powerful by larger income inequalities. Rather than being separate from all the varied indications of class and status, greater income inequality strengthens their divisive hold on us, making societies more hierarchical.

2. Inequality affects social mixing

Countries with bigger income differences tend to have less social mobility: as we saw in Chapter 6, people are more likely to remain in the classes they were born into because larger income differences increase class barriers, make the social hierarchy more rigid and opportunities for children even more unequal. Similarly, marriages across class differences become less common as income differences increase. And as part of that same picture, the residential segregation of the rich and poor also increases.[418] These three points all indicate that greater inequality means that people in different social classes are more separated from each other: the cultural, social and physical divisions all grow wider. Our lives become increasingly defined and restricted by class and status, and the social fabric damaged for everyone. Research now shows that in more unequal societies, the correlation between people's incomes and the class they feel they belong to becomes stronger. At the same time, more people identify themselves as having lower social status.[419]

3. Inequality affects social cohesion

In Chapters 1 and 2, we saw that levels of status anxiety increase in more unequal societies. We all become more worried about each other's judgements of where we stand in society, and as a result, many find social contact increasingly stressful and awkward and so become more likely to 'keep themselves to themselves'. Where there is greater inequality, community life is weaker and levels of interpersonal trust decline – almost certainly because the stress of status insecurity makes people withdraw from social engagement. And as inequality makes social life more stressful, people increasingly make use of drink and drugs to allay their anxieties so that they can relax in each other's company. Hence, drug abuse is, as we saw in Chapter 4, more common in more unequal societies.

4. Inequality increases anxieties about status

We have also discussed the evidence of the psychological responses to higher levels of anxiety about social evaluation. As people battle with their own lack of confidence and low self-esteem, depression and anxiety disorders increase. Less predictable, though understandable in the light of research into the Dominance Behavioural System, are the higher rates of schizophrenia and psychotic symptoms in more unequal countries. These conditions contribute to the link between inequality and mental illness that we first showed in *The Spirit Level* and which has since been confirmed by the numerous studies we described in Chapters 2–4. This connection shows that inequality damages social interaction and our sense of ourselves in relation to each other.

We saw in Chapter 3 that there is also a tendency for people to respond to a heightened social evaluative threat by flaunting their merits and achievements rather than being modest about them. This is shown most clearly in the higher levels of 'self-enhancement' – of rating yourself more highly than others – widespread in the more unequal societies. Internationally comparable data on narcissism are lacking, but we saw in the USA that narcissism became more prevalent as inequality increased.

5. Inequality heightens consumerism and conspicuous consumption

The fifth and final evidential link that larger income differences increase our concern with status, centres on consumerism and the importance of money. Because people tend to use money to show what they are worth, increases in status anxiety mean that money becomes even more important in more unequal societies. People work longer hours, get into debt more and are more likely to go bankrupt. Conspicuous consumption, which is, after all, self-enhancement by economic means, increases in more unequal societies.[420-422] The heightened concern with social status and desire for self-advancement is also evident in data showing that students in the more unequal US states are more likely to cheat to get good marks – by buying term papers on the internet – than are students in more equal states.[423]

The very positive reverse side of this body of evidence is that it points to important new policy levers for improving the quality of life and well-being of the vast majority of the population. We now know how to reduce the power of class and status. Whole societies could be liberated from a hierarchical social structure that encourages people at each level in the status hierarchy to exclude those below them. Much of the nastiness which feeds social anxiety and lack of confidence could be brought to an end so that social life could regenerate.

IS THERE A RIGHT AMOUNT OF INEQUALITY?

We cannot say exactly by how much income differences must be reduced to maximize well-being. What we do know is that, rather than levelling off among the more equal countries, both our own Index of Health and Social Problems and the UNICEF Index of Child Well-being show a continuous rate of improvement from the most unequal to the most equal developed countries. This suggests that the benefits of greater equality persist *at the very least* up to the levels of equality found in the Scandinavian countries, which are among the most equal developed countries. Beyond that we have no data and so cannot say what happens. However, by the time the most unequal countries have reduced income differences to those levels there will, perhaps, be examples of countries that will show if it is worth going further.

What level of equality is desirable may also differ in different contexts. For example, in societies with high levels of geographical mobility, which lack settled communities, greater equality is likely to be even more important than it is in more stable societies. The weaker community life is, the more important it becomes to avoid additional sources of social division.

In the more equal of the rich developed societies, incomes of the richest 20 per cent of the population are between three-and-a-half and four times those of the poorest 20 per cent. In the more unequal, like the USA and UK, the gap is around twice as large. The implication is that the more unequal countries should aim to at least halve the income differences between the top and bottom 20 per cent. Although this would reduce inequality only to levels experienced in the 1960s and early 1970s, it is clear that this could not be achieved quickly simply by tweaking top tax rates and social security benefits.

PREVIOUS MAJOR CHANGES
IN INEQUALITY

Given the substantial benefits, in terms of encouraging and enabling environmental sustainability and improving well-being for entire populations, you might expect that reductions in income differences would be easy to achieve. But the distribution of income and wealth reflects crucial aspects of the distribution of power in any society, and the efficacy of an idea or policy is in itself no guarantee of its implementation. To understand the task that lies before us we must first examine the forces which have led to major changes in income distribution in the past.

Figure 9.1 shows the long-term trends in income inequality among a group of rich countries. The major changes between 1930 and 2014 are illustrative of a broad pattern widely shared across the developed

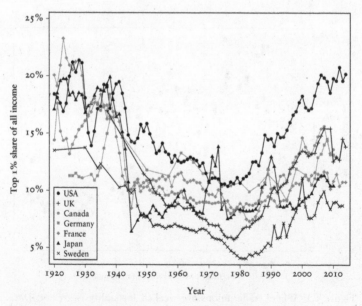

Figure 9.1: Trends in the income share of the richest 1 per cent.

world, and are not a reflection of short-term factors such as the business cycle. Inequality was high until the 1930s, when a long decline began – exactly when varies by five to ten years from country to country and from one measure of income inequality to another. The trend continued downward until sometime in the 1970s. But from around 1980, or a little later in some countries, inequality started to grow again until, by the early twenty-first century, some countries had returned to levels of inequality not seen since the 1920s.

This overall pattern – the initial long decline and later increase in inequality – reflects the strengthening, and then the weakening, of the labour movement, and the political ideology which accompanied it. If you take the proportion of the labour force in trade unions as a measure of the strength of the labour movement's influence as a countervailing voice in society, the relationship with inequality is very clear. Figure 9.2 shows the relation between inequality and the proportion of the labour force in trade unions in sixteen OECD countries at various points between 1966 and 1994.[424]

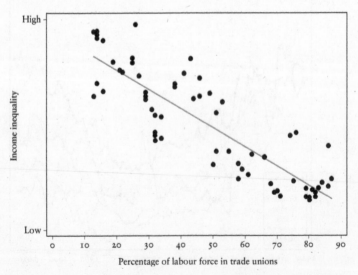

Figure 9.2: Where trade unions are weaker, inequality is greater. Data from sixteen OECD countries, 1966–94.[424]

When and wherever trade union membership is lower (towards the left-hand side of the chart), inequality is higher. This relationship has been found repeatedly in trends over time in a number of different countries. Figure 9.3 shows that as trade union strength increased in the USA, levels of inequality declined – and then rose again as trade union strength reduced.[425]

The connection between trade union membership and inequality should not, however, be seen as if it were simply a reflection of the ability of trade unions to gain higher wages for their members. Instead, the relationship indicates the wider waxing (and later waning) of the influence of progressive politics as a whole. What shaped the distribution of wealth and income was the strength of a set of values in society – most obviously expressed in the ideology and politics of the labour movement. Accompanying it was also the fear of communism and the worry that the economic depression of the 1930s would be interpreted as the collapse of capitalism that Marx had predicted. During the Great Depression, when President Roosevelt introduced the New Deal to the USA and dramatically reduced income differences, he explained to industrialists and the

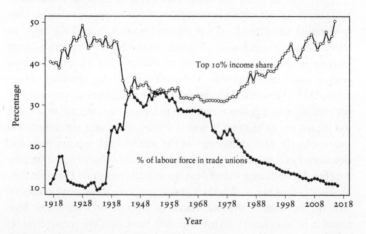

Figure 9.3: Changes in trade union strength and inequality in the USA, 1918–2008.[425]

rich that it was necessary to reform the system in order to preserve it. Indeed, he is sometimes regarded as having saved capitalism from itself. Reductions in inequality were, then, the product both of a collective movement that brought people together with some shared sense of identity and purpose, and the perceived threat that movement posed. The millions of people who suffer the effects of current inequality have so far failed to make up a progressive political force, united by a common cause, with demands which must be met.

Until the end of the 1960s, communist central planning was often thought – despite its other faults – to be more efficient, and to produce faster economic growth rates (according to CIA estimates) than capitalism. It was only with the declining economic performance of the USSR and its satellite countries in the 1970s and 1980s that this view was reversed. The rise in inequality since around 1980 is largely attributable to the political power of the neoliberal ideology espoused and promulgated by President Reagan and Margaret Thatcher. Legislation was passed in one country after another to weaken trade union power. Utilities, transport and mutual companies were privatized, leading to a rapid widening of pay differences within them, and taxes on the wealthy were dramatically cut.

There was, however, an unexpected effect of reducing – sometimes by as much as half – top tax rates from above 80 per cent. Rather than moderating the growth of top *pre-tax* incomes, it had the opposite effect. Because the rich were allowed to keep a higher proportion of any increase in their income, additions to their pre-tax incomes suddenly became much more desirable. The result was a strong tendency, shown across OECD countries, for the rich to gain faster increases in their pre-tax incomes where governments had cut top tax rates most dramatically: the bigger the reductions in top tax rates, the faster the subsequent increase in the pre-tax incomes of the rich.[426] High top tax rates had functioned as a partial wage cap; once they were removed, the wealthy benefitted from both a reduced tax burden and more rapid gains in their incomes before tax. Given their stated purpose of boosting economic growth, the irony is that reductions in top tax rates have now been found to be associated with lower growth rates. An IMF research report finds not only that inequality is bad for growth (as we pointed out in Chapter 6), but also that redistribution is not damaging to growth.[270]

The central role of politics – as opposed to 'market forces' – as the driver of the major changes in inequality (illustrated in Figure 9.3) is confirmed by experience elsewhere. The World Bank makes the same point in a 1993 report on the eight countries which used to be known as the 'tiger economies': Japan, South Korea, Taiwan, Singapore, Hong Kong, Thailand, Malaysia and Indonesia.[427] It describes how, with well-publicized programmes of 'shared growth', these countries all reduced their income differentials during the period 1960–1980. Policies variously included land reform, subsidies to reduce fertilizer prices and boost rural incomes, wealth sharing programmes, large-scale public housing programmes, and assistance to worker co-operatives. The World Bank report then considers why their governments pursued these more egalitarian policies. It says that, in each case, governments reduced inequality primarily because they faced challenges to their legitimacy, often from communist rivals, and needed to win wider popular support. South Korea faced ideological competition from North Korea, for example; Taiwan and Hong Kong faced the claims of China; and communist guerrilla forces operated widely. So here, as in the rich developed countries, it is a mistake to assume that the main changes in inequality over the last century have resulted simply from impersonal market forces driven by globalization or technical change rather than from political and ideological processes.[428] It is not a matter of impersonal economic forces beyond our control; politics and policy have played a central role in determining the distribution of income.

THE POLITICAL PENDULUM

Recent political reversals have led many to feel despondent about the prospects of progress. High levels of inequality have caused political polarization, much as they did in the 1920s. Paul Krugman describes how in the 1960s and '70s there was a large overlap in voting between Republicans and Democrats in the US Congress, but with the growth of inequality that has now completely disappeared.[428] A similar process of political polarization is also evident in Europe. The resurgence of the far right and the far left has been fuelled not only by those victims of inequality who abandoned the establishment parties of the centre left, which had long since abandoned them, but also by the development of more antisocial values across more unequal societies as a whole. Donald Trump was elected President of the United States by a minority of voters, and perhaps Bernie Sanders, despite calling himself a socialist, would have had a better chance of beating him than Hillary Clinton.

The recent rejection of centrist parties by voters on both the left and right suggests a sentiment more fundamental than the considerations that determine which way they turn in any particular election. Political commentators are united in identifying a deep-seated desire for change, although ideas as to what that change should be seem comparatively few on the ground. One of the key ideas that Marx took from his analysis of history was how the development of the industrial system of production forced fundamental changes in the social and political organization of society. It isn't necessary to be a Marxist to recognize that, while our own system has changed out of all recognition, we have been drawn into a global network of total interdependence, and that technological advances have transformed our economies and lives. Despite this we manifestly have not been ushered into a new post-capitalist, post-scarcity world. Instead, the new productive system continues to be organized in a way which would be immediately recognizable to people two centuries ago.

Despite unprecedented levels of physical comfort we suffer a huge burden of unhappiness and mental illness. The so-called meritocracy, which frames our aspirations and defines success, turns out to be an anachronism based largely on a falsehood. International relations continue to be conducted as if it was better to spend so much on military forces, whose use is so often counterproductive, rather than on developing international co-operation and mutual support. And for lack of an adequate framework, we fail to deal with a growing list of international problems, including climate change, the increasing flows of desperate refugees and migrants, the undemocratic and unbridled power of multinationals, the need for enforceable international law, and the $21–32 trillion (20–30 per cent of the world's annual product) which the Tax Justice Network estimates is hidden in tax havens. Though on each issue it is easy to see at least the direction in which progress lies, the changes we need are daunting in their enormity.

There are, however, signs that the sands are beginning to shift. World carbon emissions have at last reached their peak and ceased to rise, but because we continue to tip 36 billion tonnes of carbon dioxide into the atmosphere each year, far more than it can absorb without increasing the planet's temperature, the challenge before us remains very severe.

No doubt initiated by the financial crash of 2008, and spurred on by the Occupy movement, the cause of greater equality has also been taken up – in word though not yet in deed – by world leaders. President Obama called inequality 'the defining challenge of our time'.[429] The Pope described it as 'the root of social ills'.[430] The then UN Secretary-General, Ban Ki-moon, and the Managing Director of the International Monetary Fund, Christine Lagarde, have made equally strong statements.[431, 432] Opinion polls in most countries show that a very large majority of the population – sometimes as high as 80 per cent – think that income differences are too large, even though most people underestimate how large they actually are. In an American research project, people were shown *unlabelled* diagrams illustrating the distributions of wealth in Sweden and in the United States. Around 90 per cent of the respondents preferred the fairer Swedish distribution to the American one. Interestingly, that proportion hardly varied between Republican and Democratic voters, between rich and poor, or between men and women.[433]

Despite the weight of public opinion, only a few signs of remedial action are detectable. The Living Wage movement has led many large UK public- and private-sector institutions to raise minimum pay rates for their staff.[434] In Britain, close to 25 local authorities, almost all controlled by the Labour Party, have set up Fairness Commissions to recommend policies for reducing income differences locally.[435] At the international level, the OECD has taken action on tax avoidance by securing agreements with tax havens to share information on bank accounts with tax authorities.[436] However, since the financial crash, there has so far been no general tendency for income differences in OECD countries to narrow.

Evidently, major reductions in inequality can be induced by

political pressure, though as soon as the pressure weakens the former inequalities reassert themselves – as Figure 9.1 shows they did after 1980. As the labour movement has weakened and social democratic parties have moved to the right, much of the social progress achieved since the 1920s has been undone. Newspapers report that more UK households now employ domestic help and servants than at any time since the nineteenth century,[437, 438] soup kitchens and foodbanks have re-emerged, and those receiving inflated top incomes are founding new dynasties whose subsequent generations will enjoy inherited wealth and leisure.

These reversals indicate a failure of previous generations to make institutional changes that would have embedded progress more deeply in society. Reductions in inequality relied too much on income redistribution through taxes and social security benefits, which, with a swing of the ideological pendulum, could be undone at the stroke of a pen. Lasting progress towards greater equality will depend on building structural changes, such as greater economic democracy, which can provide firmer foundations.

ECONOMIC DEMOCRACY

The main source of widening income differences over the last generation has been the tendency for the incomes (before taxes) of the wealthiest to increase much more rapidly than everyone else's. Figure 9.4 shows the widening of income differences in the biggest 350 American companies from the mid-1960s to 2015. Differentials between the pay of the CEOs and of 'production workers' in the same companies averaged around 20:1 or 30:1 in the 1970s, but by the first decade of this century these differentials had increased tenfold, to between 200:1 and 400:1.[439] By contrast, incomes among the least well-off half of the population have stagnated over the last generation. As we have seen, this widening of the income gap has been reflected in a perception of widening differences in personal worth and ability, as well as in an increase of hubris and sense of entitlement among those at the top.

These huge income differentials occur almost entirely in the private sector. In the public sector – whether in local government, health

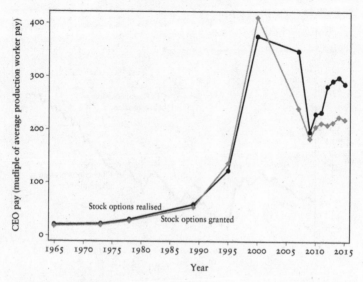

Figure 9.4: Changing ratio of CEO pay to average pay of production workers in largest 350 US companies.[439]

services, universities, the police or the military – differentials are very significantly smaller, typically no more than 20:1 and sometimes as low as 10:1. The widening contrast between public- and private-sector income differentials in the last decades of the twentieth century was starkly reflected in the pay rises which the CEOs of public utilities and mutual companies gained when they were privatized from the 1980s onwards. It is now widely accepted that executive pay in the private sector has little or no relationship with, let alone being justified by, company performance.[440] A study of 429 of the largest companies in the USA found that the returns to shareholders over a ten-year period were substantially lower among companies in which the CEO got more than the median total pay, compared to those in which they got less. This is shown in Figure 9.5.

There is also evidence that small groups of employees are more productive when the members of each group are paid the same. An experiment involving 378 manufacturing employees in India

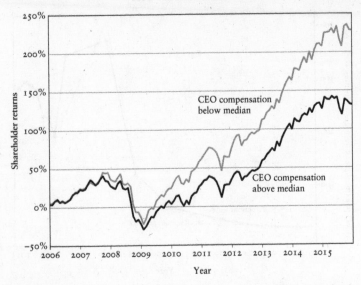

Figure 9.5: Company performance in the 429 largest US companies is better where CEOs are paid less.[441]

compared the performance of groups with and without pay differences between group members. It found that groups with pay differences between their members had substantially lower productivity and higher absences compared to groups without pay differences.[442] With all that we now know about the effects of inequality, it seems likely that this finding reflects differences in co-operation, trust and bonding between group members.

Because it is easily reversed, the redistribution of income through taxes and social security benefits is particularly vulnerable when so many people regard taxes as a kind of legalized theft of income which they feel they earned and have a right to. But the idea that we have each earned our income through our own unaided efforts would only be true if we all produced what we needed in isolation, as self-sufficient peasant farmers came close to doing, instead of through processes that actually depend on the contributions of many others. People's incomes reflect their ability to extract a larger or smaller share of what is produced jointly. Not even the difficulty of people's work bears much relation to their rewards.[443] Few wealthy individuals or CEOs would have become rich if they lived in an impoverished society, without infrastructure – transport, communications, power and water supplies – as well as skilled and well-educated employees. And as economists have always made clear, employers only employ people if they think the value of their work is greater than the amount they are paid.

The rise in inequality, driven primarily by the 'bonus culture' and the rapid rise of top incomes, marks the lack of any effective democratic constraint on the self-interest of the powerful – a lack of constraint from any source, whether through taxation, trade union power or the political influence of the rest of what was once called the 'socialist movement'. To reverse this process, effective new constraints will have to be devised and incorporated permanently into the economic system; democracy will have to be extended into the economic sphere in ways which are consistent with, but modify, the effects of the market. That all modern economic activity is now, de facto, interdependent, co-operative activity, needs to be reflected both in the division of income from it, and in how the institutions we work in are controlled.

About half the member countries of the European Union presently have some kind of legislative provision for employee representation on company boards or remuneration committees.[443-445] A 2013 survey carried out in the UK (which is, like the USA, still without a legal requirement for any employee representation) found that 76 per cent of the population were in favour of employee representation on company boards.[446] Employee surveys in the USA also show that a large majority want more participation in decision making.[447] When Theresa May took office as Conservative Prime Minister in Britain in 2016, she expressed a desire to take at least the first step in this direction. But very soon afterwards she abandoned the idea. In Germany, the 'Right of Co-determination' was established in 1951 in coal mining and steel production. In 1976 it was extended to all companies with more than 2,000 employees. In publicly quoted (but not family owned) companies with between 500 and 2,000 employees, one-third of the members of the board must be employee representatives. Though legislation differs in strength from country to country, and is often too weak to make much difference, studies suggest that companies which have employee representatives on their boards tend to have smaller income differences within them.[448] It also looks as if countries with stronger legislation of this kind have experienced smaller rises in inequality since 1980 than countries without such legislation. A large study of the effect of employee representation in Germany on company performance found that employee representation increases company efficiency and market value.[449] Employee representatives brought information and understanding to the board, enabling improved decision making and higher company values. Companies in sectors that need more intense co-ordination, integration of activities and information sharing, including 'trade, transportation, computers, pharmaceuticals, and other manufacturing', were found to benefit most from employee representation. (However, where employees were represented by an outside trade union official who was not an employee of the company, these benefits of improved flows of information were not found.) In addition to providing more information upwards, there were also benefits to workers and unions of better communication about strategy and profits across corporate hierarchies.

As well as more robust legislative provision for employee representation on company boards, we also need policies to grow the sector of the economy made up of more thoroughly democratic institutions, such as employee co-operatives and employee-owned companies. Income differences in co-operatives tend to be very much smaller than elsewhere. In the Basque region of Spain, the Mondragon group of co-operatives, founded sixty years ago and now employing nearly 80,000 people, sees top to bottom pay differences in its companies of around 5:1, and very rarely more than 6:1 – though there is a tendency for senior staff to be poached by other higher-paying corporations in Spain.

As well as reducing income differences, co-operatives and employee-owned companies also lead to a redistribution of wealth from external shareholders to employees and, simultaneously, reduce unearned income. By broadening the distribution of wealth, these companies contribute to a resolution of the problem at the centre of economist Thomas Piketty's book *Capital*.[450] His argument, that returns on capital increase inequality because they increase faster than other earnings, depends on wealth remaining concentrated in the hands of a few well-off people. Economic democracy may be the best way of spreading both the ownership and earnings of wealth more widely.

In addition, it is clear that co-operatives and employee-owned companies change working relationships and improve the experience of work: as Robert Oakeshott says in his book *Jobs and Fairness*, an employee buyout can change a company from a piece of property into a community.[451] While people in many residential areas don't know their neighbours and there is little or no active community life, it is at work that we now have most to do with each other and ought to be able to rebuild a sense of community. The main reason why most of us do not think of our place of employment as especially communal is because it is there that income differences are first created and where we are most divided by hierarchical systems of 'line management', from superior to subordinate. By reforming the nature of work hierarchies and reducing the scale of divisive income differences, more democratic economic institutions such as employee-owned companies and co-operatives can help develop social cohesion and reciprocity at work, and strengthen community life more widely.[452, 453]

Another crucial advantage of more democratic and egalitarian models of business is that they tend to have higher productivity. Most evaluations of forms of economic democracy have looked at companies which have made only very partial moves towards employee representation. But there have been a number of large and well-controlled studies – comparing before-and-after data on performance for several hundred matched pairs of companies – including ones looking at the effects of profit sharing and employee share ownership.[454] What they show is that there are only reliable improvements in productivity when these provisions are combined with participative management.[455, 456] In the words of one report:

> We can say with certainty that when ownership and participative management are combined, substantial gains result. Ownership alone and participation alone, however, have at best, spotty or short-lived results ... the impact of participation in the absence of [share]

ownership is short-lived ... Ownership seems to provide the cultural glue to keep participation going.[457]

When it comes to fully employee-owned firms, an Employee Ownership Share Index (compiled by Field Fisher Waterhouse) shows that from its initiation in 1992 to 2012 it rose 648 per cent, more than two-and-a-half times the gains made by the FTSE All Share Index, which rose by 245 per cent. A recent review of over one hundred studies confirms not only the better performance of employee-owned companies, but also that they reduce inequality among employees.[458] Not all wholly employee-owned companies are, however, owned by all their employees; some are owned by a minority of senior managers. But a review of the evidence concluded that 'broad ownership [i.e. spread across a larger proportion of employees] boosts productivity by 4% over what would otherwise have been expected'.[459] Other reviews have reached similar conclusions – including one commissioned by the British government.[456, 460, 461]

The evidence from sources such as these suggests that employee-owned companies not only raise productivity but also outperform others in terms of innovation, ability to withstand recession, sickness absence, employee satisfaction and, of course, equality. An interesting corollary to this is that while more democratic companies increase productivity *and* reduce income differences, among non-democratic companies the evidence suggests bigger income differences among employees, from the CEO downwards, are associated with lower productivity.[462] The only fly in the democratic ointment is that the advantages appear to diminish (but not to be reversed) in larger companies where genuinely participative management becomes unwieldy and requires more formal representative structures which they may lack.

By contrast, the involvement of outside shareholders in decision making can often prove an obstacle to company performance. Not only do shareholders lack detailed knowledge of the operations of the companies in whose shares they deal, but the fluctuations in share prices which draw their attention have little or no effect on the companies whose shares are traded. Shareholders are often less equipped or inclined to scrutinize the board's reports and recommendations, even when it is in the interests of the company to do so, and annual meetings frequently degenerate into exercises in rubber-stamping.

One of the most important reasons to develop the co-operative and employee-owned business sector is the connection between greater equality and sustainability. It was Murray Bookchin, an American pioneer of the environmental movement, who said that corporations 'can no more be "persuaded" to limit growth than a human being can be "persuaded" to stop breathing'.[463] This focus on growth comes both from the need to maximize returns to external shareholders and from the way businesses work to concentrate wealth and power at the top. In the absence of structural change there is little sign that either the self-aggrandizement of those at the top or the power of the profit motive is in any way self-limiting.[464]

Co-operatives, on the other hand, are more likely to act as communities and less likely to make expansion their highest priority. For the same reasons, they also seem more likely to perform well in ethical and environmental terms. A study of employees in twenty-two companies with contrasting levels of organizational democracy – in Austria, Italy and Germany – concluded that greater democracy not only improves the 'socio-moral' climate within the company, but also increases employees' 'civic virtues', 'pro-social perspective-taking' and tendencies towards mutual aid.[465, 466] But to ensure that more democratically constituted companies act in the public interest, there is no reason why their boards should not include representatives of the community and consumers, alongside employee representatives.

WHY NOW?

Unless required to do so by law, most companies make little or no gesture towards employee democracy, despite the overwhelming majority of employees who want systems that allow them more active participation and give them a louder voice in the decision-making process.[447] As a result, employees are more likely to feel disaffected, partly because they know that their role is to serve the interests of external shareholders and profit, and partly because of the annoyance caused by line management systems set up to ensure that they do.

These issues are far from trivial. The lack of a sense of control over work is now known to have a major influence on health – mainly because it increases stress.[467, 468] And, in the context of the increasing complexity of modern production, maximizing people's control over their work makes greater workplace democracy more urgent.[469] Broader issues of institutional injustice, lack of accountability and whether people feel they are treated fairly are also now known to damage health – including accelerating the decline of mental functioning with age.[470-472] Even among schoolchildren, feeling unfairly treated is a powerful stressor: a study covering children in twenty-one countries found that in nineteen of them children suffered more headaches when they felt unfairly treated by their teachers.

The evidence that employee turnover is consistently lower in more democratic companies suggests that people prefer working in them. This impression is confirmed by the tendency for these companies to be over-represented in lists of the best employers to work for. The frequent – often unspoken – animosity and friction that many employees feel towards their bosses is likely to be less common in co-operatives and employee-owned companies, particularly so where senior managers are accountable to employees who may also have a direct or indirect role in their appointment.

An additional reason for supporting all forms of economic democracy is that the existing forms of company ownership and control are becoming a counterproductive anachronism. A report called *Workers on Board*, from the British Trades Union Congress, describes how the traditional form of share ownership has become increasingly inappropriate for modern businesses.[473] It points out that in the 1960s most shares were owned by individuals with a longer-term stake in a small number of companies, which they followed and took some interest in. People would own shares in the same company for an average of seven years. But now, in many countries, the vast majority of shares are owned by financial institutions which spread their investments across hundreds or even thousands of companies. Because they make money through short-term share trading, often triggered simply by computer algorithms, the average length of time they own a share is thought to be less than a minute, so they have no long-term (or even short-term) interest in or knowledge of these companies. Even outside high-frequency trading systems, shares are on average owned for only a few months. A large listed company may now have thousands, or even tens of thousands, of shareholders and will find it difficult even to obtain full information on who its shareholders are.

At the same time, modern production increasingly involves the integration of the expertise and knowledge of many different people, so much so that the value of a company is now less a matter of its buildings and capital equipment, than of the combined skills, expertise and know-how of its employees. This means that buying and selling a company increasingly amounts to buying and selling a group of people – an appallingly anachronistic concept, especially when that group of people would be likely to run that company more successfully themselves. The purpose is of course to buy rights to the profit stream which that group of people produce.

But if companies with more democratic structures tend to have higher productivity, and modern shareholding has become an anachronism, why don't we see rapid extensions of democracy into the economic sphere? The answer is that companies do not exist simply to produce the goods and services that we all need. By their very nature, they tend to concentrate power and wealth in the hands of a few people at the top. As a result, the 'captains of industry' face a conflict of interest between what might maximize their individual private gain, and what might be best for their companies. The problem was illustrated in Figure 9.5 (page 246), which showed that the performance of companies in which the CEOs were paid less was better than in the ones where they were paid more. The danger is that very high salaries will be particularly attractive to people whose primary focus is self-advancement, rather than the interests of the company.

The turnover of many multinational corporations is larger than the GDP of many whole countries. A few are larger even than countries like Norway and New Zealand, and yet they lack democratic accountability and often pay little or no tax. In 2008, the US

Government Accountability Office reported that 83 of the USA's biggest 100 corporations used subsidiaries in tax havens to avoid tax. The Tax Justice Network said that 99 of the 100 biggest companies in Europe did the same. And yet they depend on the entire publicly funded infrastructure – from transport systems to education and the police – which others pay for.

Despite the popularity of corporate responsibility programmes, what is best for a company's bottom line often isn't in the interests of the public at large. Indeed, large corporations play an increasingly antisocial role in society. In his book *Lethal But Legal*, Nicholas Freudenberg, who is Distinguished Professor of Public Health at the City University of New York, provides copious and detailed evidence that the food, tobacco, alcohol, gun, pharmaceutical, agribusiness and automobile industries are now among the most important threats to public health.[474] Whether it is food manufacturers fighting against attempts to reduce obesity or the scandal of the falsification of emissions from diesel vehicle engines, the cost is measured in tens and hundreds of thousands of human lives. Freudenberg shows how corporations use advertising expenditure, political influence and the media to counter evidence from scientific research of the harm their products do and to fight any legislative attempts to reduce risk. They pack regulatory systems with people who will defend their interests, and spend vast sums on lobbying politicians in order to continue to sell their products in the face of massive evidence of harm. Even companies that make products which do not damage health still aim to maximize sales and consumption in the face of overwhelming evidence that carbon emissions have to be reduced by at least 80 per cent to save us from the worst effects of global warming. It should not be beyond the wit of modern societies to ensure that production is undertaken in the service of the public good, humanity and the planet.

THE GREAT TRANSITION

The existing structure of our societies imposes huge costs on us all. It is, as we have shown, an inefficient way of producing well-being;

as well as being better for everyone, a more equal society would be less, rather than more expensive. The Equality Trust calculated that if the UK reduced its inequality merely to the average of the OECD countries, it would save £39 billion a year just from the resulting improvements in physical and mental health and from the reductions in violence and rates of imprisonment.[475] Given that inequality is a powerful predictor of many other aspects of social dysfunction, the total cost reductions would be higher still.

In the 1970s, Britain was as equal as the Scandinavian countries are now. Since then the gap between the richest and poorest 20 per cent in Britain has widened so rapidly that it is now twice as big as in Scandinavia. The contribution of top incomes to increasing inequality matters just as much as poverty and low incomes. Equality can be increased by reducing income differences either before tax or by redistributing incomes through progressive taxes and more generous benefits. Judging from examples of more equal countries or American states, the specific path taken to achieve greater equality is less important than the levels of equality they achieve. Both approaches seem to bring the social benefits of greater equality, and both must be pursued.

In terms of redistributive policies, action to tackle offshore tax havens and other forms of tax avoidance is self-evidently a necessary preliminary to making taxes more progressive again. Because greater equality seems to diminish prejudice against those lower on the social ladder, greater equality might also make it easier to provide a more generous system of social security benefits. More radical proposals to reform taxes and benefit systems include plans for a basic income and for a land tax. Both have found their advocates among academics and policy experts and have a lot to recommend them.[476-479] Indeed, the increasing prospect of many jobs being replaced by automation and artificial intelligence means that a basic income may become a necessity.

On income differences before tax, a number of countries have seen campaigns to increase minimum wages or to encourage employers to pay a 'living wage' substantially above the legal minimum. But to successfully reduce income differences before tax governments will have to manage their economies to keep unemployment low enough to ensure stronger competition for labour. Historically, as Figures 9.2 and 9.3 show (pages 238 and 239), trade unions have also played a key role in reducing inequality. Although the shift from large heavy industries to small service-sector businesses means trade unions are unlikely ever to regain their former strength, their legal ability to represent and act on behalf of their members nevertheless needs to be restored. To maintain an orderly wage bargaining system now that trade unions are weaker, it is even more important to counter low incomes among the non-unionized. Part of the answer is to re-establish national wage councils, made up of trade union, employer and expert members, to set and oversee minimum wage agreements, rights and conditions of employment. This is particularly urgent in those sectors where employers have shrugged-off their responsibilities, using notions of self-employment and zero-hours contracts to avoid fulfilling their obligations to employees, leaving them without rights to holidays, pensions, sickness absence cover and more.[480]

By far the most important long-term measure, however, will be the reduction of pre-tax income differences by extending democracy into the economic sphere. Policy initiatives developed for this purpose will meet powerful resistance from business – though, as we have seen, CEOs and shareholders are not always the best champions of their companies' interests. Likewise, although many ideologically driven interpretations of the merits of growth and ills of regulation are presented as if they were concerned only with the greater good, they frequently reflect the efforts of an affluent minority to justify and protect their own interests. This is an important point because policy development will require a great deal of discussion and ideologies serving sectional interests will constantly threaten to derail it. In the past, the interests of the less well-off were partly protected by recognition that different class interests give rise to different class ideologies. But when political leaders of even progressive political parties get too close to the very wealthy, that notion is lost – and voters can start to believe that people as wealthy as President Trump will somehow serve the interests of the least well-off.

With occasional admirable exceptions, extensions to democracy are rarely supported by those whose power they would curtail. Opposition will be strong, but the democratization of the economy needs to be a publicly recognized political objective. It should be advocated and defended by all progressive politicians as the next major step in human progress. We need to create a popular understanding that this is part of a transition to a sustainable future, capable of producing a higher real quality of life than is currently possible. Rather than a revolution, what is needed is a gradual and far-reaching transformation.

To help in this process, the profile of the existing employee-owned and co-operative businesses needs to be raised in every country. They already have substantial strength. Even in the UK, where this more democratic sector of the economy is weaker than in many other countries, there are close to 500 employee-owned and co-operative businesses, with a combined annual turnover of £10.7 billion and close to 100,000 employees. According to the UK's Employee Ownership Association, this sector of the economy has been growing over the last few years at a rate of 9 per cent a year. Attention also needs to be drawn to examples of highly successful companies with more democratic business models, including large companies like Arup, Scott Bader, Swann-Morton and John Lewis. The largest employee-owned company in the USA is Publix Super Markets with 175,000 employees and a turnover of $30 billion from over 1,000 branches – which makes it one of the ten largest privately held companies in the USA. Eighty per cent of the company is owned by past and present employees, with the remaining 20 per cent owned by the family of the company's founder. There are also a number of large US companies owned wholly by their employees, including Lifetouch, a photographic services business with a staff of 20,000.

One way of raising the profile of the whole sector would be to encourage these companies to mark their greater commitment to fairness and democracy by displaying their status as part of their logo. It might be helpful to set up a 'democratic company' logo – perhaps modelled on the 'fair trade' example – to increase the visibility of these companies and make people more aware of their ethical and practical advantages. Consumer campaigns have shown that companies are very sensitive to publicity on reputational issues which might adversely affect their sales, and this could be included in the criteria used to certify businesses as meeting various other social, environmental and ethical standards.

A more direct approach to assisting the development of more democratic businesses would be to set up an internet portal to make it easier for people to do their shopping, banking and selection of utility suppliers from them: a website which would let customers select a category of goods and then connect them with democratic companies supplying those goods and services. With time and development it could work like an egalitarian version of Amazon, but without that company's record of tax avoidance and mistreatment of employees. As well as giving the more democratic sector of the economy an additional market advantage, such a website would also increase public awareness of the practical and ethical benefits of more democratic business models.

Making the case for economic democracy and placing it at the centre of the political agenda will have to be complemented by legislative change. The first objective should be to require, by law, that all but the smallest companies must have employee representatives on their boards and remuneration committees. To embed democracy into the economy, the proportions of employee representatives on company boards and remuneration committees should increase over time, moving eventually to majority control and beyond. Another way of setting up a gradual transfer of control might be to include a requirement that a small proportion of shares should be transferred each year to employee-controlled trusts. If just 2 per cent were transferred each year, employees would be in majority control after twenty-five years. The Swedish trade unions once proposed a system of Employee Investment Funds, intended to increase employees' control over their companies. It was set up, in a watered-down form, in 1983 and involved companies paying a small part of their profits into collectively controlled employee funds with voting rights in their companies.[481] They were fiercely opposed by the Swedish Employers' Federation and cancelled when the Social Democratic Party lost power in 1991, before the funds were large enough to contribute more than marginally to the stabilization and democratization of the Swedish economy. Nevertheless, in terms of financial performance and the valuable experience gained by those involved, the scheme proved that such funds could work well.

Even before legislation to increase economic democracy, forms of representation could be made a condition of gaining public-sector contracts, or lower corporation tax rates. In both Rhode Island and California, there have been legislative initiatives to reduce corporation taxes for companies with smaller pay ratios, and to give them preferential treatment when awarding government contracts. Elsewhere, there are initiatives to use public expenditure to support the development of 'community wealth building'. These initiatives funnel the expenditure of local public-sector 'anchor' institutions – such as the local hospital, university and city government – towards the local economy. The aim is to build sustainable businesses controlled by their employees and to ensure local development is under local community control. The Democracy Collaborative, in Cleveland, Ohio, established the 'Evergreen Cooperative' modelled on the hugely successful Mondragon co-operative group in Spain. So far the Ohio venture consists of Ohio Cooperative Solar, producing energy, the Green City Growers Cooperative, with five acres of greenhouses for growing vegetables, and the Evergreen Cooperative Laundry serving local hospitals and hotels. Preston in Lancashire has begun a similar initiative with agreement from local public-sector institutions willing to divert a higher proportion of their expenditure to support local wealth building and businesses.

In Britain, the Employee Ownership Association and Co-operatives UK have set out policy proposals to accelerate the growth of employee-controlled businesses. Both organizations suggest that a major obstacle to the development of this sector is the lack of awareness of these models among professional legal and financial advisers. As a result, more democratic models are not considered as options at key stages of business development: when businesses are started, when they plan major expansions, when they have to deal with succession issues when founders retire, or when a business needs to be rescued. The lack of interest and knowledge among legal and financial advisers would be diminished if public awareness was raised, but government departments responsible for business could also provide the necessary support and advice for the establishment of, or

conversion to, employee ownership. They might also provide a training and advice service on how to set up employee-owned and
co-operative companies.

Because banks are generally unfamiliar with co-operatives, there
are often difficulties in arranging loans to help fund employee buy-
outs. There is a strong case for making special loans available for this
purpose. Ideally, government should work out a complete package of
measures to grow the democratic sector, complete with tax incentives, sources of advice and support, readymade rules of governance
and sources of finance.

The constitutions of employee-owned and co-operative business
should, in all cases, be designed to prevent employees selling their
companies back to external shareholders. The absence of effective
provisions of this kind has in the past led to major waves of 'demutu-
alization' and has prevented a faster growth of the more democratic
sector.

Lastly, employees taking on new functions as members of company boards will need training in areas such as management, business
law, accountancy and economics. Options should range from very
short courses – like some of the learning schemes designed to prepare
school governors – to the provision of master's degree courses to
which people could be seconded. As well as improving the confidence and quality of decision making among elected board members,
the provision of preparatory courses would also communicate the
seriousness of a government's commitment to seeing this transition
through.

Creating a new society involves much more than pressure for
forms of workplace democracy. That has been the central subject of
this chapter because, without structural change to embed greater
income equality more fundamentally into our society, inequality will
simply rise, fall, and rise again, following orchestrated shifts in public opinion. Without the reductions in inequality which these
proposals aim to bring about, we may have to accept that we will be
defeated by climate change. There are already indications that the
195 nations that agreed in December 2015 to make voluntary reductions in carbon emissions are unlikely to achieve their goals. If they
do, then we should be on target for keeping global warming to no

more than a fairly disastrous 3°C. But unlike international trade agreements – which allow companies to sue when elected governments harm their commercial prospects by, for instance, introducing legislation to protect the environment or public health – there is no provision for their enforcement. And the longer we delay, the more sudden, difficult and traumatic the transition to low-carbon economies will have to be. A new outlook, provided by a new society, seems increasingly necessary.

CREATING A NEW SOCIETY

Greater equality is at the heart of creating a better society because it is fundamental to the quality of social relations in society at large. Social status systems among humans (like dominance ranking systems or pecking orders among animals) are orderings based on power; they ensure privileged access to resources for those at the top, regardless of the needs of others. The fact that humans, like members of any other species, all have the same basic needs means that there is always the question of whether or not to share access to scarce resources; whether to co-operate as allies or compete as rivals. Do we want to live in a society based on co-operation and reciprocity, or competition and rivalry?

In Chapter 5 we mentioned that in the seventeenth century Thomas Hobbes placed conflict avoidance – the 'warre of each against all' – at the centre of his political philosophy. He believed that the only way to keep the peace was to have a sovereign with absolute power to enforce it. What Hobbes could not know is that in human prehistory, long before the development of government, societies were based on systems of food sharing and a high degree of equality. People engaged in these activities, as Marshall Sahlins has pointed out, to keep the peace and avoid the Hobbesian conflict for scarce resources.[210] The reason he said 'gifts make friends and friends make gifts' is because gifts symbolize – in the most concrete terms – that the giver and receiver recognize, respect and respond to each other's needs.[210] The result, as we saw earlier, was that for more than 90 per cent of human existence, we lived typically in societies with a level of equality which seems to modern eyes scarcely credible.[216, 218] But people today still share food and eat together socially because it is an expression of relationships built on sharing, rather than on competing for access to basic necessities. The same message is, as we saw, also enshrined in the major world religions.

In effect, we have deep within our psyche two fundamentally different social strategies (the two sides of human nature outlined in Chapter 5): one predicated upon friendship and the other based on ideas of superiority and inferiority. We all know how to make and value friends and we all know how snobbishness, downward prejudice and social climbing work. The extent to which we deploy and are subject to these strategies has repercussions throughout the rest of social life; it colours our psychology and social customs.

The strength of the social hierarchy and the importance of status serve as indicators of how far a society departs from equality. The further the departure from mutuality, reciprocity and sharing, the stronger the basic message that we will each have to fend for ourselves. We are pushed towards more antisocial forms, becoming more concerned with status and self-advancement, while community life, trust and our willingness to help each other all decline.

At the heart of progressive politics there has always been an intuition that inequality is divisive and socially corrosive. Now we have the internationally comparable data which proves that intuition true. Moving both towards sustainability and a society liberated from class divisions and status hierarchies is part of the same process: a transition to a society which is better for all of us. The challenge is to open up a new era of improvements in well-being – no longer the diminishing returns from economic growth, but real gains from what greater equality does for our confidence, our relationships with others and for the quality of the physical and social environment. By reducing the extraordinarily wasteful status competition that drives conspicuous consumption, we will also increase our willingness to act for the common good.

Let us now summarize the four key improvements in the quality of life which can take us towards a more fulfilling and sustainable way of life. First, through greater equality, we gain a world where status matters less, where the awkward divisions of class begin to heal, where social anxieties are less inhibiting of social interaction and people are less plagued by issues of confidence, self-doubt and low self-esteem. This would, in turn, reduce our need for the drink and drugs we so often use to cope with anxiety and ease social contact. There would be less need for narcissistic self-presentation, less need to overspend for the sake of appearances. In short, we move towards a more relaxed social life, with stronger communities, in which it is easier to enjoy the pleasures of friendship and conviviality and gain a society better able to meet our basic social needs.

Second, we move from a society that maximizes consumption and status, to a society that uses each increase in productivity to gain more leisure and reduce the demands of work. The New Economics Foundation has suggested that we should aim to work only twenty-one hours a week. Large international differences in working hours do not seem to affect GNP per head.[482] We need more time for family and for our children, more time to care for each other, for friends, for the elderly and to enjoy community life. In future, increases in productivity should be translated into reductions in working hours instead of increased income and profit. If we had a long-term increase in labour productivity of 2 per cent a year, in ten years' time all could enjoy the same material standard of living as we do now but with an extra day off work a week. And given that the average age gap between parents and children is around thirty years, the lives of our children would be transformed. But with more workplace democracy and shorter hours, the productivity growth rate – which has been so poor in the UK – might rise to 3 per cent a year. That would give us an extra day off a week within seven years, and the working week could be halved within twenty-four years. If, as some studies suggest, almost half of all jobs may be vulnerable to computerization and automation,[483] cutting hours and sharing work will become increasingly important if we are to enjoy the benefits of technical progress. The alternative is likely to be a growing division between the unemployed and the overworked.

Third is the improvement in the quality of working life resulting from the extension of democracy into employment. The current anachronistic system, in which the control of companies – groups of people – can be bought and sold, must be phased out. The normal rigid ranking system, with line management and institutionalized hierarchies, excludes people from control over their work and any say in whose interests it serves. Working in democratic institutions such as co-operatives and employee-owned businesses (with or without community and consumer representatives), means that management becomes answerable to employees. Hierarchy would become overlaid with social obligations, and much smaller income differences would reduce status divisions. The next great stage in human development must therefore be the extension of democracy into working life. Work should be where we find a sense of self-worth and the experience of making a valued contribution. We can no longer accept a system of employment which reduces the lives of so many to a demeaning shadow of their potential.

Fourth are all the health and social benefits of living in a more equal society. More equal societies bring major reductions in almost all the problems that become more common lower down the social ladder. A more equal society would enjoy better physical and mental health, higher standards of child well-being, less violence, fewer people in prison, less drug addiction and more equal opportunities for children. A more equal society is conducive to the psychosocial well-being of whole populations.

As well as making real and tangible improvements to the quality of our lives, these improvements in the social functioning of our societies will put environmental sustainability within our reach. By reducing status insecurities we will reduce not only the most obvious conspicuous consumption, but also the huge volume of wasteful consumption driven more defensively by the attempts to maintain standards and avoid falling behind others. We may become more willing to repair goods instead of replacing them, and designs might facilitate that. With the decline of individualism and the strengthening of community life, we may feel less need for private cars and other forms of private provision. But above all, greater equality is likely to mean that our economic and political interests are less divergent and we find it easier to act for the common good.

The changes proposed are neither impractical nor idealistic; they are a necessary response to the damage inequality is already doing and the traumatic dislocation which climate change holds in store for us. Although recent decades have seen dramatic reductions in world poverty (those living on less than $2 a day) attributable to economic growth in developing countries, that progress will be seriously threatened if we fail to reduce carbon emissions and protect the environment. And in the rich countries, where measures of well-being are no longer responsive to economic growth, present structures are evidently not an efficient way of producing human well-being.

A shared conception of a better society gives coherence to policy. A vision of a better future can also reinvigorate some of the idealism and principle which so often seems to have become submerged in a politics driven by opportunism and expediency. Whole populations have for too long been pushed around by unrecognized but extremely powerful social forces. We hope that a better, scientific and evidence-based understanding of them will help us address the very serious human and environmental problems they have created.

Change on the scale needed, however, can only be achieved if large numbers of people commit themselves to achieving it. Some-time after the late 1970s, it seems, progressive politics either lost its conviction that a better form of society was possible or lost the ability to convince people that politics was the route to achieving it. The result was the almost uncontested rise of neoliberalism. Now, facing the evidence of global warming and calamitous climate change, the world is in need of a radical alternative, a clear vision of a future society which is not only environmentally sustainable, but in which the real quality of life is better for the vast majority. Only then will people commit themselves to the long task of bringing that society into being.

Appendices

Resources

THE EQUALITY TRUST

If we want to build a better society, it is essential we take action. In 2009, along with Bill Kerry, we co-founded The Equality Trust, now a registered charity in England and Wales, which works to improve the quality of life in the UK by reducing economic inequality. Working with others to build a social movement for change, The Equality Trust analyses and disseminates the latest research, promotes robust evidence-based arguments and supports a dynamic network of local groups. Please visit us at www.equalitytrust.org.uk. Online you can sign up for the newsletter, find information and resources, ways to get involved and news of events. Or you can find us on Facebook at https://www. facebook.com/equalitytrust, or follow us on Twitter: @equalitytrust.

THE WELLBEING ECONOMY ALLIANCE (WE-ALL)

WE-All is a new global campaigning organization set up to create a Global New Economy Movement aimed at building sustainable wellbeing, rather than maximizing GDP. Although the need for an economic transformation is widely recognized, it is not happening fast enough. Bringing together the many exemplary but often disconnected initiatives already in progress round the world, WE-All will convene seven meta-movements centred variously on businesses, faith and values groups, academia and think-tanks, civil society organizations, governments, places such as cities, regions and localities already implementing new economy initiatives, and institutional innovators. WE-All has been joined by a growing number of partner organizations and, with the leadership of the Scottish government and encouraged by the OECD, it has brought together a group of governments, including those of Costa Rica, New Zealand, Slovenia and Scotland, committed to pioneering the implementation of new economy proposals. With a global citizens' movement, it will develop and disseminate new narratives to build a Global New Economy Movement. With the growing influence of WE-All and other like-minded organizations, we look forward to seeing a more rapid transition to economic systems devoted to sustainable well-being (wellbeingeconomy.org).

OTHER USEFUL LINKS

There are many excellent websites and online resources for readers interested in inequality research and campaigning, a few of the best are:

- Inequality.org A project of the Institute for Policy Studies, a think-tank based in Washington, DC.
- http://toomuchonline.org/ A monthly exploration of excess and inequality, in the United States and throughout the world, also from the Institute for Policy Studies.
- http://www.resolutionfoundation.org/ A UK think-tank that works to improve the living standards of people on low to middle incomes.
- http://highpaycentre.org/ A UK think-tank focused on pay at the top of the income scale; campaigns to reduce the income gap between the super-rich and the rest of the population.
- http://policy-practice.oxfam.org.uk/our-work/inequality International poverty charity Oxfam now campaigns to reduce extreme inequality.

For links between inequality, climate change and alternative economic policy, try:

- The New Economics Foundation: http://www.neweconomics.org
- The Alliance for Sustainability and Prosperity: http://www.asap4all.com

A List of Health and Social Outcomes
Affected by Income Inequality

This table lists some of the different health problems and social issues that researchers have found to be significantly linked to income inequality, published in peer-reviewed journal papers. The references are *examples* of such studies – for some outcomes there are hundreds of examples, for others only one published study. This is neither a comprehensive list of outcomes nor a comprehensive list of studies, but is to help readers who want to explore the academic research; where possible the citations are to relevant reviews, which cover numerous studies.

Health/social outcome	Shown in international comparisons	Shown in comparisons of US states	Shown in longitudinal or time series analyses
Physical Health (for a causal review of the health-inequality literature, see Pickett and Wilkinson 2015[3])			
Life expectancy	Wilkinson and Pickett 2006[2] Babones 2008[484]	Clarkwest 2008[485]	Zheng 2012[486] Pickett and Wilkinson 2015[3]
Infant mortality	Ram 2005[490] Ram 2006[488] Kim and Saada 2013[487]	Kim and Saada 2013[487]	Torre and Myrskyla 2014[489]
Mortality (adult)	Wilkinson and Pickett 2006[2]	Ram 2005[490]	Zheng 2012[486] Torre and Myrskyla 2014[489]

Health/social outcome	Shown in international comparisons	Shown in comparisons of US states	Shown in longitudinal or time series analyses
Obesity	Pickett, Kelly et al. 2005[171]	Pickett and Wilkinson 2012[491]	
HIV infection	Drain, Smith et al. 2004[492]	Buot, Docena et al. 2014[493]	
Mental Health and Well-being			
Mental illness (all)	Pickett and Wilkinson 2010[59] Ribeiro et al. 2017[60]	Ribeiro, Bauer et al. 2017[60]	
Depression/ depressive symptoms	Steptoe, Tsuda et al. 2007[94] Patel, Burns et al. 2018[512]	Messias, Eaton et al. 2011[96] Patel, Burns et al. 2018[512]	
Schizophrenia	Burns, Tomita et al. 2014[101]		
Psychotic symptoms	Johnson, Wibbels et al. 2015[102]		
Status anxiety	Layte and Whelan 2014[57]		
Self-enhancement	Loughnan, Kuppens et al. 2011[112]		
Narcissism			Wilkinson and Pickett 2017[123]
Substance use or deaths	Wilkinson and Pickett 2009[494] Cutright and Fernquist 2011[168]	Wilkinson and Pickett 2007[496] Gray 2016[495]	

Table (*continued*)

Health/social outcome	Shown in international comparisons	Shown in comparisons of US states	Shown in longitudinal or time series analyses
Problem gambling	Wilkinson and Pickett 2017[123]		
Social Cohesion			
Trust/social capital	Freitag and Bühlmann 2009[497] Elgar and Aitken 2011[73]	Kawachi and Kennedy 1997[498]	Uslaner and Brown 2005[40]
Solidarity	Paskov and Dewilde 2012[39]		
Agreeableness		de Vries, Gosling et al. 2011[105]	
Civic participation	Lancee and Van de Werfhorst 2012[37]		
Cultural participation	Szlendak and Karwacki 2012[377]		
Ambiguous stereotyping	Durante, Fiske et al. 2013[154]		
Social comparisons		Cheung and Lucas 2016[499]	
Homicides	Ouimet 2012[500] Daly 2016*[38]	Glaeser, Resseger et al. 2008[501] Daly 2016*[38]	Rufrancos, Power et al. 2013[410] Daly 2016*[38]
Imprisonment	Wilkinson and Pickett 2007[496]	Wilkinson and Pickett 2007[496]	

Health/social outcome	Shown in international comparisons	Shown in comparisons of US states	Shown in longitudinal or time series analyses
Women's status	Wilkinson and Pickett 2009[494]	Kawachi and Kennedy 1999[502]	
Children's Life Chances			
Child well-being	Pickett and Wilkinson 2007[189]	Pickett and Wilkinson 2007[189]	Pickett and Wilkinson 2015[190]
Bullying	Elgar, Craig et al. 2009[233]		
Child maltreatment		Eckenrode, Smith et al. 2014[247]	
Educational attainment	Wilkinson and Pickett 2007[496]	Wilkinson and Pickett 2007[496]	
Dropping out of school		Wilkinson and Pickett 2007[496]	
Social mobility	Corak 2016[341]	Chetty, Hendren et al. 2014[503]	
Teenage pregnancy	Pickett, Mookherjee et al. 2005[335]	Kearney and Levine 2012[504]	
Environmental Issues (for comprehensive analysis and review, see Boyce 1994[505] and Cushing, Morello-Frosch et al. 2015[506])			
Biodiversity	Mikkelson, Gonzalez et al. 2007[508] Holland, Peterson et al. 2009[507]		

Table (*continued*)

Health/social outcome	Shown in international comparisons	Shown in comparisons of US states	Shown in longitudinal or time series analyses
Water/meat/ petrol consumption	Stotesbury and Dorling 2015[509]		
CO_2 emissions/ air pollution	Drabo 2011[510] Cushing, Morello-Frosch et al. 2015[506]	Jorgenson, Schor et al. 2015[511]	
Status consumption	Walasek and Brown 2015[421]	Walasek and Brown 2015[422]	
Compliance with international environmental agreements	Wilkinson, Pickett et al. 2010[414]		

*Martin Daly's book *Killing the Competition* summarizes and references his own and others' research over more than thirty-five years.

References

1. Wilkinson, R. G. and Pickett, K., *The Spirit Level: Why Equality is Better for Everyone.* London: Penguin, 2010.
2. Wilkinson, R. G. and Pickett, K. E., 'Income inequality and population health: a review and explanation of the evidence', *Social Science & Medicine* 2006; 62 (7): 1768–84.
3. Pickett, K. E. and Wilkinson, R. G., 'Income inequality and health: a causal review', *Social Science & Medicine* 2015; 128: 316–26.
4. Popper, K., *Conjectures and Refutations: The Growth of Scientific Knowledge.* Abingdon: Routledge, 2014.
5. Cooley, C. H., *Human Nature and the Social Order.* Piscataway, NJ: Transaction Books, 1992.
6. Beck, M., 'Party on: a survival guide for social-phobes', *O Magazine,* 23 November 2011, http://marthabeck.com/page/48/.
7. Adler, A., *What Life Should Mean To You.* 1931.
8. Zimbardo, P. G., *Shyness: What It Is, What To Do About It.* Boston, Mass.: Da Capo Press, 1990.
9. Burstein, M., Ameli-Grillon, L. and Merikangas, K. R., 'Shyness versus social phobia in US youth', *Pediatrics* 2011; 128 (5): 917–25.
10. Henderson, L. and Zimbardo, P., 'Shyness, social anxiety, and social anxiety disorder', *Social Anxiety: Clinical, Developmental, and Social Perspectives* 2010; 2: 65–92.
11. Kessler, R. C., Chiu, W. T., Demler, O., Merikangas, K. R. and Walters, E. E., 'Prevalence, severity, and comorbidity of 12-month DSM-IV disorders in the National Comorbidity Survey Replication', *Archives of General Psychiatry* 2005; 62 (6): 617–27.
12. Cox, B. J., MacPherson, P. S. and Enns, M. W., 'Psychiatric correlates of childhood shyness in a nationally representative sample', *Behaviour Research and Therapy* 2005; 43 (8): 1019–27.
13. Kessler, R. C., Angermeyer, M., Anthony, J. C., et al., 'Lifetime prevalence and age-of-onset distributions of mental disorders in the World Health Organization's World Mental Health Survey Initiative', *World Psychiatry* 2007; 6 (3): 168–76.

14. Twenge, J. M., 'The age of anxiety? Birth cohort change in anxiety and neuroticism, 1952–1993', *Journal of Personality & Social Psychology* 2000; 79 (6): 1007–21.

15. Collishaw, S., Maughan, B., Natarajan, L. and Pickles, A., 'Trends in adolescent emotional problems in England: a comparison of two national cohorts twenty years apart', *Journal of Child Psychology & Psychiatry* 2010; 51 (8): 885–94.

16. American Psychological Association, 'Stress in America: coping with change', *Stress in America Survey*, 2017.

17. Luttmer, E. F., 'Neighbors as negatives: relative earnings and well-being', *The Quarterly Journal of Economics* 2005; 120 (3): 963–1002.

18. Ferrer-i-Carbonell, A., 'Income and well-being: an empirical analysis of the comparison income effect', *Journal of Public Economics* 2005; 89 (5): 997–1019.

19. Brooks, D., 'The epidemic of worry', *New York Times* 25 October 2016.

20. Greenfeld, L., 'The maddening of America', *Project Syndicate* 25 July 2013.

21. Manger, W., 'The anxiety epidemic sweeping Britain – are you at risk and what can you do?' *Daily Mirror* 6 June 2016.

22. Kelley, M., 'An anxiety epidemic is sweeping the US', *The Atlantic* 2012.

23. Angell, M., 'The epidemic of mental illness: Why', *New York Review of Books* 2011; 58 (11): 20–22.

24. Hutton, W., 'Only fundamental social change can defeat the anxiety epidemic', *Observer* 8 May 2016.

25. Angell, M., 'The epidemic of mental illness: Why', *New York Review of Books* 2011; 58 (11): 20–22.

26. Swinton Insurance, 'No place like home. Manchester', reported on Mumsnet.com, 19 November 2013.

27. Findley, A., 'Do you do a special clean up for visitors or just go with the flow?' *Apartment Therapy*, http://www.apartmenttherapy.com/do-quickly-clean-for-guests-179438, 2012.

28. Holt-Lunstad, J., Smith, T. B. and Layton, J.B., 'Social relationships and mortality risk: a meta-analytic review', *PLoS Medicine* 2010; 7 (7): e1000316.

29. Kiecolt-Glaser, J. K., Loving, T. J., Stowell, J. R., et al., 'Hostile marital interactions, proinflammatory cytokine production, and

wound healing', *Archives of General Psychiatry* 2005; 62 (12): 1377–84.

30. Cohen, S., 'Keynote presentation at the Eight International Congress of Behavioral Medicine: the Pittsburgh common cold studies: psychosocial predictors of susceptibility to respiratory infectious illness', *International Journal of Behavioral Medicine* 2005; 12 (3): 123–31.

31. Russ, T. C., Stamatakis, E., Hamer, M., et al., 'Association between psychological distress and mortality: individual participant pooled analysis of 10 prospective cohort studies', *British Medical Journal* 2012; 345: e4933.

32. Holahan, C. J. and Moos, R. H., 'Social support and psychological distress: a longitudinal analysis', *Journal of Abnormal Psychology* 1981; 90 (4): 365–70.

33. Saltzman, K. M. and Holahan, C. J., 'Social support, self-efficacy, and depressive symptoms: an integrative model', *Journal of Social & Clinical Psychology* 2002; 21 (3): 309–22.

34. Layard, R., *Happiness: Lessons from a New Science*. London: Allen Lane, 2005.

35. Rodríguez-Pose, A. and von Berlepsch, V., 'Social capital and individual happiness in Europe', *Journal of Happiness Studies* 2014; 15 (2): 357–86.

36. Powdthavee, N., 'Putting a price tag on friends, relatives, and neighbours: using surveys of life satisfaction to value social relationships', *Journal of Socio-Economics* 2008; 37 (4): 1459–80.

37. Lancee, B. and Van de Werfhorst, H. G., 'Income inequality and participation: a comparison of 24 European countries', *Social Science Research* 2012; 41 (5): 1166–78.

38. Daly, M., *Killing the Competition: Economic Inequality and Homicide*. New Brunswick, NJ: Transaction, 2016.

39. Paskov, M. and Dewilde, C., 'Income inequality and solidarity in Europe', *Research in Social Stratification and Mobility* 2012; 30 (4): 415–32.

40. Uslaner, E. M. and Brown, M., 'Inequality, trust, and civic engagement', *American Politics Research* 2005; 33 (6): 868–94.

41. Sonenscher, M., *Sans-culottes: An Eighteenth-century Emblem in the French Revolution*. Princeton, NJ: Princeton University Press, 2008.

42. Diamond, J. M., *The World Until Yesterday: What Can We Learn From Traditional Societies?* New York: Viking, 2012.

43. Scott, J. C., *Against the Grain*. New Haven, Conn.: Yale University Press, 2017.

44. Boehm, C., *Hierarchy in the Forest: The Evolution of Egalitarian Behavior*. Cambridge, Mass.: Harvard University Press, 1999.

45. Karnehed, N. E., Rasmussen, F., Hemmingsson, T. and Tynelius, P., 'Obesity in young adulthood is related to social mobility among Swedish men', *Obesity* 2008; 16 (3): 654–8.

46. Harper, B., 'Beauty, stature and the labour market: a British cohort study', *Oxford Bulletin of Economics and Statistics* 2000; 62 (s1): 771–800.

47. Bourdieu, P., *Distinction: A Social Critique of the Judgement of Taste*. London: Routledge, 1984.

48. Veblen, T., *The Theory of The Leisure Class*. Oxford: Oxford University Press, 2007.

49. Heffetz, O., 'A test of conspicuous consumption: visibility and income elasticities', *Review of Economics and Statistics* 2011; 93 (4): 1101–17.

50. Wilkinson, R. and Pickett, K., 'The poison of inequality was behind last summer's riots', *Guardian* 5 August 2012.

51. Carroll, D., Ring, C., Hunt, K., Ford, G. and Macintyre, S., 'Blood pressure reactions to stress and the prediction of future blood pressure: effects of sex, age, and socioeconomic position', *Psychosomatic Medicine* 2003; 65 (6): 1058–64.

52. Matthews, K. A., Katholi, C. R., McCreath, H., et al., 'Blood pressure reactivity to psychological stress predicts hypertension in the CARDIA study', *Circulation* 2004; 110 (1): 74–8.

53. Dressler, W. W., 'Modernization, stress, and blood pressure: new directions in research', *Human Biology* 1999: 583–605.

54. Rodriguez, B. L., Labarthe, D. R., Huang, B. and Lopez-Gomez, J., 'Rise of blood pressure with age. New evidence of population differences', *Hypertension* 1994; 24 (6): 779–85.

55. Waldron, I., Nowotarski, M., Freimer, M., Henry, J. P., Post, N. and Witten, C., 'Cross-cultural variation in blood pressure: a quantitative analysis of the relationships of blood pressure to cultural characteristics, salt consumption and body weight', *Social Science & Medicine* 1982; 16 (4): 419–30.

56. Timio, M., Verdecchia, P., Venanzi, S., et al., 'Age and blood pressure changes. A 20-year follow-up study in nuns in a secluded order', *Hypertension* 1988; 12 (4): 457–61.

57. Layte, R. and Whelan, C., 'Who feels inferior? A test of the status anxiety hypothesis of social inequalities in health', *European Sociological Review* 2014; 30: 525–35.

58. Dickerson, S. S. and Kemeny, M. E., 'Acute stressors and cortisol responses: a theoretical integration and synthesis of laboratory research', *Psychological Bulletin* 2004; 130 (3): 355–91.

59. Pickett, K. E. and Wilkinson, R. G., 'Inequality: an underacknowledged source of mental illness and distress', *British Journal of Psychiatry* 2010; 197: 426–8.

60. Ribeiro, W. S., Bauer, A., Andrade, M. C. R., et al., 'Income inequality and mental illness-related morbidity and resilience: a systematic review and meta-analysis', *Lancet Psychiatry* 2017; 4 (7): 554–62.

61. Summerfield, D. A., 'Income inequality and mental health problems', *British Journal of Psychiatry* 2011; 198 (3): 239.

62. Demyttenaere, K., Bruffaerts, R., Posada-Villa, J., et al., 'Prevalence, severity, and unmet need for treatment of mental disorders in the World Health Organization World Mental Health Surveys', *Journal of the American Medical Association* 2004; 291 (21): 2581–90.

63. Australian Bureau of Statistics, *National Health Survey, Mental Health, 2001*. Canberra: Australian Bureau of Statistics, 2003.

64. WHO International Consortium in Psychiatric Epidemiology, 'Cross-national comparisons of the prevalences and correlates of mental disorders', *Bulletin of the World Health Organization* 2000; 78 (4): 413–26.

65. Office for National Statistics, *Psychiatric Morbidity Among Adults Living in Private Households, 2000*. London: HMSO, 2001.

66. Case, A. and Deaton, A., 'Rising morbidity and mortality in midlife among white non-Hispanic Americans in the 21st century', *Proceedings of the National Academy of Sciences of the USA* 2015; 112 (49): 15078–83.

67. Minton, J. W., Pickett, K. E., Shaw, R., Vanderbloemen, L., Green, M. and McCartney, G. M., 'Two cheers for a small giant? Why we need better ways of seeing data: a commentary on: "Rising morbidity and mortality in midlife among white non-Hispanic Americans in the 21st century"', *International Journal of Epidemiology* 2016; doi: 10.1093/ije/dyw095.

68. Brugha, T. S., 'The end of the beginning: a requiem for the categorization of mental disorder?' *Psychological Medicine* 2002; 32 (7): 1149–54.

69. McManus, S., Meltzer, H., Brugha, T., Bebbington, P. and Jenkins, R., *Adult Psychiatric Morbidity in England, 2007: Results of a Household Survey*. Leeds: NHS Information Centre, 2009.

70. Johnson, S. L., Leedom, L. J. and Muhtadie, L., 'The dominance behavioral system and psychopathology: evidence from self-report, observational, and biological studies', *Psychological Bulletin* 2012; 138 (4): 692–743.

71. Dabbs, J. M., Carr, T. S., Frady, R. L. and Riad, J. K., 'Testosterone, crime, and misbehavior among 692 male prison inmates', *Personality and Individual Differences* 1995; 18 (5): 627–33.

72. Layte, R., 'The association between income inequality and mental health: testing status anxiety, social capital, and neo-materialist explanations', *European Sociological Review* 2012; 28 (4): 498–511.

73. Elgar, F. J. and Aitken, N., 'Income inequality, trust and homicide in 33 countries', *European Journal of Public Health* 2011; 21 (2): 241–6.

74. Brunner, E., Marmot, M., Canner, R., Beksinska, M., Davey Smith, G. and O'Brien, J., 'Childhood social circumstances and psychosocial and behavioural factors as determinants of plasma fibrinogen', *Lancet* 1996; 347 (9007): 1008–13.

75. Staugaard, S. R., 'Threatening faces and social anxiety: a literature review', *Clinical Psychology Review* 2010; 30 (6): 669–90.

76. Gilbert, P., *The Compassionate Mind*. London: Constable, 2010.

77. World Health Organization. Fact sheet - depression: http://www.who.int/mediacentre/factsheets/fs369/en/, 2017.

78. Gilbert, P., Broomhead, C., Irons, C., et al., 'Development of a striving to avoid inferiority scale', *British Journal of Social Psychology* 2007; 46 (Pt 3): 633–48.

79. Gilbert, P., McEwan, K., Bellew, R., Mills, A. and Gale, C., 'The dark side of competition: how competitive behaviour and striving to avoid inferiority are linked to depression, anxiety, stress and self-harm', *Psychology & Psychotherapy* 2009; 82 (Pt 2): 123–36.

80. Brooks, F., Magnusson, J., Klemera, E., et al., *HBSC England National Report: Health Behaviour in School-aged Children (HBSC)*. World Health Organization Collaborative Cross National Study, University of Hertfordshire, 2015.

81. Martin, G., Swannell, S. V., Hazell, P. L., Harrison, J. E. and Taylor, A. W., 'Self-injury in Australia: a community survey', *Medical Journal of Australia* 2010; 193 (9): 506–10.

82. Muehlenkamp, J. J., Claes, L., Havertape, L. and Plener, P. L., 'International prevalence of adolescent non-suicidal self-injury and deliberate self-harm', *Child & Adolescent Psychiatry & Mental Health* 2012; 6 (10): 1–9.

83. Gilbert, P., McEwan, K., Irons, C., et al., 'Self-harm in a mixed clinical population: the roles of self-criticism, shame, and social rank', *British Journal of Clinical Psychology* 2010; 49 (Pt 4): 563–76.

84. Eisenberger, N. I., Lieberman, M. D. and Williams, K. D., 'Does rejection hurt? An fMRI study of social exclusion', *Science* 2003; 302 (5643): 290–92.

85. DeWall, C. N., MacDonald, G., Webster, G. D., et al., 'Acetaminophen reduces social pain: behavioral and neural evidence', *Psychological Science* 2010; 21 (7): 931–7.

86. Sherman, G. D., Lee, J. J., Cuddy, A. J., et al., 'Leadership is associated with lower levels of stress', *Proceedings of the National Academy of Sciences of the USA* 2012; 109 (44): 17903–7.

87. Wood, A. M., Boyce, C. J., Moore, S. C. and Brown, G. D., 'An evolutionary based social rank explanation of why low income predicts mental distress: a 17 year cohort study of 30,000 people', *Journal of Affective Disorders* 2012; 136 (3): 882–8.

88. Wetherall, K., Daly, M., Robb, K. A., Wood, A. M. and O'Connor, R. C., 'Explaining the income and suicidality relationship: income rank is more strongly associated with suicidal thoughts and attempts than income', *Social Psychiatry & Psychiatric Epidemiology* 2015; 50 (6): 929–37.

89. Osafo Hounkpatin, H., Wood, A. M., Brown, G. D. A. and Dunn, G., 'Why does income relate to depressive symptoms? Testing the income rank hypothesis longitudinally', *Social Indicators Research* 2015; 124 (2): 637–55.

90. Daly, M., Boyce, C. and Wood, A., 'A social rank explanation of how money influences health', *Health Psychology* 2015; 34 (3): 222.

91. Elgar, F. J., De Clercq, B., Schnohr, C. W., et al, 'Absolute and relative family affluence and psychosomatic symptoms in adolescents', *Social Science & Medicine* 2013; 91: 25–31.

92. Bannink, R., Pearce, A. and Hope, S., 'Family income and young adolescents' perceived social position: associations with self-esteem

and life satisfaction in the UK Millennium Cohort Study', *Archives of Disease in Childhood* 2016; 101 (10): 917–21.

93. Melgar, N. and Rossi, M., 'A cross-country analysis of the risk factors for depression at the micro and macro level', *IDB Working Paper Series*. Inter-American Development Bank, 2010.

94. Steptoe, A., Tsuda, A., Tanaka, Y. and Wardle, J., 'Depressive symptoms, socio-economic background, sense of control, and cultural factors in university students from 23 countries', *International Journal of Behavioral Medicine* 2007; 14 (2): 97–107.

95. Cifuentes, M., Sembajwe, G., Tak, S., Gore, R., Kriebel, D. and Punnett, L. 'The association of major depressive episodes with income inequality and the human development index', *Social Science & Medicine* 2008; 67 (4): 529–39.

96. Messias, E., Eaton, W. W. and Grooms, A. N., 'Economic grand rounds: income inequality and depression prevalence across the United States: an ecological study', *Psychiatric Services* 2011; 62 (7): 710–12.

97. Fan, A. Z., Strasser, S., Zhang, X., et al., 'State-level socioeconomic factors are associated with current depression among US adults in 2006 and 2008', *Journal of Public Health & Epidemiology* 2011; 3 (10): 462–70.

98. Muramatsu, N., 'County-level income inequality and depression among older Americans', *Health Services Research* 2003; 38 (6p2): 1863–84.

99. Paskov, M. and Richards, L., 'Is social status inequality bad for the mental health of nations?' 3rd International European Social Survey Conference Blog Post, 11 July 2016, https://essconf2016.wordpress.com/2016/07/11/is-social-status-inequality-bad/.

100. Johnson, S. L. and Carver, C. S., 'The dominance behavioral system and manic temperament: motivation for dominance, self-perceptions of power, and socially dominant behaviors', *Journal of Affective Disorders* 2012; 142(1-3): 275–82.

101. Burns, J. K., Tomita, A. and Kapadia, A. S., 'Income inequality and schizophrenia: increased schizophrenia incidence in countries with high levels of income inequality', *International Journal of Social Psychiatry* 2014: 60 (2): 185–96.

102. Johnson, S. L., Wibbels, E. and Wilkinson, R., 'Economic inequality is related to cross-national prevalence of psychotic symptoms', *Social Psychiatry & Psychiatric Epidemiology* 2015; 50 (12): 1799–807.

103. Twenge, J. M., Zhang, L. and Im, C., 'It's beyond my control: a cross-temporal meta-analysis of increasing externality in locus of control, 1960–2002', *Personality & Social Psychology Review* 2004; 8 (3): 308–19.

104. Haushofer, J., 'The psychology of poverty: evidence from 43 countries', Massachusetts Instititute of Technology Working Paper, 2013, http://web.mit.edu/joha/www/publications/Haushofer_Psychology_of_Poverty/ 2013.09.14.pdf.

105. de Vries, R., Gosling, S. and Potter, J., 'Income inequality and personality: are less equal U.S. states less agreeable?' *Social Science & Medicine* 2011; 72 (12): 1978–85.

106. Paskov, M., Gërxhani, K. and Van der Werfhorst, G., 'Giving up on the Joneses? The relationship between income inequality and status-seeking', *European Sociological Review* 2016, doi: https://doi.org/ 10.1093/esr/jcw052.

107. Kawachi, I., Kennedy, B. P., Lochner, K. and Prothrow-Stith, D., 'Social capital, income inequality, and mortality', *American Journal of Public Health* 1997; 87 (9): 1491–8.

108. 'Local health outcomes predict Trumpward swings', *The Economist* 19 November 2016.

109. Darvas, Z. and Efstathiou, K., 'Income inequality boosted Trump vote', Bruegel, 2016, http://bruegel.org/2016/11/income-inequality-boosted-trump-vote/.

110. Barford, A., Dorling, D. and Pickett, K., 'Re-evaluating self-evaluation. A commentary on Jen, Jones, and Johnston (68:4, 2009)', *Social Science & Medicine* 2010; 70 (4): 496–7; discussion 98–500.

111. Abdallah, S., Thompson, S. and Marks, N., 'Estimating worldwide life satisfaction', *Ecological Economics* 2008; 65 (1): 35–47.

112. Loughnan, S., Kuppens, P., Allik, J., et al., 'Economic inequality is linked to biased self-perception', *Psychological Science* 2011; 22 (10): 1254–8.

113. Cross, K. P., 'Not can, but will college teaching be improved?' *New Directions for Higher Education* 1977; 17: 1–15.

114. Alicke, M. D. and Govorun, O., 'The better-than-average effect', in M. D. Alicke, D. Dunning and J. Krueger (eds.), *The Self in Social Judgment*. New York: Psychology Press, 2005, pp. 85–106.

115. Svenson, O., 'Are we all less risky and more skillful than our fellow drivers?' *Acta Psychologica* 1981; 47 (2): 143–8.

116. Hughes, B. L. and Beer, J. S., 'Protecting the self: the effect of social-evaluative threat on neural representations of self', *Journal of Cognitive Neuroscience* 2013; 25 (4): 613–22.

117. Campbell, W. K. and Sedikides, C., 'Self-threat magnifies the self-serving bias: a meta-analytic integration', *Review of General Psychology* 1999; 3 (1): 23–43.

118. Brown, J. D., 'Understanding the better than average effect: motives (still) matter', *Personality and Social Psychology Bulletin* 2012; 38 (2): 209–19.

119. Twenge, J. M. and Campbell, W. K., *The Narcissism Epidemic: Living in the Age of Entitlement.* New York: Simon and Schuster, 2009.

120. *Washington Post*-Kaiser Family Foundation. Poll, 2011, http://www.washingtonpost.com/wp-srv/politics/polls/postkaiserpoll_110211.html.

121. Twenge, J. M., Konrath, S., Foster, J. D., Campbell, W. K. and Bushman, B. J., 'Egos inflating over time: a cross-temporal meta-analysis of the Narcissistic Personality Inventory', *Journal of Personality* 2008; 76 (4): 875–902.

122. Piketty, T. and Saez, E., 'Income and wage inequality in the US 1913–2002', in A. Atkinson and T. Piketty (eds.), *Top Incomes Over The Twentieth Century.* Oxford: Oxford University Press, 2007.

123. Wilkinson, R. G. and Pickett, K. E., 'The enemy between us: the psychological and social costs of inequality', *European Journal of Social Psychology* 2017; 47: 11–24.

124. Martin, S. R., Côté, S. and Woodruff, T., 'Echoes of our upbringing: how growing up wealthy or poor relates to narcissism, leader behavior, and leader effectiveness', *Academy of Management Journal* 2016; 59 (6): 2157–77.

125. Schor, J. B., *The Overspent American: Why We Want What We Don't Need.* New York: HarperCollins, 1999.

126. Twenge, J. M., Campbell, W. K. and Freeman, E. C., 'Generational differences in young adults' life goals, concern for others, and civic orientation, 1966–2009', *Journal of Personality and Social Psychology* 2012; 102 (5): 1045–62.

127. Twenge, J. M. and Donnelly, K., 'Generational differences in American students' reasons for going to college, 1971–2014: the rise of extrinsic motives', *Journal of Social Psychology* 2016: 1–10.

128. Tanenbaum, L., *Catfight: Women and Competition.* New York: Seven Stories Press, 2002.

129. Patalay, P. and Fitzsimons, E., *Mental Ill-health Among Children of the New Century: Trends across Childhood with a Focus on Age 14.* London: Centre for Longitudinal Studies, 2017.

130. Bhatia, R., 'Why women aren't the only ones pressured into looking good any more as their male counterparts are now lurking closer than ever', *Daily Mail* 12 February 2012.

131. American Society of Plastic Surgeons, '2013 cosmetic plastic surgery statistics', *Plastic Surgery Statistics Report*, 2014, www.plasticsurgery.org.

132. American Society for Aesthetic Plastic Surgery, 'Quick facts: highlights of the ASAPS 2013 statistics on cosmetic surgery', 2014, www.surgery.org.

133. British Association of Aesthetic Plastic Surgeons, 'Britain sucks', 2014, http://baaps.org.uk/about-us/press-releases/1833-britain-sucks.

134. von Soest, T., Kvalem, I. L. and Wichstrom, L., 'Predictors of cosmetic surgery and its effects on psychological factors and mental health: a population-based follow-up study among Norwegian females', *Psychological Medicine* 2012; 42 (3): 617–26.

135. Sarwer, D. B., Zanville, H. A., LaRossa, D., et al., 'Mental health histories and psychiatric medication usage among persons who sought cosmetic surgery', *Plastic and Reconstructive Surgery* 2004; 114 (7): 1927–33.

136. Grubb, J., Exline, J., McCain, J. and Campbell, W. K., 'Of course we're narcissistic: emerging adult reactions to generational differences in trait narcissism and entitlement', Society for Personality and Social Psychology, 17th Annual Convention. San Diego, 2016.

137. Babiak, P. and Hare, R. D., *Snakes in Suits: When Psychopaths Go to Work*: New York: HarperCollins, 2007.

138. Ronson, J., *The Psychopath Test*. London: Picador, 2011.

139. Byrne, J. A., *Chainsaw: The Notorious Career of Al Dunlap In The Era of Profit-At-Any-Price*. New York: HarperBusiness, 1999.

140. Board, B. J. and Fritzon, K., 'Disordered personalities at work', *Psychology, Crime & Law* 2005; 11 (1): 17–32.

141. Bakan, J., *The Corporation: The Pathological Pursuit of Profit and Power*. New York: Simon and Schuster, 2003.

142. Blackburn, S., *Mirror, Mirror: The Uses and Abuses of Self-love*. Oxford: Princeton University Press, 2014.

143. Piff, P. K., Kraus, M. W., Côté, S., Cheng, B. H. and Keltner, D., 'Having less, giving more: the influence of social class on prosocial behavior', *Journal of Personality and Social Psychology* 2010; 99 (5): 771–84.

144. Stern, K., 'Why the rich don't give to charity', *The Atlantic* April 2013.

145. Piff, P. K., Stancato, D. M., Côté, S., Mendoza-Denton, R. and Keltner, D., 'Higher social class predicts increased unethical behavior', *Proceedings of the National Academy of Sciences* 2012; 109 (11): 4086–91.

146. Piff, P. K., 'Wealth and the inflated self: class, entitlement, and narcissism', *Personality & Social Psychology Bulletin* 2014; 40 (1): 34–43.

147. Côté, S., House, J. and Willer, R., 'High economic inequality leads higher-income individuals to be less generous', *Proceedings of the National Academy of Sciences of the USA* 2015; 112 (52): 15838–43.

148. Paulhus, D. L., 'Interpersonal and intrapsychic adaptiveness of trait self-enhancement: a mixed blessing?' *Journal of Personality and Social Psychology* 1998; 74 (5): 1197.

149. Derue, D. S., Nahrgang, J.D., Wellman, N. and Humphrey, S. E., 'Trait and behavioral theories of leadership: an integration and meta-analytic test of their relative validity', *Personnel Psychology* 2011; 64 (1): 7–52.

150. De Waal, F. B., *Good Natured: The Origins of Right and Wrong in Humans and Other Animals*. Cambridge, Mass.: Harvard University Press, 1996.

151. Clark, M. E., *In Search of Human Nature*. London: Routledge, 2002.

152. Baron-Cohen, S., *Zero Degrees of Empathy: A New Theory of Human Cruelty*. London: Penguin, 2011.

153. Fiske, S. T., *Envy Up, Scorn Down: How Status Divides Us*. New York: Russell Sage Foundation, 2011.

154. Durante, F., Fiske, S. T., Kervyn, N., et al., 'Nations' income inequality predicts ambivalence in stereotype content: how societies mind the gap', *British Journal of Social Psychology* 2013; 52 (4): 726–46.

155. Uslaner, E. M., *Segregation and Mistrust: Diversity, Isolation, and Social Cohesion*. Cambridge: Cambridge University Press, 2012.

156. Alexander, B. K., *The Globalization of Addiction: A Study in Poverty of the Spirit*. Oxford: Oxford University Press, 2008.

157. Erikson, E. H., 'Identity and the life cycle: selected papers', *Psychological Issues* 1959.

158. Bourgois, P., 'Lumpen abuse: the human cost of righteous neoliberalism', *City & Society* 2011; 23 (1): 2–12.

159. Baumeister, R. F., *Escaping the Self: Alcoholism, Spirituality, Masochism, and Other Flights From the Burden of Selfhood*. New York: Basic Books, 1991.

160. Thompson, D., *The Fix*. London: Collins, 2013.

161. Barton, A. and Husk, K., ' "I don't really like the pub [. . .]": reflections on young people and pre-loading alcohol', *Drugs and Alcohol Today* 2014; 14 (2): 58–66.

162. McCreanor, T., Lyons, A., Moewaka Barnes, H., et al., 'Drink a 12 box before you go': pre-loading among young people in Aotearoa New Zealand. *Kōtuitui: New Zealand Journal of Social Sciences Online* 2015: 1–11.

163. Bolton, J. M., Robinson, J. and Sareen, J., 'Self-medication of mood disorders with alcohol and drugs in the National Epidemiologic Survey on Alcohol and Related Conditions', *Journal of Affective Disorders* 2009; 115 (3): 367–75.

164. Robinson, J., Sareen, J., Cox, B. J. and Bolton, J., 'Self-medication of anxiety disorders with alcohol and drugs: results from a nationally representative sample', *Journal of Anxiety Disorders* 2009; 23 (1): 38–45.

165. Galea, S., Ahern, J., Tracy, M. and Vlahov, D., 'Neighborhood income and income distribution and the use of cigarettes, alcohol, and marijuana', *American Journal of Preventive Medicine* 2007; 32 (6 Suppl): S195–S202.

166. Galea, S., Ahern, J., Vlahov, D., et al., 'Income distribution and risk of fatal drug overdose in New York City neighborhoods', *Drug & Alcohol Dependency* 2003; 70 (2): 139–48.

167. Elgar, F. J., Roberts, C., Parry-Langdon, N. and Boyce, W., 'Income inequality and alcohol use: a multilevel analysis of drinking and drunkenness in adolescents in 34 countries', *European Journal of Public Health* 2005; 15 (3): 245–50.

168. Cutright, P. and Fernquist, R. M., 'Predictors of per capita alcohol consumption and gender-specific liver cirrhosis mortality rates: thirteen European countries, circa 1970–1984 and 1995–2007', *OMEGA – Journal of Death and Dying* 2011; 62 (3): 269–83.

169. Dietze, P. M., Jolley, D. J., Chikritzhs, T. N., et al., 'Income inequality and alcohol attributable harm in Australia', *BMC Public Health* 2009; 9 (1): 70.

170. Karriker-Jaffe, K. J., Roberts, S. C. and Bond, J. 'Income inequality, alcohol use, and alcohol-related problems', *American Journal of Public Health* 2013; 103 (4): 649–56.

171. Pickett, K. E., Kelly, S., Brunner, E., Lobstein, T. and Wilkinson, R. G., 'Wider income gaps, wider waistbands? An ecological study of obesity and income inequality', *Journal of Epidemiology & Community Health* 2005; 59 (8): 670–74.

172. Bratanova, B., Loughnan, S., Klein, O., Claassen, A. and Wood, R., 'Poverty, inequality, and increased consumption of high calorie food: experimental evidence for a causal link', *Appetite* 2016; 100: 162–71.

173. Groesz, L. M., McCoy, S., Carl, J., et al., 'What is eating you? Stress and the drive to eat', *Appetite* 2012; 58 (2): 717–21.

174. Williams, R. J., Volberg, R. A. and Stevens, R. M. G., 'The population prevalence of problem gambling: methodological influences, standardized rates, jurisdictional differences and worldwide trends'. Ontario, Canada: Ontario Problem Gambling Research Centre & the Ontario Ministry of Health and Long Term Care, 2012.

175. Gentile, D., 'Pathological video-game use among youth ages 8 to 18. A national study', *Psychological Science* 2009; 20 (5): 594–602.

176. Gentile, D. A., Choo, H., Liau, A., et al., 'Pathological video game use among youths: a two-year longitudinal study', *Pediatrics* 2011; 127 (2): e319–e29.

177. Mentzoni, R. A., Brunborg, G. S., Molde, H., et al., 'Problematic video game use: estimated prevalence and associations with mental and physical health', *Cyberpsychology, Behavior, and Social Networking* 2011; 14 (10): 591–6.

178. Kuss, D. J., 'Internet gaming addiction: current perspectives', *Psychology Research and Behavior Management* 2013; 6: 125–37.

179. Metzner, R., 'Psychedelic, psychoactive, and addictive drugs and states of consciousness', in M. Earleywine (ed.), *Mind-altering Drugs: The Science of Subjective Experience*. New York: Oxford University Press, 2005, pp. 25–48.

180. Li, D. X. and Guindon, G. E., 'Income, income inequality and youth smoking in low- and middle-income countries', *Addiction* 2013; 108 (4): 799–808.

181. Lawson, N., *All Consuming*. London: Penguin, 2009.

182. Wallop, H., *Consumed*. London: Collins, 2013.

183. Fox, K., *Watching the English: The Hidden Rules of English Behaviour*. London: Hodder and Staughton, 2004.

184. Wallace, M. and Spanner, C., *Chav!: A User's Guide to Britain's New Ruling Class*. London: Random House, 2004.

185. Trentmann, F., *Empire of Things: How We Became a World of Consumers, From The Fifteenth Century to the Twenty-First*. London: Penguin, 2016.

186. Briggs, D., *Deviance and Risk on Holiday: An Ethnography of British Tourists in Ibiza*. New York: Springer, 2013.

187. James, O., *Affluenza*. London: Vermilion, 2007.

188. UNICEF Innocenti Research Centre, *Child Poverty in Perspective: An Overview of Child Well-being in Rich Countries*. Florence: Innocenti Report Card 7, 2007.

189. Pickett, K. E. and Wilkinson, R. G., 'Child wellbeing and income inequality in rich societies: ecological cross sectional study', *British Medical Journal* 2007; 335 (7629): 1080.

190. Pickett, K. E. and Wilkinson, R. G., 'The ethical and policy implications of research on income inequality and child well-being', *Pediatrics* 2015; 135 Suppl 2: S39–47.

191. Boseley, S., 'British children: poorer, at greater risk and more insecure', *Guardian* 14 February 2007.

192. Ipsos-Mori and Nairn, A., *Children's Well-being in UK, Sweden and Spain: The role of Inequality and Materialism*. London: UNICEF UK, 2011.

193. Kasser, T., *The High Price of Materialism*. Cambridge, Mass.: MIT Press, 2003.

194. Kasser, T., 'Cultural values and the well-being of future generations: a cross-national study', *Journal of Cross-Cultural Psychology* 2011; 42 (2): 206–15.

195. Twenge, J. M. and Kasser, T., 'Generational changes in materialism and work centrality, 1976–2007: associations with temporal changes in societal insecurity and materialistic role modeling', *Personality and Social Psychology Bulletin* 2013; 39 (7): 883–97.

196. Weale, S., 'English children among the unhappiest in the world at school due to bullying', *Guardian* 19 August 2015.

197. Monbiot, G., 'Materialism: a system that eats us from the inside out', *Guardian* 9 December 2013, https://www.theguardian.com/commentisfree/2013/dec/09/materialism-system-eats-us-from-inside-out.

198. Earwicker, R., 'The impact of problem debt on health – a literature review', Equity Action – the EU Joint Action Programme on Health Inequalities, 2014, http://www.equityaction-project.eu/.

199. Iacoviello, M., 'Household debt and income inequality, 1963–2003', *Journal of Money, Credit and Banking* 2008; 40 (5): 929–65.

200. Klein, N., *No Logo*. London: Flamingo, 2001.

201. Schor, J. and White, K. E., *Plenitude: The New Economics of True Wealth*. New York: Penguin Press, 2010.

202. Skidelsky, E. and Skidelsky, R., *How Much is Enough?: Money and the Good Life*. London: Penguin, 2012.

203. Costanza, R., 'How to build a lagomist economy', *Guardian* 6 April 2015, https://www.theguardian.com/sustainable-business/2015/apr/06/lagomist-economy-consumerism-quality-of-life.

204. Scheff, T. J., 'Shame and the social bond: a sociological theory', *Sociological Theory* 2000; 18 (1): 84–99.

205. Lewis, H. B., 'Shame and guilt in neurosis', *Psychoanalytic Review* 1971; 58 (3): 419.

206. Nathanson, D. L., *The Many Faces of Shame*. New York: Guilford Press, 1987.

207. Dunbar, R. I. M., 'Brains on two legs: group size and the evolution of intelligence', in F. B. de Waal (ed.), *Tree of Origin: What Primate Behavior Can Tell Us About Human Social Evolution*. Cambridge, Mass.: Harvard University Press, 2001.

208. Dunbar, R. I. M. and Shultz, S., 'Evolution in the social brain', *Science* 2007; 317 (5843): 1344–7.

209. MacLean, E. L., Sandel, A. A., Bray, J., et al., 'Group size predicts social but not nonsocial cognition in lemurs', *PLoS One* 2013; 8 (6): e66359.

210. Sahlins, M., *Stone Age Economics*. London: Routledge, 2003.

211. Hobbes, T., *Leviathan*. Oxford: Oxford University Press, 1998.

212. Richmond, B. G. and Jungers, W. L., 'Size variation and sexual dimorphism in *Australopithecus afarensis* and living hominoids', *Journal of Human Evolution* 1995; 29 (3): 229–45.

213. Mitani, J. C., Gros-Louis, J. and Richards, A. F., 'Sexual dimorphism, the operational sex ratio, and the intensity of male competition in polygynous primates', *The American Naturalist* 1996; 147 (6): 966–80.

214. Sapolsky, R. M., *Why Zebras Don't Get Ulcers: The Acclaimed Guide To Stress, Stress-Related Diseases, And Coping*. New York: Henry Holt, 2004.

215. Woodburn, J., 'Egalitarian societies', *Man* 1982; 17: 431–51.

216. Erdal, D. and Whiten, A., 'Egalitarianism and Machiavellian intelligence in human evolution', in P. Mellars and K. Gibson (eds.), *Modelling the Early Human Mind*. Cambridge: McDonald Institute Monographs, 1996.

217. Boehm, C., 'Egalitarian behavior and reverse dominance hierarchy', *Current Anthropology* 1993; 34: 227–54.

218. Boehm, C., *Moral Origins: The Evolution of Virtue, Altruism, and Shame*. New York: Basic Books, 2012.

219. Fehr, E., Bernhard, H. and Rockenbach, B., 'Egalitarianism in young children', *Nature* 2008; 454 (7208): 1079.

220. Gintis, H., Van Schaik, C., Boehm, C., et al., 'Zoon politikon: the evolutionary origins of human political systems', *Current Anthropology* 2015; 56 (3): 340–41.

221. Erdal, D., Whiten, A., Boehm, C. and Knauft, B., *On Human Egalitarianism: An Evolutionary Product of Machiavellian Status Escalation?* Chicago: University of Chicago Press, 1994.

222. Price, T. D. and Feinman, G. M., *Foundations of Social Inequality.* New York: Springer Science & Business Media, 1995.

223. Price T. D. and Bar-Yosef, O., 'Traces of inequality at the origins of agriculture in the ancient Near East', in T. D. Price and G. M. Feinman (eds.), *Pathways to Power.* New York: Springer, 2010, pp. 147–68.

224. Bowles, S., Smith, E. A. and Borgerhoff Mulder, M., 'The emergence and persistence of inequality in premodern societies: introduction to the special section', *Current Anthropology* 2010; 51 (1): 7–17.

225. Hastorf, C. A., *Agriculture and the Onset of Political Inequality before the Inka.* Cambridge: Cambridge University Press, 1993.

226. Brosnan, S. F. and de Waal, F. B., 'Evolution of responses to (un) fairness', *Science* 2014; 346 (6207): 1251776.

227. Naito, T. and Washizu, N., 'Note on cultural universals and variations of gratitude from an East Asian point of view', *International Journal of Behavioral Science* 2015; 10 (2): 1–8.

228. McCullough, M. E., Kimeldorf, M. B. and Cohen, A. D., 'An adaptation for altruism: the social causes, social effects, and social evolution of gratitude', *Current Directions in Psychological Science* 2008; 17 (4): 281–5.

229. Mauss, M. and Halls, W. D., *The Gift: Forms and Functions of Exchange in Archaic Societies.* New York: W. W. Norton & Co., 1954.

230. Oosterbeek, H., Sloof, R. and Van De Kuilen, G., 'Cultural differences in ultimatum game experiments: evidence from a meta-analysis', *Experimental Economics* 2004; 7 (2): 171–88.

231. Frank, R. H., *Passions Within Reason: The Strategic Role of the Emotions.* New York: W. W. Norton & Co., 1988.

232. Fehr, E. and Gachter, S., 'Altruistic punishment in humans', *Nature* 2002; 415 (6868): 137–40.

233. Elgar, F. J., Craig, W., Boyce, W., Morgan, A. and Vella-Zarb, R., 'Income inequality and school bullying: multilevel study of adolescents in 37 countries', *Journal of Adolescent Health* 2009; 45 (4): 351–9.

234. DeBruine, L. M., Jones, B. C., Crawford, J. R., Welling, L. L. and Little, A. C., 'The health of a nation predicts their mate preferences: cross-cultural variation in women's preferences for masculinized male faces', *Proceedings of the Royal Society of London B: Biological Sciences* 2010; 277 (1692): 2405–10.

235. Brooks, R., Scott, I. M., Maklakov, A. A., et al., 'National income inequality predicts women's preferences for masculinized faces better than health does', *Proceedings of the Royal Society of London B: Biological Sciences* 2011; 278 (1707): 810–12.

236. Brooks, R., Scott, I. M., Maklakov, A. A., et al., 'National income inequality predicts women's preferences for masculinized faces better than health does', *Proceedings of the Royal Society of London B: Biological Sciences* 2011; 278 (1707): 810–12; discussion 13–14.

237. Kim, D. A., Benjamin, E. J., Fowler, J. H. and Christakis, N. A., 'Social connectedness is associated with fibrinogen level in a human social network', *Proceedings of the Royal Society of London B: Biological Sciences* 2016; 283: 20160958.

238. Wilkinson, G. S., 'Reciprocal altruism in bats and other mammals', *Ethology and Sociobiology* 1988; 9 (2–4): 85–100.

239. Hauser, M. D., Chen, M. K., Chen, F. and Chuang, E., 'Give unto others: genetically unrelated cotton-top tamarin monkeys preferentially give food to those who altruistically give food back', *Proceedings of the Royal Society of London B: Biological Sciences* 2003; 270 (1531): 2363–70.

240. Kolominsky, Y., Igumnov, S. and Drozdovitch, V., 'The psychological development of children from Belarus exposed in the prenatal period to radiation from the Chernobyl atomic power plant', *Journal of Child Psychology and Psychiatry* 1999; 40 (2): 299–305.

241. Provençal, N. and Binder, E. B., 'The effects of early life stress on the epigenome: from the womb to adulthood and even before', *Experimental Neurology* 2015; 268: 10–20.

242. Anacker, C., O'Donnell, K. J. and Meaney, M. J., 'Early life adversity and the epigenetic programming of hypothalamic-pituitary-adrenal function', *Dialogues in Clinical Neuroscience* 2014; 16 (3): 321.

243. Lutz, P.-E., Almeida, D. M., Fiori, L. and Turecki, G., 'Childhood maltreatment and stress-related psychopathology: the epigenetic memory hypothesis', *Current Pharmaceutical Design* 2015; 21 (11): 1413–17.

244. Golldack, D., Lüking, I. and Yang, O., 'Plant tolerance to drought and salinity: stress regulating transcription factors and their

functional significance in the cellular transcriptional network', *Plant Cell Reports* 2011; 30 (8): 1383–91.

245. Slavich, G. M. and Cole, S. W., 'The emerging field of human social genomics', *Clinical Psychological Science* 2013; 1 (3): 331–48.

246. Sapolsky, R. M., 'Stress, stress-related disease, and emotional regulation', in J. J. Gross (ed.), *Handbook of Emotion Regulation*. New York: Guilford Press, 2007, pp. 606–15.

247. Eckenrode, J., Smith, E. G., McCarthy, M. E. and Dineen, M., 'Income inequality and child maltreatment in the United States', *Pediatrics* 2014; 133 (3): 454–61.

248. Yehuda, R., Daskalakis, N. P., Bierer, L. M., et al., 'Holocaust exposure induced intergenerational effects on FKBP5 methylation', *Biological Psychiatry* 2016; 80 (5): 372–80.

249. McGuinness, D., McGlynn, L. M., Johnson, P. C., et al., 'Socioeconomic status is associated with epigenetic differences in the pSoBid cohort', *International Journal of Epidemiology* 2012; 41 (1): 151–60.

250. Tung, J., Barreiro, L. B., Johnson, Z. P., et al., 'Social environment is associated with gene regulatory variation in the rhesus macaque immune system', *Proceedings of the National Academy of Sciences of the USA* 2012; 109 (17): 6490–95.

251. Sapolsky, R. M., Romero, L. M. and Munck, A. U., 'How do glucocorticoids influence stress responses? Integrating permissive, suppressive, stimulatory, and preparative actions', *Endocrine Reviews* 2000; 21 (1): 55–89.

252. Sen, A., 'Poor, relatively speaking', *Oxford Economic Papers* 1983: 153–69.

253. Walker, R., Kyomuhendo, G. B., Chase, E., et al., 'Poverty in global perspective: is shame a common denominator?' *Journal of Social Policy* 2013; 42 (2): 215–33.

254. Chance, M. R. A., 'Attention structure as the basis of primate rank orders', *Man* 1967; 2 (4): 503–18.

255. Pannozzo, P. L., Phillips, K. A., Haas, M. E. and Mintz, E. M., 'Social monitoring reflects dominance relationships in a small captive group of brown capuchin monkeys (*Cebus apella*)', *Ethology* 2007; 113 (9): 881–8.

256. Kalma, A., 'Hierarchisation and dominance assessment at first glance', *European Journal of Social Psychology* 1991; 21 (2): 165–81.

257. Brown, P. H., Bulte, E. and Zhang, X., 'Positional spending and status seeking in rural China', *Journal of Development Economics* 2011; 96 (1): 139–49.

258. Huberman, B. A., Loch, C. H. and Önçüler, A., 'Status as a valued resource', *Social Psychology Quarterly* 2004; 67 (1): 103–14.

259. Frey, B. S., 'Knight fever – towards an economics of awards', CESifo Working Paper No. 1468, IEW Working Paper No. 239, May 2005, https://ssrn.com/abstract=717302.

260. Runciman, W. G., *Relative Deprivation and Social Justice: A Study of Attitudes to Social Inequality in 20th Century England.* Berkeley, Calif.: University of California Press, 1966.

261. Sapolsky, R. M., *A Primate's Memoir: A Neuroscientist's Unconventional Life Among The Baboons.* New York: Simon and Schuster, 2007.

262. Gilligan, J., *Preventing Violence.* New York: Thames and Hudson, 2001.

263. Dawes, C. T., Fowler, J. H., Johnson, T., McElreath, R. and Smirnov, O., 'Egalitarian motives in humans', *Nature* 2007; 446 (7137): 794–6.

264. Keyes, C. L. M. and Waterman, M. B., 'Dimensions of well-being and mental health in adulthood', in M. H. Bornstein, L. Davidson, C. L. M. Keyes and K. A. Moore (eds.), *Crosscurrents in Contemporary Psychology. Well-Being: Positive Development Across the Life Course.* Mahwah, NJ: Lawrence Erlbaum Associates, 2003, pp. 477–97.

265. Russ, T. C., Stamatakis, E., Hamer, M., et al., 'Association between psychological distress and mortality: individual participant pooled analysis of 10 prospective cohort studies', *British Medical Journal* 2012; 345: e4933.

266. Johnson, B., The Third Margaret Thatcher Lecture, Centre for Policy Studies, 2013, http://www.cps.org.uk/events/q/date/2013/11/27/the-2013-margaret-thatcher-lecture-boris-johnson/.

267. Stiglitz, J. E., *The Price of Inequality: How Today's Divided Society Endangers Our Future.* New York: W. W. Norton & Co., 2012.

268. Krugman, P., 'Why inequality matters', *New York Times* 15 December 2013.

269. Cingano, F., 'Trends in income inequality and its impact on economic growth', OECD Social, Employment and Migration Working Papers, No. 163, OECD Publishing, 2014, http://dx.doi.org/10.1787/5jxrjncwxv6j-en.

270. Ostry, M. J. D., Berg, M. A. and Tsangarides, M. C. G., *Redistribution, Inequality, and Growth.* Washington, DC: International Monetary Fund, 2014.

271. Smith, G. D., 'Epidemiology, epigenetics and the "Gloomy Prospect": embracing randomness in population health research and practice', *International Journal of Epidemiology* 2011; 40 (3): 537–62.

272. Plato, *The Republic*. London: Penguin Classics, 3rd edition, 2007.

273. Holtzman, N. A., 'Genetics and social class', *Journal of Epidemiology and Community Health* 2002; 56 (7): 529–35.

274. Flynn, J. R., *Are We Getting Smarter? Rising IQ in the Twenty-First Century*. New York: Cambridge University Press, 2012.

275. Dhuey, E. and Lipscomb, S., 'What makes a leader? Relative age and high school leadership', *Economics of Education Review* 2008; 27 (2): 173–83.

276. Sprietsma, M., 'Effect of relative age in the first grade of primary school on long-term scholastic results: international comparative evidence using PISA 2003', *Education Economics* 2010; 18 (1): 1–32.

277. Baker, J. and Logan, A. J., 'Developmental contexts and sporting success: birth date and birthplace effects in national hockey league draftees 2000–2005', *British Journal of Sports Medicine* 2007; 41 (8): 515–17.

278. Cobley, S., Baker, J., Wattie, N. and McKenna, J., 'Annual age-grouping and athlete development', *Sports Medicine* 2009; 39 (3): 235–56.

279. Helsen, W. F., Van Winckel, J. and Williams, A. M., 'The relative age effect in youth soccer across Europe', *Journal of Sports Sciences* 2005; 23 (6): 629–36.

280. Vestberg, T., Gustafson, R., Maurex, L., Ingvar, M. and Petrovic, P., 'Executive functions predict the success of top-soccer players', *PLoS One* 2012; 7 (4): e34731.

281. Plomin, R., Asbury, K. and Dunn, J., 'Why are children in the same family so different? Nonshared environment a decade later', *The Canadian Journal of Psychiatry* 2001; 46 (3): 225–33.

282. Woollett, K. and Maguire, E. A., 'Acquiring "the Knowledge" of London's layout drives structural brain changes', *Current Biology* 2011; 21 (24–2): 2109–14.

283. Gaser, C. and Schlaug, G., 'Gray matter differences between musicians and nonmusicians', *Annals of the New York Academy of Sciences* 2003; 999: 514–17.

284. Draganski, B., Gaser, C., Kempermann, G., et al., 'Temporal and spatial dynamics of brain structure changes during extensive learning', *Journal of Neuroscience* 2006; 26 (23): 6314–17.

285. Mora, F., Segovia, G. and del Arco, A., 'Aging, plasticity and environmental enrichment: structural changes and neurotransmitter dynamics in several areas of the brain', *Brain Research Reviews* 2007; 55 (1): 78–88.

286. Boyke, J., Driemeyer, J., Gaser, C., Büchel, C. and May, A., 'Training-induced brain structure changes in the elderly', *Journal of Neuroscience* 2008; 28 (28): 7031–5.

287. Mahncke, H. W., Bronstone, A. and Merzenich, M. M., 'Brain plasticity and functional losses in the aged: scientific bases for a novel intervention', *Progress in Brain Research* 2006; 157: 81–109.

288. Hanson, J. L., Hair, N., Shen, D. G., et al., 'Family poverty affects the rate of human infant brain growth', *PLoS One* 2013; 8 (12): e80954.

289. Dickerson, A. and Popli, G. K., 'Persistent poverty and children's cognitive development: evidence from the UK Millennium Cohort Study', *Journal of the Royal Statistical Society: Series A (Statistics in Society)* 2016; 179 (2): 535–58.

290. Brooks-Gunn, J. and Duncan, G. J., 'The effects of poverty on children', *The Future of Children* 1997; 7 (2): 55–71.

291. Korenman, S., Miller, J. E. and Sjaastad, J. E., 'Long-term poverty and child development in the United States: Results from the NLSY', *Children and Youth Services Review* 1995; 17 (1–2): 127–55.

292. Kiernan, K. E. and Mensah, F. K., 'Poverty, maternal depression, family status and children's cognitive and behavioural development in early childhood: a longitudinal study', *Journal of Social Policy* 2009; 38 (4): 569–88.

293. Blair, C., Granger, D. A., Willoughby, M., et al., 'Salivary cortisol mediates effects of poverty and parenting on executive functions in early childhood', *Child Development* 2011; 82 (6): 1970–84.

294. Guo, G. and Harris, K. M., 'The mechanisms mediating the effects of poverty on children's intellectual development', *Demography* 2000; 37 (4): 431–47.

295. Ayoub, C., O'Connor, E., Rappolt-Schlictmann, G., et al., 'Cognitive skill performance among young children living in poverty: risk, change, and the promotive effects of Early Head Start', *Early Childhood Research Quarterly* 2009; 24 (3): 289–305.

296. Hart, B. and Risley, T. R., *Meaningful Differences in the Everyday Experience of Young American Children.* Baltimore, Md: Paul H. Brookes Publishing, 1995.

297. Heckman, J. J., 'Creating a more equal and productive Britain', Young Foundation Lecture, 2011, www.youngfoundation.org/files/images/Heckman_Lecture_19_May_2011.pdf.

298. Crawford, C., Macmillan, L. and Vignoles, A., 'When and why do initially high-achieving poor children fall behind?' *Oxford Review of Education* 2017; 43 (1): 88–108.

299. OECD, *Equity and Quality in Education Supporting Disadvantaged Students and Schools.* Paris: OECD Publishing, 2012, http://dx.doi.org/10.1787/9789264130852-en.

300. Burgess, S. and Greaves, E., 'Test scores, subjective assessment, and stereotyping of ethnic minorities', *Journal of Labor Economics* 2013; 31 (3): 535–76.

301. Ferguson, R. F., 'Teachers' perceptions and expectations and the Black–White test score gap', *Urban Education* 2003; 38 (4): 460–507.

302. Rosenthal, R. and Jacobson, L., 'Pygmalion in the classroom', *The Urban Review* 1968; 3 (1): 16–20.

303. Hanna, R. N. and Linden, L. L., 'Discrimination in grading', *American Economic Journal: Economic Policy* 2012; 4 (4): 146–68.

304. Reay, D., 'The zombie stalking English schools: social class and educational inequality', *British Journal of Educational Studies* 2006; 54 (3): 288–307.

305. Blanden, J., 'Essays on intergenerational mobility and its variation over time' [PhD Thesis], University of London, 2005.

306. Reay, D., *Miseducation: Inequality, Education and the Working Classes.* Bristol: Policy Press, 2017.

307. Bradley, R. H. and Corwyn, R. F., 'Socioeconomic status and child development', *Annual Review of Psychology* 2002; 53: 371–99.

308. Barnett, W. S., Jung, K., Yarosz, D. J., et al., 'Educational effects of the Tools of the Mind curriculum: a randomized trial', *Early Childhood Research Quarterly* 2008; 23 (3): 299–313.

309. Barnett, W. S. and Masse, L. N., 'Comparative benefit–cost analysis of the Abecedarian program and its policy implications', *Economics of Education Review* 2007; 26 (1): 113–25.

310. Heckman, J. J., 'Skill formation and the economics of investing in disadvantaged children', *Science* 2006; 312 (5782): 1900–902.

311. Heckman, J. J., 'The economics, technology, and neuroscience of human capability formation', *Proceedings of the National Academy of Sciences* 2007; 104 (33): 13250–55.

312. Magnuson, K. A., Ruhm, C. and Waldfogel, J., 'Does prekindergarten improve school preparation and performance?' *Economics of Education Review* 2007; 26 (1): 33–51.

313. Magnuson, K. A., Ruhm, C. and Waldfogel, J., 'The persistence of preschool effects: Do subsequent classroom experiences matter?' *Early Childhood Research Quarterly* 2007; 22 (1): 18–38.

314. Hoff, K. and Pandey, P., 'Belief systems and durable inequalities: an experimental investigation of Indian caste', Policy Research Working Paper. Washington, DC: World Bank, 2004.

315. Stroessner, S. and Good, C., 'Stereotype threat: an overview', www.diversity.arizona.edu/sites/diversity/files/stereotype_threat_overview.pdf.

316. Nguyen, H.-H. D. and Ryan, A. M., 'Does stereotype threat affect test performance of minorities and women? A meta-analysis of experimental evidence', *Journal of Applied Psychology* 2008; 93 (6); 1314–34.

317. Croizet, J.-C. and Dutrévis, M., 'Socioeconomic status and intelligence: why test scores do not equal merit', *Journal of Poverty* 2004; 8 (3): 91–107.

318. Steele, C. M. and Aronson, J., 'Stereotype threat and the intellectual test performance of African-Americans', *Journal of Personality and Social Psychology* 1995; 69: 797–811.

319. Davies, P. G., Spencer, S. J., Quinn, D. M. and Gerhardstein, R., 'Consuming images: how television commercials that elicit stereotype threat can restrain women academically and professionally', *Personality and Social Psychology Bulletin* 2002; 28 (12): 1615–28.

320. Hess, T. M., Auman, C., Colcombe, S. J. and Rahhal, T. A., 'The impact of stereotype threat on age differences in memory performance', *The Journals of Gerontology Series B: Psychological Sciences and Social Sciences* 2003; 58 (1): P3–P11.

321. Aronson, J., Lustina, M. J., Good, C., et al., 'When white men can't do math: necessary and sufficient factors in stereotype threat', *Journal of Experimental Social Psychology* 1999; 35 (1): 29–46.

322. Brown, R. P. and Pinel, E. C., 'Stigma on my mind: individual differences in the experience of stereotype threat', *Journal of Experimental Social Psychology* 2003; 39 (6): 626–33.

323. Blascovich, J., Spencer, S. J., Quinn, D. and Steele, C., 'African Americans and high blood pressure: the role of stereotype threat', *Psychological Science* 2001; 12 (3): 225–9.

324. Schmader, T., Johns, M. and Forbes, C., 'An integrated process model of stereotype threat effects on performance', *Psychological Review* 2008; 115 (2): 336.

325. Schmader, T. and Johns, M., 'Converging evidence that stereotype threat reduces working memory capacity', *Journal of Personality and Social Psychology* 2003; 85 (3): 440.

326. Damme, D. V., 'How closely is the distribution of skills related to countries' overall level of social inequality and economic prosperity?' *OECD Education Working Papers* 2014; 105.

327. OECD and Statistics Canada, *Literacy in the Information Age: Final Report of the International Adult Literacy Survey.* Paris: Organization for Economic Co-operation and Development, 2000.

328. Wilkinson, R. and Pickett, K. E., 'Health inequalities and the UK presidency of the EU', *Lancet* 2006; 367 (9517): 1126–8.

329. OECD, *OECD Skills Outlook 2013: First Results from the Survey of Adult Skills.* Paris: OECD Publishing, 2013.

330. OECD, *PISA 2009 Results, Volume V. Learning Trends: Changes in Student Performance Since 2000.* Paris: OECD, 2010.

331. Bird, P. K., 'Social gradients in child health and development in relation to income inequality. Who benefits from greater income equality?' [PhD Thesis], University of York, 2014.

332. Bradbury, B., Corak, M., Waldfogel, J. and Washbrook, E., 'Inequality during the early years: child outcomes and readiness to learn in Australia, Canada, United Kingdom, and United States', IZA [Institute for the Study of Labor] Discussion Paper No. 6120, 2011.

333. UNICEF Innocenti Research Centre, *Child Well-being in Rich Countries: A Comparative Overview.* Florence: Innocenti Report Card 11, 2013.

334. Elgar, F. J., Pickett, K. E., Pickett, W., et al., 'School bullying, homicide and income inequality: a cross-national pooled time series analysis', *International Journal of Public Health* 2013; 58 (2): 237–45.

335. Pickett, K. E., Mookherjee, J. and Wilkinson, R. G., 'Adolescent birth rates, total homicides, and income inequality in rich countries', *American Journal of Public Health* 2005; 95 (7): 1181–3.

336. UNICEF Innocenti Research Centre, *Fairness for Children. A League Table of Inequality in Child Well-being in Rich Countries.* Florence: UNICEF Innocenti Centre, 2016.

337. Corak, M., 'Income inequality, equality of opportunity, and intergenerational mobility', *Journal of Economic Perspectives* 2013; 27 (3): 79–102.

338. Krueger, A., 'The rise and consequences of inequality'. Presentation made to the Center for American Progress, 12 January 2012. Available at http://www.americanprogress. org/events/2012/01/12/17181/ the-rise-and-consequences-of-inequality.

339. Aaronson, D. and Mazumder, B., 'Intergenerational economic mobility in the United States, 1940 to 2000', *Journal of Human Resources* 2008; 43 (1): 139–72.

340. Blanden, J., Goodman, A., Gregg, P. and Machin, S., *Changes in Intergenerational Mobility in Britain*. Bristol: University of Bristol, Centre for Market and Public Organisation, 2001.

341. Corak, M., 'Inequality from generation to generation: the United States in comparison', IZA [Institute for the Study of Labor] Discussion Paper No. 9929, 2016.

342. Evans, G. W. and English, K., 'The environment of poverty: multiple stressor exposure, psychophysiological stress, and socioemotional adjustment', *Child Development* 2002; 73 (4): 1238–48.

343. McLoyd, V. C., 'The impact of economic hardship on black families and children: psychological distress, parenting, and socioemotional development', *Child Development* 1990; 61 (2): 311–46.

344. McLoyd, V. C. and Wilson, L., 'Maternal behavior, social support, and economic conditions as predictors of distress in children', *New Directions for Child Development* 1990 (46): 49–69.

345. Garrett, P., Ng'andu, N. and Ferron, J., 'Poverty experiences of young children and the quality of their home environments', *Child Development* 1994; 65 (2 Spec No): 331–45.

346. Levine, A. S., Frank, R. H. and Dijk, O., 'Expenditure cascades', *SSRN Electronic Journal* Sept 2010; 1.

347. Bowles, S. and Park Y., 'Emulation, inequality, and work hours: was Thorstein Veblen right?' *The Economic Journal* 2005; 115: F397–F412.

348. Simmons, R. G. and Rosenberg, M., 'Functions of children's perceptions of the stratification system', *American Sociological Review* 1971; 36: 235–49.

349. Tudor, J. F., 'The development of class awareness in children', *Social Forces* 1971; 49: 470–76.

350. Dorling, D., 'Danny Dorling on education and inequality', *Times Higher Education* 25 September 2014.

351. Popham, F., 'Deprivation is a relative concept? Absolutely!', *Journal of Epidemiology and Community Health* 2015; 69 (3): 199–200.

352. Joseph Rowntree Foundation, *UK Poverty 2017: A Comprehensive Analysis of Poverty Trends and Figures*. York: Joseph Rowntree Foundation, 2017.

353. Child Poverty Action Group, 'Child poverty facts and figures', 2014. Retrieved from http://www.cpag.org.uk/child-poverty-facts-and-figures.

354. Rank, M. R. and Hirschl, T. A., 'The likelihood of experiencing relative poverty over the life course', *PLoS One* 2015; 10 (7): e0133513.

355. US Census Bureau, *Current Population Survey Annual Social and Economic Supplement*. Washington, DC: US Census Bureau, 2016.

356. Siddiqi, A., Kawachi, I., Berkman, L., Hertzman, C. and Subramanian, S. V., 'Education determines a nation's health, but what determines educational outcomes? A cross-national comparative analysis', *Journal of Public Health Policy* 2012; 33 (1): 1–15.

357. Benn, M. and Millar, F., *A Comprehensive Future: Quality and Equality For All Our Children*. London: Compass, 2006.

358. OECD, *Improving Schools in Sweden: An OECD Perspective*. Paris: OECD, 2015, http://www.oecd.org/edu/school/improving-schools-in-sweden-an-oecd-perspective.htm.

359. Elias, N. and Jephcott, E., *The Civilizing Process*. Oxford: Blackwell, 1982.

360. Erickson, C., *To the Scaffold: The Life of Marie Antoinette*. London: Macmillan, 2004.

361. Ashenburg, K., *The Dirt on Clean: An Unsanitized History*. Toronto: Vintage Canada, 2010.

362. Szreter, S., 'Rapid economic growth and "the four Ds" of disruption, deprivation, disease and death: public health lessons from nineteenth-century Britain for twenty-first-century China?' *Tropical Medicine & International Health* 1999; 4 (2): 146–52.

363. Hanley, L., *Respectable: Crossing the Class Divide*. London: Allen Lane, 2016.

364. Hanson, W., *The Bluffer's Guide to Etiquette*. London: Bluffer's, 2014.

365. Crompton, R., 'Consumption and class analysis', *The Sociological Review* 1997; 44 (1 suppl): 113–32.

366. Deutsch, N. L. and Theodorou, E., 'Aspiring, consuming, becoming: youth identity in a culture of consumption', *Youth & Society* 2010; 42 (2): 229–54.

367. Institute for Public Policy Research, 'Modern women marrying men of the same or lower social class', IPPR, 5 April 2012.

368. Merrill, D. M., *Mothers-in-law and Daughters-in-law: Understanding the Relationship and What Makes Them Friends or Foe.* Westport, Conn.: Greenwood Publishing Group, 2007.

369. Neumann, J., *Poor Kids*, BBC1, 7 June 2011.

370. Tippett, N. and Wolke, D., Socioeconomic status and bullying: a meta-analysis', *American Journal of Public Health* 2014; 104 (6): e48–e59.

371. Odgers, C. L., Donley, S., Caspi, A., Bates, C. J. and Moffitt, T. E., 'Living alongside more affluent neighbors predicts greater involvement in antisocial behavior among low-income boys', *Journal of Child Psychology & Psychiatry* 2015; 56 (10): 1055–64.

372. Goldstein, R., Almenberg, J., Dreber, A., et al., 'Do more expensive wines taste better? Evidence from a large sample of blind tastings', *Journal of Wine Economics* 2008; 3 (1): 1–9.

373. Atkinson, W., 'The context and genesis of musical tastes: omnivorousness debunked, Bourdieu buttressed', *Poetics* 2011; 39 (3): 169–86.

374. Savage, M., *Social Class in the 21st Century.* London: Penguin, 2015.

375. Hobsbawm, E., *Fractured Times: Culture and Society in the Twentieth Century.* London: Little, Brown, 2013.

376. Toronyi-Lalic, I., 'Sceptic's Sistema', *Classical Music* June 2012.

377. Szlendak, T. and Karwacki, A., 'Do the Swedes really aspire to sense and the Portuguese to status? Cultural activity and income gap in the member states of the European Union', *International Sociology* 2012; 27 (6): 807–26.

378. Brown, R., *Prejudice: Its Social Psychology.* Chichester: John Wiley & Sons, 2011.

379. Prandy, K., 'The revised Cambridge scale of occupations', *Sociology* 1990; 24 (4): 629–55.

380. Sayer, A., *The Moral Significance of Class.* Cambridge: Cambridge University Press, 2005.

381. de Tocqueville, A., *Democracy in America.* London: Penguin, 2003.

382. Child Rights International Network, *Minimum Ages of Criminal Responsibility Around the World,* 2017, https://www.crin.org/en/home/ages.

383. Rifkin, J., *The Empathic Civilization: The Race to Global Consciousness in a World in Crisis.* New York: Penguin, 2009.

384. Major, J., *Today,* 24 November 1990.

385. Ross, L., 'The intuitive psychologist and his shortcomings: distortions in the attribution process', *Advances in Experimental Social Psychology* 1977; 10: 173–220.

386. Jones, O., *Chavs: The Demonization of the Working Class*. London: Verso Books, 2012.

387. Jayaratne, T. E., Gelman, S. A., Feldbaum, M., et al., 'The perennial debate: nature, nurture, or choice? Black and white Americans' explanations for individual differences', *Review of General Psychology* 2009; 13 (1): 24–33.

388. Christensen, K. D., Jayaratne, T., Roberts, J., Kardia, S. and Petty, E., 'Understandings of basic genetics in the United States: results from a national survey of black and white men and women', *Public Health Genomics* 2010; 13 (7–8): 467–76.

389. Jorde, L. B. and Wooding, S. P., 'Genetic variation, classification and "race"', *Nature Genetics* 2004; 36: S28–S33.

390. Olalde, I., Allentoft, M. E., Sanchez-Quinto, F., et al., 'Derived immune and ancestral pigmentation alleles in a 7,000-year-old Mesolithic European', *Nature* 2014; 507 (7491): 225–8.

391. Montagu, A., *Man's Most Dangerous Myth: The Fallacy of Race*. Lanham, Md: AltaMira Press, 2001.

392. Kubiszewski, I., Costanza, R., Franco, C., et al., 'Beyond GDP: measuring and achieving global genuine progress', *Ecological Economics* 2013; 93: 57–68.

393. Cutler, D., Deaton, A. and Lleras-Muney, A., 'The determinants of mortality', *Journal of Economic Perspectives* 2006; 20 (3): 97–120.

394. Jackson, T., *Prosperity Without Growth. Economics for a Finite Planet*. Abingdon: Earthscan, 2009.

395. Hansen, J., Sato, M., Kharecha, P., et al., 'Target atmospheric CO_2: where should humanity aim?' *Open Atmospheric Science Journal* 2008; 2: 217–31.

396. World Health Organization. *Quantitative Risk Assessment of the Effects of Climate Change on Selected Causes of Death, 2030s and 2050s*. Geneva: World Health Organization, 2014.

397. Rahmstorf, S., 'Modeling sea level rise', *Nature Education Knowledge* 2012; 3 (10): 4.

398. Parry, M., Palutikof, J., Hanson, C. and Lowe, J., 'Squaring up to reality', *Nature Reports Climate Change* 2008; 2: 68–70.

399. Osterreichisches Institut fur Wirtschaftsforschung, *Economics, Reality and the Myths of Growth*. Vienna, 2013.

400. Jolly, A., *Lucy's Legacy: Sex and Intelligence in Human Evolution*. Cambridge, Mass.: Harvard University Press, 2001.
401. Bird-David, N., Abramson, A., Altman, J., et al., 'Beyond "The Original Affluent Society": a culturalist reformulation [and Comments and Reply]', *Current Anthropology* 1992; 33 (1): 25–47.
402. Sahlins, M., 'The original affluent society', in J. Gowdy (ed.), *Limited Wants, Unlimited Means: A Hunter-Gatherer Reader on Economics and the Environment*. Washington, DC: Island Press, 1998, pp. 5–41.
403. Wilkinson, R. G., *Poverty and Progress: An Ecological Model of Economic Development*. London: Methuen, 1973.
404. Lee, R. B. and DeVore, I., *Man the Hunter*: Piscataway, NJ: Transaction Publishers, 1968.
405. Larsen, C. S., 'The agricultural revolution as environmental catastrophe: implications for health and lifestyle in the Holocene', *Quaternary International* 2006; 150 (1): 12–20.
406. Mummert, A., Esche, E., Robinson, J. and Armelagos, G. J., 'Stature and robusticity during the agricultural transition: evidence from the bioarchaeological record', *Economics & Human Biology* 2011; 9 (3): 284–301.
407. Dittmar, H., Bond, R., Hurst, M. and Kasser, T., 'The relationship between materialism and personal well-being: a meta-analysis', *Journal of Personality and Social Psychology* 2014; 107 (5): 879–924.
408. Meltzer, H., Bebbington, P., Brugha, T., Farrell, M. and Jenkins, R., 'The relationship between personal debt and specific common mental disorders', *European Journal of Public Health* 2013; 23 (1): 108–13.
409. Kwon, R. and Cabrera, J. F., 'Socioeconomic factors and mass shootings in the United States', *Critical Public Health* 2017: 1–8.
410. Rufrancos, H., Power, M., Pickett, K. E. and Wilkinson, R., 'Income inequality and crime: a review and explanation of the time-series evidence', *Sociology and Criminology* 2013; 1: 103.
411. Jayadev, A. and Bowles, S., 'Guard labor', *Journal of Development Economics* 2006; 79 (2): 328–48.
412. Bowles, S. and Jayadev, A., 'Garrison America', *Economists' Voice* 2007; 4 (2): 1–7.
413. World Economic Forum, *The Global Competitiveness Report, 2000–2001*. New York: Oxford University Press, 2002.
414. Wilkinson, R. G., Pickett, K. E. and De Vogli, R., 'Equality, sustainability, and quality of life', *British Medical Journal* 2010; 341: c5816.

415. Motesharrei, S., Rivas, J. and Kalnay, E., 'Human and nature dynamics (HANDY): modeling inequality and use of resources in the collapse or sustainability of societies', *Ecological Economics* 2014; 101: 90–102.

416. Wilkinson, R. G. and Pickett, K. E., 'Income inequality and socioeconomic gradients in mortality', *American Journal of Public Health* 2008; 98 (4): 699–704.

417. Jutz, R., 'The role of income inequality and social policies on income-related health inequalities in Europe', *International Journal for Equity in Health* 2015; 14: 117.

418. Lobmayer, P. and Wilkinson, R. G., 'Inequality, residential segregation by income, and mortality in US cities', *Journal of Epidemiology & Community Health* 2002; 56 (3): 183–7.

419. Andersen, R. and Curtis, J., 'The polarizing effect of economic inequality on class identification: evidence from 44 countries', *Research in Social Stratification and Mobility* 2012; 30 (1): 129–41.

420. Jaikumar, S. and Sarin, A., 'Conspicuous consumption and income inequality in an emerging economy: evidence from India', *Marketing Letters* 2015; 26 (3): 279–92.

421. Walasek, L. and Brown, G. D., 'Income inequality, income, and internet searches for status goods: a cross-national study of the association between inequality and well-being', *Social Indicators Research* 2015; doi:10.1007/s11205-015-1158-4.

422. Walasek, L. and Brown, G. D., 'Income inequality and status seeking, searching for positional goods in unequal US states', *Psychological Science* 2015; 26 (4): 527–33.

423. Neville, L., 'Do economic equality and generalized trust inhibit academic dishonesty? Evidence from state-level search-engine queries', *Psychological Science* 2012; 23 (4): 339–45.

424. Gustafsson, B. and Johansson, M., 'In search of smoking guns: what makes income inequality vary over time in different countries?' *American Sociological Review* 1999: 585–605.

425. Eisenbrey, R. G. and Gordon, C., 'As unions decline, inequality rises'. *Economic Policy Institute* 2012, http://www.epi.org/publication/unions-decline-inequality-rises/.

426. Piketty, T., Saez, E. and Stantcheva, S., 'Optimal taxation of top labor incomes: a tale of three elasticities', National Bureau of Economic Research, 2011.

427. World Bank, *The East Asian Miracle*. Oxford: Oxford University Press, 1993.

428. Krugman, P., *The Conscience of a Liberal*. New York: W. W. Norton & Co., 2009.

429. Obama, B., State of the Union address, 2014, http://www.whitehouse.gov/the-press-office/2014/01/28/president-barack-obamas-state-union-address.

430. Pope Francis, *Evangelii Gaudium*. Vatican City: Vatican Press, 2013.

431. Lagarde, C., Speech at World Economic Forum, Davos, 2013, https://www.imf.org/external/np/speeches/2013/012313.htm.

432. Ban K.-m., Remarks at Informal General Assembly Thematic Debate on Inequality, United Nations, 2013, http://www.un.org/apps/news/story.asp?NewsID=45361#.WdNCPFu3zcs.

433. Norton, M. I. and Ariely, D., 'Building a better America – one wealth quintile at a time', *Perspectives on Psychological Science* 2011; 6 (1): 9–12.

434. Living Wage Commission, *Work That Pays*. London, 2014.

435. Bunyan, P. and Diamond, J., *Approaches to Reducing Poverty and Inequality in the UK. A Study of Civil Society Initiatives and Fairness Commissions*. Edge Hill University/Webb Memorial Trust, 2014.

436. Houlder, V., 'Switzerland pledges to lift veil on tax secrecy', *Financial Times* 6 May 2014.

437. Gibbons, K., 'Extra home help gives Britain that Downton feeling', *The Times* 31 January 2014.

438. Mount, H., 'Are you being served?' *Daily Telegraph* 28 April 2013.

439. Mishel, L. and Sabadish, N., 'Pay and the top 1%: how executive compensation and financial-sector pay have fuelled income inequality', *Issue Brief*, Economic Policy Institute, 2012.

440. Tosi, H. L., Werner, S., Katz, J. P. and Gomez-Mejia, L. R., 'How much does performance matter? A meta-analysis of CEO pay studies', *Journal of Management* 2000; 26 (2): 301–39.

441. Marshall, L., 'Are CEOs paid for performance?' MSCI Inc., 2016.

442. Breza, E., Kaur, S. and Shamdasani, Y., 'The morale effects of pay inequality', National Bureau of Economic Research, 2016.

443. Chang, H.-J., *23 Things They Don't Tell You About Capitalism*. New York: Bloomsbury Publishing, 2012.

444. Conchon, A. K., Kluge, N. and Stollt, M., 'Worker board-level partici-
pation in the 31 European Economic Area countries', European Trade
Union Institute, 2013, http://www.worker-participation.eu/National-
Industrial-Relations/Across-Europe/Board-level-Representation2/TABLE-
Worker-board-level-participation-in-the-31-European-Economic-Area-
countries:

445. Schulten, T. and Zagelmeyer, S., 'Board-level employee representation in Europe', *EIR Observer* 1998; 5: 1–4, https://www.eurofound.
europa.eu/sites/default/files/ef_files/eiro/pdf/eo98-5.pdf.

446. Survation, Employment Survey II, 6 February 2013, http://survation.
com/wp-content/uploads/2014/04/Employment-II-Full-Tables.pdf.

447. Freeman, R. B. and Rogers, J., *What Workers Want*. Ithaca, NY:
Cornell University Press, 2006.

448. Vitols, S., 'Board level employee representation, executive remuneration and firm performance in large European companies', European Corporate Governance Institute and European Trade Union
Institute, 2010.

449. Fauver, L. and Fuerst, M. E., 'Does good corporate governance
include employee representation? Evidence from German corporate
boards', *Journal of Financial Economics* 2006; 82 (3): 673–710.

450. Piketty, T., trans. A. Goldhammer, *Capital in the Twenty-first Century*. Cambridge, Mass.: Harvard University Press, 2014.

451. Oakeshott, R., *Jobs and Fairness: The Logic and Experience of
Employee Ownership*. Norwich: Michael Russell, 2000.

452. Azevedo, A. and Gitahy, L., 'The cooperative movement, self-
management, and competitiveness: the case of Mondragon Corpo-
racion Cooperativa', *Working USA* 2010; 13 (1): 5–29.

453. Zeuli, K. and Radel, J., 'Cooperatives as a community development
strategy: linking theory and practice', *Journal of Regional Analysis
and Policy* 2005; 35 (1): 43–54.

454. Blasi, J., Kruse, D., Sesil, J. and Kroumova, M., 'Broad-based stock
options and company performance: what the research tells us', *Journal
of Employee Ownership, Law, and Finance* 2000; 12 (3): 69–102.

455. Kardas, P. A., Scharf, A. L., Keogh, J. and Rodrick, S. S., *Wealth
and Income Consequences of Employee Ownership: A Comparative Study for Washington State*. Oakland, Calif.: National Center
for Employee Ownership, 1998.

456. Lampel, J., Bhalla, A. and Jha, P., *Model Growth: Do Employee-
owned Businesses Deliver Sustainable Performance?* London: Cass
Business School, City University, 2010.

457. NCEO, *Employee Ownership and Corporate Performance: A Comprehensive Review of the Evidence.* Oakland, Calif.: National Center for Employee Ownership, 2004.

458. Kruse, D., 'Does employee ownership improve performance?' *IZA World of Labor* 2016; 311.

459. Blasi, J., Kruse, D. and Bernstein, A., *In the Company of Owners.* New York: Basic Books, 2003.

460. Nuttall, G., 'Sharing success: the Nuttall review of employee ownership', Department of Business, Innovation and Skills, BIS/12/933, 4 July 2012.

461. Matrix Knowledge Group, *The Employee Ownership Effect: A Review of the Evidence.* London: Matrix Evidence, a division of Matrix Knowledge Group, 2010.

462. Martins, P. S., 'Dispersion in wage premiums and firm performance', *Economics Letters* 2008; 101 (1): 63–5.

463. Bookchin, M., *Remaking Society: Pathways to a Green Future.* Cambridge, Mass.: South End Press, 1990.

464. Kelly, M., 'The next step for CSR: building economic democracy', *Business Ethics* 2002; 16: 2–7.

465. Verdorfer, A. P., Weber, W. G., Unterrainer, C. and Seyr, S., 'The relationship between organizational democracy and socio-moral climate: exploring effects of the ethical context in organizations', *Economic and Industrial Democracy* 2012: 0143831X12450054.

466. Weber, W. G., Unterrainer, C. and Schmid, B. E., 'The influence of organizational democracy on employees' socio-moral climate and prosocial behavioral orientations', *Journal of Organizational Behavior* 2009; 30 (8): 1127–49.

467. Ruiz, J. I., Nuhu, K., McDaniel, J. T., et al., 'Inequality as a powerful predictor of infant and maternal mortality around the world', *PLoS One* 2015; 10 (10): e0140796.

468. Bosma, H., Marmot, M. G., Hemingway, H., et al., 'Low job control and risk of coronary heart disease in Whitehall II (prospective cohort) study', *British Medical Journal* 1997; 314 (7080): 558–65.

469. Theorell, T., 'Democracy at work and its relationship to health', *Research in Occupational Stress and Well-being* 2003; 3: 323–57.

470. De Vogli, R., Brunner, E. and Marmot, M. G., 'Unfairness and the social gradient of metabolic syndrome in the Whitehall II study', *Journal of Psychosomatic Research* 2007; 63 (4): 413–19.

471. De Vogli, R., Ferrie, J. E., Chandola, T., Kivimaki, M. and Marmot, M. G., 'Unfairness and health: evidence from the Whitehall II

study', *Journal of Epidemiology & Community Health* 2007; 61 (6): 513–18.

472. Elovainio, M., Singh-Manoux, A., Ferrie, J. E., et al., 'Organisational justice and cognitive function in middle-aged employees: the Whitehall II study', *Journal of Epidemiology & Community Health* 2012; 66 (6): 552–6.

473. Williamson, J. and the TUC, *Workers on Board: The Case For Workers' Voice in Corporate Governance*. London: Trades Union Congress, 2013.

474. Freudenberg, N., *Lethal But Legal: Corporations, Consumption, and Protecting Public Health*. New York: Oxford University Press, 2014.

475. The Equality Trust, *The Cost of Inequality*. London: The Equality Trust, 2014.

476. Bregman R., *Utopia for Realists: The Case for a Universal Basic Income, Open Borders, and a 15-hour Workweek*. Originally published in Dutch online on *De Correspondent*, 2016; English edition published 2017 by Bloomsbury.

477. Dye, R. F. and England, R. W., 'Assessing the theory and practice of land value taxation', Lincoln Institute of Land Policy, 2010.

478. Gilroy, B. M., Heimann, A. and Schopf, M., 'Basic income and labour supply: the German case', *Basic Income Studies* 2012; 8 (1): 43–70.

479. Widerquist, K. and Sheahen, A., 'The United States: the basic income guarantee – past experience, current proposals', *Basic Income Worldwide: Horizons of Reform* 2012: 11.

480. Dickens, R., Gregg, P., Machin, S., Manning, A. and Wadsworth, J., 'Wages councils: was there a case for abolition?' *British Journal of Industrial Relations* 1993; 31 (4): 515–29.

481. Burkitt, B. and Whyman, P., 'Employee investment funds in Sweden: their past, present and future', *European Business Review* 1994; 94 (4): 22–9.

482. Coote, A., Franklin, J., Simms, A. and Murphy, M., *21 Hours: Why a Shorter Working Week Can Help Us All to Flourish in the 21st Century*. London: New Economics Foundation, 2010.

483. Frey, C. B. and Osborne, M., *The Future of Employment: How Susceptible Are Jobs to Computerisation?* Oxford Martin School, University of Oxford, 2013.

484. Babones, S. J., 'Income inequality and population health: correlation and causality', *Social Science & Medicine* 2008; 66 (7): 1614–26.

485. Clarkwest, A., 'Neo-materialist theory and the temporal relationship between income inequality and longevity change', *Social Science & Medicine* 2008; 66 (9): 1871–81.

486. Zheng, H., 'Do people die from income inequality of a decade ago?' *Social Science & Medicine* 2012; 75 (1): 36–45.

487. Kim, D. and Saada, A., 'The social determinants of infant mortality and birth outcomes in western developed nations: a cross-country systematic review', *International Journal of Environmental Research & Public Health* 2013; 10 (6): 2296.

488. Ram, R., 'Further examination of the cross-country association between income inequality and population health', *Social Science & Medicine* 2006; 62 (3): 779–91.

489. Torre, R. and Myrskyla, M., 'Income inequality and population health: an analysis of panel data for 21 developed countries, 1975–2006', *Population Studies* 2014; 68 (1): 1–13.

490. Ram, R., 'Income inequality, poverty, and population health: evidence from recent data for the United States', *Social Science & Medicine* 2005; 61 (12): 2568–76.

491. Pickett, K. E. and Wilkinson, R. G., 'Income inequality and psychosocial pathways to obesity', in A. Offer, R. Pechey and S. Ulijaszek (eds.), *Insecurity, Inequality, and Obesity in Affluent Societies.* Oxford: British Academy, 2012.

492. Drain, P. K., Smith, J. S., Hughes, J. P., Halperin, D. T. and Holmes, K. K., 'Correlates of national HIV seroprevalence: an ecologic analysis of 122 developing countries', *Journal of Acquired Immune Deficiency Syndrome* 2004; 35 (4): 407–20.

493. Buot, M.-L. G., Docena, J. P., Ratemo, B. K., et al., 'Beyond race and place: distal sociological determinants of HIV disparities', *PLoS One* 2014; 9 (4): e91711.

494. Wilkinson, R. G. and Pickett, K. E., 'Income inequality and social dysfunction', *Annual Review of Sociology* 2009; 35: 493–512.

495. Gray, N., 'Income inequality, alcoholism and high blood pressure prevalence in the U.S.', posted at the 6th Biennial Conference of the American Society of Health Economists, University of Pennsylvania, June 2016.

496. Wilkinson, R. G. and Pickett, K. E., 'The problems of relative deprivation: why some societies do better than others', *Social Science & Medicine* 2007; 65 (9): 1965–78.

497. Freitag, M. and Bühlmann, M., 'Crafting trust: the role of political institutions in a comparative perspective', *Comparative Political Studies* 2009; 42 (12): 1537–66.

498. Kawachi, I. and Kennedy, B. P., 'The relationship of income inequality to mortality: does the choice of indicator matter?' *Social Science & Medicine* 1997; 45 (7): 1121–7.

499. Cheung, F. and Lucas, R. E., 'Income inequality is associated with stronger social comparison effects: the effect of relative income on life satisfaction', *Journal of Personality & Social Psychology* 2016; 110 (2): 332–41.

500. Ouimet, M., 'A world of homicides: the effect of economic development, income inequality, and excess infant mortality on the homicide rate for 165 countries in 2010', *Homicide Studies* 2012; 16 (3): 238–58.

501. Glaeser, E. L., Resseger, M. G. and Tobio, K., 'Urban inequality', National Bureau of Economic Research, 2008.

502. Kawachi, I. and Kennedy, B. P., 'Income inequality and health: pathways and mechanisms', *Health Services Research* 1999; 34 (1 Pt 2): 215–27.

503. Chetty, R., Hendren, N., Kline, P. and Saez, E., 'Where is the land of opportunity? The geography of intergenerational mobility in the United States', National Bureau of Economic Research, 2014.

504. Kearney, M. S. and Levine, P. B., 'Why is the teen birth rate in the United States so high and why does it matter?' *Journal of Economic Perspectives* 2012; 26 (2): 141–66.

505. Boyce, J. K., 'Inequality as a cause of environmental degradation', *Ecological Economics* 1994; 11 (3): 169–78.

506. Cushing, L., Morello-Frosch, R., Wander, M. and Pastor, M., 'The haves, the have-nots, and the health of everyone: the relationship between social inequality and environmental quality', *Annual Review of Public Health* 2015; 36 (1): 193–209.

507. Holland, T. G., Peterson, G. D. and Gonzalez, A., 'A cross-national analysis of how economic inequality predicts biodiversity loss', *Conservation Biology* 2009; 23 (5): 1304–13.

508. Mikkelson, G. M., Gonzalez, A. and Peterson, G. D., 'Economic inequality predicts biodiversity loss', *PLoS One* 2007; 2 (5): e444.

509. Stotesbury, N. and Dorling, D., 'Understanding income inequality and its implications: why better statistics are needed', *Statistics Views* 2015; 21.

510. Drabo, A., 'Impact of income inequality on health: does environment quality matter?' *Environment and Planning - Part A* 2011; 43 (1): 146.

511. Jorgenson, A., Schor, J., Huang, X. and Fitzgerald, J., 'Income inequality and residential carbon emissions in the United States: a preliminary analysis', *Human Ecology Review* 2015; 22 (1): 93–105.
512. Patel, V., Burns, J. K., Dhingra, M., et al., 'Income inequality and depression: a systematic review and meta-analysis of the association and a scoping review of mechanisms', *World Psychiatry* 2018; 17: 76–89.

Index

Note: Page numbers in italics refer to Figures; those in bold refer to the Appendices